TEACHING AND MARKETING ELECTRONIC INFORMATION LITERACY PROGRAMS

A How-To-Do-It Manual for Librarians

DONALD A. BARCLAY

HOW-TO-DO-IT MANUALS FOR LIBRARIANS

NUMBER 124

NEAL-SCHUMAN PUBLISHERS, INC.
New York, London

Published by Neal-Schuman Publishers, Inc.
100 William Street
Suite 2004
New York, NY 10038

Printed and bound in the United States of America.

Library of Congress Cataloging-in-Publication Data

Barclay, Donald A.
    Teaching and marketing electronic information literacy programs : a how-to-do-it manual for librarians / Donald A. Barclay.
        p. cm. — (How-to-do-it manuals for librarians ; no. 124)
    Includes bibliographical references.
    ISBN 1-55570-470-0 (alk. paper)
    1. Electronic information resource literacy—Study and teaching. I. Title. II. How-to-do-it manuals for libraries ; no. 124.

    ZA4065.B37 2003
    025.04'071—dc21
                                                                2003052744

CONTENTS

List of Figures   v

Preface   vii

Acknowledgments   xi

How to Use the 12 Ready-to-Go PowerPoint Presentations   xiii

Part I:
Teaching Electronic Information Literacy:
   Key Concepts and Strategies   1

1. Teaching Students Electronic Information Literacy   3
2. Teaching Students (and Others) Why Information Is Not
   All "Just a Click Away"   15
3. Teaching Students the Economics and the Ethics of
   Electronic Information   21
4. Teaching Students the Essentials of Electronic Searching
   and Information Retrieval   41
5. Teaching Students How to Evaluate Electronic Information   65

Part II:
12 Ready-to-Go PowerPoint Presentations for
   Teaching Electronic Information Literacy   91

   1. Boolean Logic   93
   2. Economics of Electronic Information   96
   3. Electronic Searching Essentials   98
   4. Electronic Searching Essentials 2   102
   5. Ethics of Electronic Information   105
   6. Evaluating Information   109
   7. Information Roadblocks   116
   8. Iterative Search Process   120
   9. Precision Versus Recall   123
  10. Strategies for Evaluation   125
  11. Web Search Engines   129
  12. Why It's All Not "Just a Click Away"   133

Part III:
Becoming a Master Electronic Information Literacy Instructor   135

6. Mastering the "One-Shot" 50–Minute Class   137

iii

7. Tackling the Extended Electronic Information Literacy
   Course   153
8. Becoming an Effective Instructor of Electronic
   Information Literacy   167
9. Extending Your Reach with Print Publications,
   Online Tutorials, and Web-casting   173

Part IV:
Managing the Successful Electronic Information Literacy Program   **193**

10. Designing and Equipping the Electronic Classroom   195
11. Marketing Electronic Information Literacy Instruction   217
12. Assessing Electronic Information Literacy Instruction   227

Appendix: Useful Resources for Information Literacy   237

Index   249

About the Author   255

LIST OF FIGURES

Figure 1-1: Hands-On Skills or Critical-Thinking Ability Exercise   6

Figure 4-1: Information Roadblocks   45

Figure 4-2: Precision Versus Recall   49

Figure 4-3: Sample Iterative Search   52

Figure 4-4: Web Search Engines (and their Limitations)   62

Figure 5-1: Scholarly Versus Nonscholarly Information   69

Figure 5-2: The Scholarly Information Process   73

Figure 5-3: Galen's Writings   78

Figure 5-4: Reviewing Reviews   83

Figure 6-1: The Three-to-Four-Point Rule   139

Figure 6-2: Formal Lesson Plan   140

Figure 6-3: Sample Outline Handout   142

Figure 6-4: Connection Between Things A and B   149

Figure 7-1: Sample Syllabus   158

Figure 10-1: Electronic Classroom Layout 1   199

Figure 10-2: Electronic Classroom Layout 2   200

Figure 10-3: Electronic Classroom Layout 3   201

Figure 10-4: Electronic Classroom Layout 4   202

Figure 10-5: Wireless Standards   210

PREFACE

Teaching electronic information is a demanding business, in part because the field is in a state of constant change. When I edited *Teaching Electronic Information Literacy* less than 10 years ago, I clearly remember making the decision that we should squeeze in a paragraph or two about this new thing called the World Wide Web. Just consider how quickly the world of computers and electronic literacy has changed since Neal-Schuman published my earlier book. In 1995:

- The average person had never sent an e-mail message or seen a Web page.
- For most people, the word "spam" conjured up images of a canned meat product.
- The Pentium chip had yet to be introduced.
- The size of the most cutting-edge, and costly, consumer hard drives was approaching .5 GB.
- The first online banks and Internet radio stations were only just debuting.
- Sun Microsystems was introducing the Java programming language.
- Buying anything online was a novelty and the now-busted dot.com bubble had hardly begun to grow.

Today, personal computers and the Web are so much a part of everyday life (in the industrialized world, anyway) that some might question the need to teach electronic information literacy. Don't babies grow up with a bottle in one hand and a mouse in the other? Don't eight-year-olds routinely solve computer glitches that tie their parents in knots? While it is true that computer skills are much more widespread (and acquired at a younger age) than they were 30 years ago, it is also true that knowing how to burn MP3s to a CD or install RedHat 7.2 does not make one literate in electronic information.

Certainly, computer skills are one element of electronic information literacy, but they are just part of the story. Many computer-savvy people are not information literate because they lack an understanding of information economics or cannot formulate an effective search strategy (skills, by the way, that are not necessarily honed by hours spent bidding for knickknacks on *eBay* or hanging out in a Backstreet Boys chat room).

Perhaps nothing legitimizes information literacy more than the fact that educational-accrediting bodies are now requiring schools and colleges to include information literacy in the curriculum. This mandate presents two golden opportunities: one, for libraries and librarians to seek administrative support for information-literacy programs, and, two, to better integrate library-centered instruction into the curriculum. When the accrediting body says that students must be information literate, library-centered instruction is no longer a nice little service for faculty who want their students to be able to complete a specific research assignment; it has become crucial to the institution's credibility and standards.

A BRIEF TOUR OF THE BOOK

The first two parts of *Teaching and Marketing Electronic Information Literacy Programs* comprises key concepts, teaching notes, and 12 PowerPoint presentations for the fundamental electronic information literacy concepts contained in the chapters. The first chapter, "Teaching Students Electronic Information Literacy," delineates in concrete terms the very abstract concepts of electronic information literacy. Chapter 2, "Teaching Students (and Others) Why Information Is Not All 'Just a Click Away,'" dispels many myths about electronic information they have picked up as members of our (mis)information society. Chapter 3, "Teaching Students the Economics and the Ethics of Electronic Information," focuses on two crucial areas of electronic information literacy that often get lost in the rush to get students pushing the right key and left clicking the correct link. Chapter 4, "Teaching Students the Essentials of Electronic Searching and Information Retrieval," brings together in a single chapter all the most important tools needed by efficient searchers. Chapter 5, "Teaching Students How to Evaluate Electronic Information," deals with what is, arguably, the most important characteristic of anyone who can call themselves information literate.

Part II, "12 Ready-to-Go PowerPoint Presentations for Teaching Electronic Information Literacy," provides instructors with slide presentations that they can use as is or modify to suit their needs. The presentations include:

1. Boolean Logic
2. Economics of Electronic Information
3. Electronic Searching Essentials
4. Electronic Searching Essentials 2
5. Ethics of Electronic Information

6. Evaluating Information
7. Information Roadblocks
8. Iterative Search Process
9. Precision Versus Recall
10. Strategies for Evaluation
11. Web Search Engines
12. Why It's All Not "Just a Click Away"

Instructors are welcome to be as creative as they wish to be in using the slide presentations that accompany this book. The presentations need not be used in any particular order, nor is it necessary to use all of the presentations. Some instructors may wish to copy and paste selected slides from the various presentations in order to create a single presentation, and customizing individual slides is perfectly fine.

Each presentation comes in both a plain-vanilla and a dressed-up version. The plain-vanilla presentations are intended for instructors who are handy with PowerPoint and wish to brand the presentations with their favorite logos, design layouts, images, and so on. The dressed-up presentations are intended for instructors who want something they can show right out of the box. In either case, instructors may edit, add to, or update these slides to create customized slide shows.

For example, the "Boolean Logic" presentation uses plants and animals to illustrate the principles of AND, OR, and NOT. If, however, you felt that your students might respond better to automobiles than to plants and animals, you could change the search statement to something like:

sedan AND four doors

and replace the images of plants and animals with images of automobiles. Just about any category of things with which a particular group of students identifies—from video-game characters to classical-music composers—could be used in this presentation.

A note of clarification: The PowerPoint slides were created for fair use. The slides may be copied for noncommercial educational use within an organization only. No part of this book or CD-ROM may be published in any form for wider distribution (including publication via the Internet) without written permission from the publisher.

For more information and instruction on this part of the book see the section "How to Use the 12 Ready-to-Go PowerPoint Presentations" on page xiii.

Part III, "Becoming a Master Electronic Information Literacy Instructor," begins with Chapter 6, "Mastering the 'One-Shot' 50–Minute Class," which helps instructors make the best of a staple that most would rather do without but with which most have to live on a day-to-day basis. Chapter 7, "Tackling the Extended Electronic Information Literacy Course," offers strategies for developing and teaching a graded, for-credit information literacy course. Chapter 8, "Becoming an Effective Instructor of Electronic Information Literacy," outlines strategies an instructor follows to become more effective in the classroom. Chapter 9, "Extending Your Reach with Print Publications, Online Tutorials, and Web-casting," reviews techniques for reaching the largest possible audience by taking instruction beyond the wall of the traditional classroom.

Part IV, "Managing the Successful Electronic Information Literacy Program," consists of three chapters that focus on building institutional support for information literacy. Chapter 10, "Designing and Equipping the Electronic Classroom," deals with developing an effective electronic classroom—an important step in building a successful electronic information literacy program. Chapter 11, "Marketing Electronic Information Literacy Instruction," focuses on "selling" the concept of information literacy to students, faculty, and administrators. Chapter 12, "Assessing Electronic Information Literacy Instruction," provides specific techniques for carrying out effective assessment in order to both improve learning outcomes while also justifying electronic information literacy programs to administrators and others.

Teaching and Marketing Electronic Information Literacy Programs ends with an appendix featuring an annotated list of more than 75 useful resources and recommendations for further reading and Web sites.

The electronic revolution of the end of the twentieth century has turned into a constant electronic literacy evolution in the twenty-first century. For librarians the challenge is designing, implementing, and promoting the instruction that will best teach students the skills necessary to master it. I hope *Teaching and Marketing Electronic Information Literacy Programs* will help the profession fulfill its vital responsibility to teach our students about this complex and important new world.

ACKNOWLEDGMENTS

If it is true that books do not write themselves, it is equally true that authors do not write books all by themselves. For their friendship and good counsel, I wish to thank my University of California, Merced Library colleagues Joyce Parham and Bruce Miller. I also owe a debt of gratitude to my friends and editors at Neal-Schuman Publishers, the dauntless Charles Harmon and the relentless (in a good way) Michael G. Kelley. Finally, I dedicate this book with love to Darcie and Tess.

HOW TO USE THE 12 READY-TO-GO POWERPOINT PRESENTATIONS

The following presentations accompany *Teaching and Marketing Electronic Information Literacy Programs*:

1. Boolean Logic
2. Economics of Electronic Information
3. Electronic Searching Essentials
4. Electronic Searching Essentials 2
5. Ethics of Electronic Information
6. Evaluating Information
7. Information Roadblocks
8. Iterative Search Process
9. Precision Versus Recall
10. Strategies for Evaluation
11. Web Search Engines
12. Why It's All Not "Just a Click Away"

ANIMATING SLIDES

Most of the bullet slides in the presentations included with this book are not animated; that is, when bullet slides are shown, all the text appears at once instead of point by point. If you would like the text on any slide to appear point by point, the easiest way to do this is to:

1. Highlight the bulleted text you would like to appear point by point.
2. From the PowerPoint toolbar choose Slide Show.
3. From the drop-down menu choose Preset Animation.
4. Click on the type of preset animation you would like to use.

Of course the bullet slides can also be animated using PowerPoint's custom animation features.

TECHNICAL DETAILS

Each presentation included with this book was created using Microsoft PowerPoint 2000. This version of PowerPoint is compatible with earlier versions of PowerPoint (such as PowerPoint 4.0 and PowerPoint 95) and should be compatible with future versions.

POWERPOINT PRESENTATION TIPS

1. PowerPoint should not be used as a teleprompter, so avoid reading every word on every slide unless you have a good reason to do so (e.g., some members of the audience are visually impaired, too far away to see the screen, or not literate).
2. Brevity is the soul of wit. Most PowerPoint presentations include too many slides and go on far too long.
3. Use PowerPoint bells and whistles sparingly. That high-tech whoosh sound may be clever if you use it once; it is perfectly annoying if you use it every time you advance to a new slide. Similarly, do not overdo it with images that fly, dance, swivel, or perform other visual stunts.
4. Avoid using text smaller than 24 point. For fancy fonts, such as those that mimic handwriting, the smallest text size may need to be much bigger than 24 point.
5. Avoid putting more than 50 words on one slide. If you need more than 50 words to say something, either break it into multiple slides or make paper copies to hand out to your audience. Better yet, find a way to express the idea graphically instead of in words—always remember that PowerPoint is a largely visual medium.
6. Detailed tables do not work well on PowerPoint. If your audience needs to see a table with lots of numbers on it, give each person in the audience a paper copy of the table. That way, if you must put the table on a slide, the audience can follow along without eyestrain.

7. Do not use too many different typefaces or overuse exotic typefaces.
8. Large blocks of centered text are hard to read. So are large blocks of justified text.
9. Too many colors can be distracting or difficult to read.
10. Make sure there is good color contrast between text and background.
11. Use images to keep readers interested and informed, but do not use images that are inappropriate for your topic or audience.
12. Make sure the design template you choose is appropriate for your audience and your topic.
13. Rehearse your presentation many times before giving it.
14. When timing your presentation, allow for questions, technical problems, and delays.
15. Keep in mind the size of the screen, your audience's distance from it, the quality of your projector, and room lighting.

PART I

TEACHING ELECTRONIC INFORMATION LITERACY: KEY CONCEPTS AND STRATEGIES

1 TEACHING STUDENTS ELECTRONIC INFORMATION LITERACY

You cannot begin to define *electronic information literacy* until you have defined the broader concept of *information literacy*. And information literacy, for better or worse, is one of those terms that has been defined within an inch of its life. Conservatively, information literacy is most often defined as some combination of basic information-seeking skills coupled with at least a minimal ability to think critically about information; on the other end of the scale, information literacy is defined as a new liberal art that employs elements of sociology, history, economics, information technology, composition, and possibly other fields of study—it all depends on who is doing the defining. Such divergence of opinion is not unique to the study of information literacy. Traditional historians, for example, tend to define the study of history as the accumulation of historical facts coupled with the ability to interpret them, while those who take a more postmodern approach define the field in philosophical terms that, in the extreme, have little to do with such petty details as what year Columbus sailed the ocean blue or who (if anyone) won the Battle of Gettysburg.

Whether your view of information literacy is conservative, cutting edge, or somewhere in between, it is not a big leap to recognize that because electronic information literacy is a subset (albeit an ever increasingly important one) of information literacy, any definitions of electronic information literacy one might generate are going to sound a lot like definitions of information literacy.

A working definition of information literacy is useful, if not flat-out necessary, when rallying others (such as teaching faculty) to the cause of information literacy or when asking administrators to pump resources into an information literacy program. A definition also makes a good polestar when planning an information literacy program. In a break with tradition—and in recognition of the fact that a one-size-fits-all definition will fit no one perfectly—this chapter will not conclude with a nailed-down definition of electronic information literacy; rather, the intent here is to bring together elements that might go into a definition while leaving the final definition to readers who, it is hoped, will come up with appropriate definitions that will best meet the needs of their specific situations.

WHAT ELECTRONIC INFORMATION LITERACY IS NOT

One way to define something is to decide what it is not.

- Electronic information literacy is neither bibliographic instruction nor library instruction. While anyone who is truly electronic information literate can make use of a library, electronic information literacy extends into realms of information that lie well beyond the boundaries of the brick-and-mortar library.
- Electronic information literacy does not fall under the realm of computer skills. While computer skills are necessary to become literate about electronic information (see below), such skills are tools toward an end, not an end unto themselves.
- Electronic information literacy is not an educational extra. Choose your cliché—"Information Age," "Information Economy," "Information Is Power"—they all point to the fact that to be a fully educated person in the twenty-first century, you must be electronic information literate.

SKILLS VERSUS CRITICAL THINKING

Definitions of electronic information literacy typically refer to both skills and critical-thinking abilities. Because critical thinking is so valued in academia it is easy to undervalue skills, yet to do so is a serious mistake.

Just as you could not become a literary scholar without being able to read or a mathematician without being able to add two plus two, so, too, you cannot become electronic information literate if you cannot use a mouse to scroll down a Web page or cannot type keywords into an on-screen search box. When you spend a good part of your time in front of computers, it is easy to forget that basic electronic information skills need to be learned

Defining Information Literacy: A Selected Bibliography

The following resources will aid anyone who is interested in developing a definition of *information literacy* and, by extension, a definition of *electronic information literacy*.

American Association of School Librarians. "Nine Information Literacy Standards for Student Learning." Chicago: ALA/AASL. (February 2003) Available: www.ala.org/aasl/ip_nine.html.

Association of College & Research Libraries. "Information Literacy Competency Standards for Higher Education." Chicago: ACRL. (February 2003) Available: www.ala.org/acrl/ilcomstan.html.

Behrens, Shirley J. 2002. "A Conceptual Analysis and Historical Overview of Information Literacy." *College & Research Libraries* 55: 309–322.

Bundy, Alan L. 1999. "Information Literacy: The 21st Century Educational Smartcard." *Australian Academic and Research Libraries* 30, no.4: 233–250.

Institute for Information Literacy. "Information Literacy in a Nutshell: Basic Information for Academic Administrators and Faculty." Chicago: ACRL. (February 2003) Available: www.ala.org/acrl/nili/whatis.html.

Loertscher, David, and Blanche Wool. 2002. *Information Literacy: A Review of the Research.* 2nd ed. San Jose, CA: Hi Willow.

Maughan, Patricia Davitt. 2002. "Assessing Information Literacy Among Undergraduates: A Discussion of the Literature and the University of California-Berkeley Assessment Experience." *College and Research Libraries* 62, no.1: 71–85.

Plotnick, Eric. 2000. "Definitions/Perspectives: Information Literacy." *Teacher Librarian* 21, no.1: 27–29.

Shapiro, Jeremy J., and Shelley K. Hughes. "Information Literacy as a Liberal Art." *Educom Review.* (February 2003) Available: www.educause.edu/pub/er/review/reviewarticles/31231.html.

Snavely, Loanne, and Natasha Cooper. 1997. "The Information Literacy Debate." *Journal of Academic Librarianship* 23 (January): 9–14.

Sonntag, Gabriela. 2001. "Report on the National Information Literacy Survey: Documenting Progress throughout the United States." *College and Research Libraries News* 62, no.10: 996–1001.

Figure 1–1: Hands-on Skills or Critical-Thinking Ability Exercise

This is a good exercise to do with a group, but you can try it on your own as well.

Step 1
Brainstorm a list of things that a person needs to be numbered among the electronic information literate. Items that go on the list can be skills, critical-thinking abilities, or whatever items the group generates. Do not put the items on the list into any kind of category during the brainstorming session. As with any brainstorming session, free association should rule, and no one (including the moderator) should overrule, ignore, or otherwise suppress any idea brought up by a participant, no matter how off the wall it may seem. Once the brainstorming is complete, the moderator and group may agree to combine any redundant items on the list.

Step 2
Working individually, each participant should put the items on the list into one of two categories listed below.

Hands-On Skills	Critical-Thinking Abilities

Step 3
The group should compare their lists to see how much agreement and disagreement there is. Ideally, disagreements will surface, generating group debate on what constitutes skills versus critical thinking and the relative importance of each.

just as the skills of reading and arithmetic are learned. While it may be true that students *should* have mastered basic computer skills by the time they are _____ (fill in the blank with the age or grade level of your choice), the fact is that they often have not. Students may have attended school at a time before such skills were taught or attended schools where technology simply was not available. Whatever the case, it is a good idea for those teaching electronic information literacy to develop a sense of what basic skills students have—or lack. After all, how much learning goes on when a instructor says, "You just click here and scroll down through the results," if half the students do not know how to click or scroll?

ASSESSING BASIC SKILLS

Assessing students' basic computer skills is easiest when the instructor has multiple contacts with the same group of students and sufficient time to conduct a thorough assessment. Of course this is not always the case in library settings where one-shot instruction is common. Simple observation is one way to assess basic skills, but if time allows you may want to test students' basic skills with a formal instrument (see below). Simply asking questions of the group such as, "Has everyone used a Web browser?" or "Does everyone know how to click onto a hyperlink?" is not an effective way to access basic skills because most students (especially adults) are reluctant to admit that they do not know how to start up Netscape or where to type www.whatever.com—especially when everyone else in the group knows (or acts like they know) how to do it already.

Taking time to bring students up to speed on basic skills is important; how to do it depends on the situation. In a group where skill levels are mixed, it may be best to allow those students who already have the basic skills to teach those who do not. Creating your own basic-skills exercise can be helpful. You might also take advantage of Chris Rippel's *Mouserobics* (www.ckls.org/~crippel/computerlab/tutorials/mouse/page1.html), a widely available online tutorial that gives students practice moving a mouse and teaches them to use:

- Radio buttons.
- Check boxes.
- Drop-down menus.

- Scroll arrows.
- Scroll-bar menus.
- Pop-up windows.
- Forms.
- Copy and paste commands.

A simple computer game such as solitaire can be another effective way to help students learn basic computer skills.

DEVELOPING AN INSTRUMENT FOR ASSESSING BASIC SKILLS

It is helpful to have on hand an instrument for accessing students' basic electronic information literacy skills. A few important points to consider when developing such an assessment:

- Create a testing-and-learning tool rather than just a testing tool. In the perfect scenario, students who start with no basic skills will have mastered the skills being assessed by the time they finish using the tool.
- Keep it short. Short assessment tools can be used even when contact time with students is limited, as is often the case in libraries.
- Design the assessment so it can be administered by anyone. That way a classroom teacher could, for example, give the assessment to her class and pass the results on to you before the class comes to the library for a one-shot instruction session.
- As much as possible, make the assessment tool fun and relevant. This will help keep those students who have already mastered basic skills from being completely bored. The treasure-hunt format is an old standby, but tools that incorporate humor, focus on topics of local or pressing interest, or lead students to amazing facts and/or entertaining trivia are also effective.
- Having students tackle the assessment in pairs can work well, though you need to be careful that a partner for whom basic skills are old hat does not take the wheel and whip through the assessment before a less skilled partner has had a chance to put so much as one finger on the keyboard.

- If the assessment produces some sort of score telling how the students did, this data can be useful for evaluation purposes. In many cases, the data will show that computer skills are not as universal among the young as the popular imagination would have it.

WHAT ARE BASIC ELECTRONIC INFORMATION LITERACY SKILLS?

Of course just about every information professional has an idea of what constitutes basic electronic information literacy skills, and it is unlikely that any two lists of such skills will agree completely. Consider the list that follows, then, as a starting point to which you can add and delete as you desire.

Someone who has mastered basic electronic information literacy skills can:

- Turn on a computer and properly shut it down.
- Use a keyboard.
- Use a mouse.
- Use other input devices if necessary (scanners, bar coders, etc.).
- Copy, cut, and paste text.
- Launch software programs (spread sheets, e-mail programs, Web browsers, etc.) and close them when done.
- Name and save files to a hard drive or disk.
- Open saved files from a hard drive or disk.
- Print electronic information in a usable format.
- Follow hyperlinks on a Web page.
- Scroll up or down to see information not immediately visible on screen.
- Connect to the Internet via modem or network connection.
- Send and receive e-mail (including attachments).
- Download and install any software needed for accessing electronic information (e.g., a helper application such as Adobe Acrobat Reader).
- Use basic Web browser commands (back arrow, home, reload, etc.).
- Use standard Web interface tools (radio buttons, drop-down menus, textboxes, forms, etc.).

- Understand basic conventions for navigating Web pages (underlined and/or blue text usually means a link, changed color means a visited link, navigation bars usually appear on top or left-hand side of a page, etc.).
- Access a specific Web page by typing a given URL into a Web browser.
- Understand what computer viruses are and be able to take at least some measures to avoid them.

WHAT CRITICAL-THINKING ABILITIES ARE NECESSARY FOR ELECTRONIC INFORMATION LITERACY?

Just as information professionals disagree about exactly what skills are necessary for electronic information literacy, so too they disagree about critical-thinking abilities. The one thing everyone seems to agree on is that critical-thinking abilities are part of the information literacy mix and that these abilities contribute to life-long learning. After all, a person could know everything there is to know about computer hardware and software and still not have a clue when it comes to thinking critically about information. In synthesis, most lists of critical-thinking abilities mention the ability to:

- Define your information need.
- Formulate a strategy for locating appropriate information.
- Evaluate information.
- Apply information in order to write a paper, complete a project, or serve some other purpose.

Almost all of the library literature that touches on the subject of critical-thinking skills is practice oriented—there are many articles that describe methods for teaching specific critical-thinking skills, and many which bemoan the lack of such skills among students, but very few articles take a broadly theoretical approach to critical thinking. You will find a detailed outline of critical-thinking abilities in the Association of College & Research Libraries' "Information Literacy Competency Standards for Higher Education: Standards, Performance Indicators, and Outcomes." (www.ala.org/acrl/ilcomstan.html) The five standards spelled out in this document are:

- The information literate student determines the nature and extent of the information needed.
- The information literate student accesses needed information effectively and efficiently.
- The information literate student evaluates information and its sources critically and incorporates selected information into his or her knowledge base and value system.
- The information literate student, individually or as a member of a group, uses information effectively to accomplish a specific purpose.
- The information literate student understands many of the economic, legal, and social issues surrounding the use of information and accesses and uses information ethically and legally.

While some of the performance indicators and outcomes included in the full document describe basic skills rather than critical-thinking abilities, critical thinking is covered in full.

For a similar example, the American Association of School Librarians' "Nine Information Literacy Standards for Student Learning" (www.ala.org/aasl/ip) covers much the same ground as the five standards given above:

Information Literacy
Standard 1: The student who is information literate accesses information efficiently and effectively.
Standard 2: The student who is information literate evaluates information critically and competently.
Standard 3: The student who is information literate uses information accurately and creatively.

Independent Learning
Standard 4: The student who is an independent learner is information literate and pursues information related to personal interests.
Standard 5: The student who is an independent learner is information literate and appreciates literature and other creative expressions of information.
Standard 6: The student who is an independent learner is information literate and strives for excellence in information seeking and knowledge generation.

Social Responsibility
Standard 7: The student who contributes positively to the learning community and to society is information literate and recognizes the importance of information to a democratic society.

Standard 8: The student who contributes positively to the learning community and to society is information literate and practices ethical behavior in regard to information and information technology.

Standard 9: The student who contributes positively to the learning community and to society is information literate and participates effectively in groups to pursue and generate information.

No doubt similar lists can be found in other print and online sources and that more such lists will continue to appear in the future. Perusing several such lists can be a great aid in drawing up a list that best suits the specific needs of your institution and your students.

ONCE YOU HAVE A DEFINITION

As mentioned above, one of the most important reasons to have a definition of information literacy is that it can help guide your planning as you develop an information literacy program. For a definition to be useful in this way, however, it must be a definition all the players agree upon, and this means that it must be reached through a group process. That process should include some people from outside the library. Adding outside voices slows down the process, but on the other hand it helps prevent the agreed-upon definition from being so library-centric that it has no legitimacy outside the library.

No matter who is involved, arriving at an agreed-upon definition of information literacy can be a frustrating process, with one of the most frustrating things about it being that a group can spend ages arguing and debating and word smithing only to find, in the end, the definition they arrived at sounds just like every other definition of information literacy. Indeed, when the process is all over someone is likely to say, "We could have just used _____'s definition of information literacy and saved all this work." This is true, of course, but it is also true that the process of defining information literacy has value in and of itself. Ideally, the process will clarify thinking, bring people together, and get them excited about the whole idea of information literacy. While, for these reasons, you should not short-circuit the process in the name of expediency, do your best to keep the process from turning into so huge a task that, once it is over, no one has any energy left to do the really important work that follows defining information literacy—formulating goals and outcomes.

How does a definition of information literacy lead to goals and outcomes? Let's say, for example, part of your agreed-upon definition of information literacy says something about the ability to apply information. From such a statement you can formulate a goal:

> When students graduate they will be able to effectively apply information in written and oral communications regardless of whether those communications are for educational, business, civic, or personal purposes.

While the above goal is likely more specific than what would be stated in a definition of information literacy, it is still somewhat general. That is all right, however, because from such a goal planners can produce a list of concrete, measurable outcomes. A few sample outcomes that could emerge from the above goal include:

- Students will understand why research and the citing of sources is an important part of effective written and oral communication.
- Students will be able to effectively employ quotations and paraphrases to support positions they take in their written and oral communications.
- Students will be able to properly cite any sources used in their written and oral communications.

Although the list of outcomes could go on, the point here is that concrete outcomes like those listed here have real meaning to frontline instructors. Supplied with a list of expected outcomes, instructors know exactly what their students need to learn and can develop lesson plans that will make that learning a reality.

2 TEACHING STUDENTS (AND OTHERS) WHY INFORMATION IS NOT ALL "JUST A CLICK AWAY"

Years ago Charles Schultz drew a *Peanuts* cartoon in which know-it-all Lucy leads Linus around the neighborhood filling his head with all sorts of misinformation. Charlie Brown ruefully observes that Linus is going to have to go to school for an extra 12 years just to unlearn everything Lucy has taught him. Sometimes it seems like the biggest part of teaching electronic information literacy is un-teaching all the misinformation about information that students have absorbed from the media, from their peers, and, yes, even from their teachers.

If the forces of misinformation about information had a banner under which to rally, it would no doubt sport the cyberspace bromide "Just a Click Away." To see just how pervasive the "Just A Click Away" mythology has become, go to your favorite Web search engine and search *"Just a Click Away"* as a phrase. How many tens of thousand of hits do you get? Next, think about what "just a click away" implies when applied to serious research. It reduces research—which ranks among the most challenging and stimulating parts of any intellectual endeavor—to not much more than an involuntary muscle twitch, something that anyone not actually in a coma could probably manage. Specifically, the "Just a Click Away" mythology implies:

- All information is easily findable and instantly available on the Web.
- All information is freely available to everybody (or at least available for a small fee *if* you subscribe to *our* ISP, database, homework-helper service, online library, etc.).
- Accessing information requires next-to-no effort (mental or physical).
- Once you have accessed information, there is no need to evaluate it or think about how you will apply it to fill your information need.

Why do students (and others) latch on to the "Just a Click Away" mythology and all the other unreal notions about information this phrase embodies?

Wishful Thinking: Shouldn't I be able to sit down at my computer at 10 p.m. and, before Dave has done his top-ten list, gather all the information I need to write my term paper. Which, like, isn't even due until tomorrow?

Hype: Ads for Internet-service providers, computer manufacturers, and online-information services promise that whatever it is they are selling will be my ticket to all the information I'll ever need. That's true, right?

Hubris: I'm a rebel. I'm a rule breaker. I've been using computers since I was two. I could probably hack into the Pentagon if I wanted to. Libraries? I don't need no stinking libraries.

Convenience: Going to the library to check out books or to use electronic resources that are unavailable from my home computer is a time-consuming pain in the neck. Plus, with information I find on Web sites I can search for keywords and cut and paste quotations—try doing that with a book or magazine.

Appearance of Thoroughness: If I type "euthanasia" into my favorite search engine, I get over 90,000 hits. Surely that's everything there is to know on the subject and more than enough for a lousy ten-page paper?

Ignorance (Type One): You mean that there is lots of information that is not on the Web and that some of what *is* on the Web is not available to everybody?

Ignorance (Type Two): I use the Web because I don't know how to do research any other way.

Making the Grade with the Web

Students sometimes make the following argument:

I do all my research by surfing the Web. The grades I get are acceptable to me. Why should I change the way I do research?

In responding to this argument, instructors could remind students that they might get *better* grades if they expanded their research repertoires (though this line of reasoning does not work on students who get straight A's). But an even better counter argument is to point out to students that what is good enough for making the grade in school may not be good enough for real life. Illustrative examples:

You are an engineering major who is able to pass your course work using whatever information you can pull up in search of *Google*. Great. After graduation, you become a structural engineer involved in the design of a mile-long suspension bridge. Are you willing to trust the lives of the people who will drive on that bridge to whatever information you happen to pull up on a Web search engine?

For your Introduction to Health Sciences class, you are assigned a five-page paper about breast cancer. Your research consists of 15 minutes of scanning through sites listed on *Yahoo!* You get an A on your paper. Congratulations. A few years later your mother is diagnosed with breast cancer. Would you want her to make life-or-death health choices based on what you can find on *Yahoo!?*

WHAT CAN LIBRARIANS DO TO COUNTERACT ALL THIS MISINFORMATION?

FIRST, DO NOT APPEAR TO BE ANTI-NET

It is crucial that librarians not come off as neo-Luddites who favor the hard old way of doing things over the easy new way. Of course most librarians are anything but anti-Net, but it is easy to sound like an enemy of progress when you do not buy the hype and express genuine concern about such phenomena as:

- Student researchers using whatever information they find on the Web with no more discrimination than PacMan gobbling up power dots.
- Student work that is supported by unreliable sources and/or rife with cut-and-paste plagiarism.
- The rumblings of politicians and administrators who say things like "Why do we need the library when everything is on the Internet?"

One way to not sound anti-Net is to emphasize just how important the Net is to libraries. Some examples you might point to include:

- Librarians were Internet pioneers, developing some of the earliest Web sites and making library public-access catalogs freely accessible on the Internet long before there was such a thing as the Web.
- The phrase (and metaphor of) "surfing the Net" was coined in 1992 by Jean Armour Polly, a librarian.
- Many "free" databases and full-text resources available to end users are, in fact, paid for out of library budgets and maintained by library staff. You can impress and amaze students by simply informing them of the actual subscription rates for a few of the pricier databases and full-text resources the library provides at no charge to the end user.
- Librarians actively contribute useful content to the Web. You might illustrate this by pointing to various library-based digitization projects such as *American Memory* (memory.loc.gov/), *JSTOR* (www.jstor.org/), or perhaps some digitization project that is the work of a library in your local area.
- Librarians and library associations are strong opponents of Net censorship and advocates for the free-flow of electronic information. To illustrate this point (and educate your students at the same time), you could point to something like the American Library Association's stand on UCITA (www.ala.org/washoff/ucita/index.html).
- Many librarians are very good at finding information on the Web, so consulting with a librarian may not only save you time, but also result in better information.

USE SPECIFIC EXAMPLES TO DEMYTHOLOGIZE THE NET

Perhaps the best way to help students develop a realistic concept of the Net is to present specific, up-to-date examples that expose the "just a click away" mythology as the fraud that it is. The following examples are merely illustrative. When using specific examples, it is essential to choose examples that are up-to-date and also relevant to your students' information needs.

Exhibit A: Not All Information on the Web Is Free

Pay a visit to the pricing information found at the *Lexis-Nexis Web Site* (www.lexis-nexis.com) so that students can see that even if the information really is just a click (or two) away, they may have to break out the credit card before making that final click.

For another example of information that is not free, access the home page of a proprietary journal or magazine to which your library does not have full-text access. Try to access one or more articles to illustrate that, even though the publication is on the Web, the full text is not just a click away. The more desirable this publication is to your audience, the better. This kind of example makes a good segue into such topics as copyright, the cost of information, and how your library decides what it can or cannot subscribe to in electronic format.

Exhibit B: Some Information Is Secret

The pharmaceutical company Pfizer makes hundreds of millions of dollars every year on the popular drug Viagra. Is it likely that the formula for making Viagra would be "just a click away"? If you search the Web and happen to find something that purports to be the formula for Viagra, how likely would it be that the information you find is the real formula?

The government, as well as corporations, keeps some information secret. For years, the government put information about nuclear power plants on various Web sites. Some months after the September 11, 2001 attacks on New York and Washington, President Bush ordered this information removed on the grounds that it might aid terrorists. (Some critics suggested that the information was really removed out of fear that it might aid environmentalists.) Obviously, there are unknown amounts of secret government information that will never be "just a click away."

Exhibit C: Not All Information on the Web Is Good Information

Of course there is plenty of bad information on the Web, and the best way to illustrate this is to find a site with information that flies in the face of an established, universally accepted fact. A visit to sites that provide "evidence" that the Earth is flat or that "prove" that the manned Moon landings were faked provide good examples of bad information.

Exhibit D: What Is Free Today May Not Be Free Tomorrow
This is not such an easy one to demonstrate, but almost everyone who has used the Web for a few years knows of a Web site that once provided information free of charge but which now requires some type of payment. One recent example is *Vindigo* (www.vindigo.com), which at one time allowed users of palm-top devices to download Zagat restaurant reviews for free but which now charges for that information. Another example is found on the Web site of *CNN* (www.cnn.com), a site which at one time provided free access to news video but which now requires visitors to subscribe before they can access video.

Horses, Putting the Cart Before

In an article entitled "'Education' Governor Axes State Library," Michael Schuyler reports on an ultimately unsuccessful attempt to close the Washington State Library as part of a budget-cutting exercise. Schuyler writes:

> When talking with a library staff member, one legislator said he never used the library anymore because everything was online anyway. When asked how he got his online information he proudly showed how he could go to the *Find-It* Web site and get everything he needed. This is a Government Information Locator Service (GILS), so that's probably true. However, Find-It was invented, funded, and is run by the Washington State Library.

Schuyler's anecdote is a powerful illustration of the way in which unrealistic notions about the electronic information can totally flip-flop reality and is reminiscent of an older (and possibly apocryphal) story of a library patron who, while complaining to a librarian about government waste, gripes: "Why does the government spend all that tax money to conduct a census every ten years when you can just look up the data in the *Statistical Abstract*?" (Schuyler, Michael. "Education Governor Axes State Library." *Computers in Libraries*. April 2002. 22:4, 36–37.)

3 TEACHING STUDENTS THE ECONOMICS AND THE ETHICS OF ELECTRONIC INFORMATION

ECONOMICS

As suggested in Chapter 2, "Teaching Students (and Others) Why It Is Not All 'Just a Click Away,'" a lack of understanding of the economic realities of electronic information contributes to an overall unrealistic view of electronic information. Providing a good dose of economic reality is, therefore, an important part of promoting electronic information literacy.

THE MYTH OF FREE INFORMATION

The existence of huge amounts of "free electronic information" on the Net is the number one reason why unrealistic ideas about the economics of information are so prevalent. When you can go on the Net and find seemingly limitless amounts of information there for the taking, it fosters a mindset that undervalues information. This is unfortunate, though understandable: If we lived in a world where you could walk out your door any day of the year and gather up all the apples you wanted, it would be difficult to imagine why anyone would pay for an apple.

However, there are quotation marks around the words *free electronic information* in the above paragraph because it can be demonstrated that there is no such thing as free information, electronic or otherwise. Take the following hypothetical example:

> Jane decides to interview her grandmother about her homefront experiences as a teenager during World War II. Jane then writes up the results of the interview, scans

several photographs of her grandmother from the war period, and puts the whole thing on the Web for any and all to access. Isn't this free information? Free to the end user, yes. Free in the economic sense, no. First of all, both Jane and her grandmother did the work of turning memories into information; Jane then did the work of putting this information on the Web. Work has economic value even if, as in this case, it is freely donated. Secondly, somebody has to pay the cost of keeping Jane's site on the Web. If Jane's site is on a commercial ISP, then either Jane or a benefactor has to pay ISP fees; if Jane's site is on a free ISP, then the provider of the free service (school, government agency, etc.) has to pay. Even if Jane owns and maintains her own Web server, there are such costs as obtaining a domain name and paying the electric bill that must be met. In any of these scenarios, if all the sundry costs of keeping Jane's site viable are not paid by *someone*, her site, along with the "free information" it contains, will vanish.

Instead of thinking of the information found on so many Web sites as free information, it would be more accurate to take a cue from the open-source software movement and think of such information as "open-access information." Since such a paradigm shift is unlikely, it is important that instructors use real-world examples to demonstrate that open-access information is not really free information. Just a few prominent examples include:

American Memory (memory.loc.gov)
This marvelous site—filled with documents, photographs, artwork, and sound recordings relating to the history of the United States—is absolutely free to end users, but the Library of Congress (which is supported by U.S. tax dollars) pays the cost of digitizing the information contained on the site and serving it over the Web. Even with the support of tax dollars, *American Memory* is economically feasible only because the information contained on the site is free of copyright restrictions.

Project Gutenberg (promo.net/pg)
Through the use of volunteers, *Project Gutenberg* makes available the texts of thousands of books at no charge to the end user. The texts are typed or scanned by volunteers and then served over the Web through the gen-

erosity of the several dozen mirror sites that support *Project Gutenberg*. The texts made available through *Project Gutenberg* are copyright free because (with very few exceptions) they are old enough to be in the public domain. Although there is no charge to access the *Project Gutenberg* texts, the dollar value of the work done by volunteers plus the value of the computer services donated by the mirror sites runs well into the millions of dollars.

Ford Motor Company (www.ford.com)

Ford Motor Company (just one example of thousands of similar corporate Web sites) provides information about Ford products and the company itself. Though free to end users, the cost of this site and the information it provides is paid for by the Ford Motor Company (which, of course, obtains its funds from consumers and investors). Ford Motor Company takes on the cost of providing open-access information on its Web site in the hope that the availability of this information will increase sales of Ford products and increase investment in Ford stock to an extent that more than pays for the cost of the Web site.

Encyclopaedia Britannica (www.britannica.com)

Supported in part by advertising, the online version of *Encyclopaedia Britannica* provides open access to information on a variety of topics. In addition to its open-access service, *Encyclopaedia Britannica* also offers a fee-based service that is available by subscription. The fee-based service is free of advertisements and provides access to additional information not available to users of the open-access service. Interestingly, the pop-up advertisements on *Encyclopaedia Britannica* serve the dual purpose of bringing in advertising revenue while, at the same time, motivating users to subscribe in order to rid themselves of the annoyance the pop-up ads create.

The Dot.Com Bust

Unlike the examples above, this is a generic example. In the late 1990s, hundreds of Internet start-up companies were launched using the following business model:

1. Our Web site will draw visitors by offering some type of free information.

2. We will make millions selling advertisements on our Web site.

The fact that nearly every start-up based on this model was out of business by the end of 2000 should be proof enough to anyone that free information is not free. It certainly is proof enough to the thousands who invested in these short-lived, poorly thought-out companies.

PROPRIETARY INFORMATION RESOURCES

Key to understanding the economics of information is understanding the difference between proprietary and nonproprietary information resources. Privately owned and controlled, proprietary-information resources require some type of payment before they may be accessed. Though proprietary information resources employ a variety of payment schemes (with new schemes cropping up all the time), payments are typically made either in the form of subscriptions or on a per-item-accessed basis. These payments may be made by individuals acting on their own behalf or by an institution (such as a library) acting on behalf of a designated group of authorized end users. Examples of proprietary information resources include:

- **Electronic full-text books and periodicals**
  These may be for-profit commercial publications (typically books, newspapers, magazines, and some scholarly journals), or they may be nonprofit publications (typically journals published by scholarly societies). It is worth noting that nonprofit electronic information is not necessarily low-cost information: some nonprofit electronic journals have stunningly high subscription fees.
- **For-profit bibliographic or full-text databases**
  Well-known examples include the *Ovid* databases, *LexisNexis*, *ScienceDirect*, *Ideal*, *EBSCOhost*, *MD Consult*, and so on. Information resources of this type typically require a subscription.
- **Fee-based information services**
  This category includes Web sites selling everything from personal credit histories to term papers. Fee-based information services typically charge end users for each transaction, though subscription-based access may also be available.

Proprietary vs. Nonproprietary Electronic Information: The *MEDLINE* Example

Produced by the National Library of Medicine (an agency of the United States government), *MEDLINE* indexes over 4,600 biomedical journals and is the premier database for the health sciences.

Since 1996, the National Library of Medicine has offered open access to *MEDLINE* through its *PubMed* service. By going to the *PubMed* home page (www.pubmed.gov), anyone may search the complete, up-to-date *MEDLINE* database with no restrictions and at no charge. (Please note: While the information on *PubMed* is open access, it is not free. United States tax dollars pay for *PubMed*.)

Even though *PubMed* provides open access to everyone, there still exist several proprietary versions of *MEDLINE* which require a paid subscription, the leading example of which is *Ovid MEDLINE*. Since the *MEDLINE* database is virtually the same in both the *Ovid* and *PubMed* versions, why would anyone (or any library) pay to use the proprietary *Ovid MEDLINE*? The key argument in favor of *Ovid MEDLINE* is that it adds value to the *MEDLINE* database; in particular, advocates argue that the *Ovid MEDLINE* search interface is more powerful than the *PubMed* interface.

Which version is better is not really important to the issue at hand. What is important is that *PubMed* and *Ovid MEDLINE* can be used by instructors to illustrate the difference between proprietary and nonproprietary electronic information resources.

For example, instructors at institutions with access to *Ovid MEDLINE* can do identical searches in both *Ovid MEDLINE* and *PubMed* to demonstrate that the two databases are, with very few exceptions, identical in content. Then, the instructor can tell students how much the institution pays for *Ovid MEDLINE* access and use this as a jumping-off point to discuss the difference between proprietary and nonproprietary information.

For a different example, instructors at institutions without access to *Ovid MEDLINE* can demonstrate that, while it is not possible to access *Ovid MEDLINE* from their institution, access to *PubMed* is freely available. Again, this can be a jumping-off point for discussion.

Although institutions such as schools and libraries often subscribe to proprietary electronic information resources on behalf of their clienteles, their clients are frequently unaware that the resources they routinely access are 1) proprietary, and 2) not available to everyone, everywhere. The survival of libraries may well depend on information literacy instructors making library clients aware of the fact that many of their favorite resources are proprietary as well as aware of the fact that some institution (often the library) is paying for their "free" access. While they are at it, instructors should also indulge in a bit of Econ-101 by explaining that having an institution (such as a library) purchase and manage one online subscription for everyone is more cost effective than everyone going out and buying individual subscriptions.

DO YOU GET WHAT YOU PAY FOR?

Is electronic information that you pay for better than open-access information? The answer to this question is: Sometimes yes, sometimes no.

In the case of the online *Encyclopaedia Britannica* discussed above, just about everyone would agree that the proprietary service (no advertising and more information) is better than the open-access service. On the other hand, with the *Ovid MEDLINE* (proprietary) versus *PubMed* (open access) example discussed in the sidebar, no one can argue that the information in the proprietary version is better (both databases are virtually identical), though of course some do argue that the *Ovid MEDLINE* interface is the better of the two and therefore worth the cost of a subscription. The *Project Gutenberg* e-texts provide yet another interesting example because the answer depends on the end user's information need. While the quality of the *Project Gutenberg* e-texts is good enough for the casual reader, no professional scholar would use a *Project Gutenberg* e-text as the basis for serious research. The reason for this is that the quality control practiced by *Project Gutenberg*'s volunteer editors is extremely unlikely to equal the quality control exercised by professional scholarly editors working for established publishing houses. Any serious scholar, therefore, would be willing to pay for an authoritative text (whether in print or electronic format) rather than settling for a free (but unauthoritative) *Project Gutenberg* e-text.

As you look at more examples of proprietary versus open-access electronic information resources, it becomes clear that the question of which is better must be answered on a case-by-case basis. Indeed, answering this question is yet another step in the overall process of evaluating electronic information, a subject which is covered in depth in Chapter 5, "Teaching Students How to Evaluate Electronic Information."

ELECTRONIC INFORMATION IS BIG BUSINESS

Money talks, and one way to catch the attention of those who underestimate the economic value of information is to "show them the money." As any librarian who writes checks to electronic information providers can testify, electronic information is expensive. The examples which follow give some sense of how much money is being made by those who sell electronic information. (Please note: Though the dollar figures given below give a good sense of just how valuable electronic information is, in some cases the figures represent income generated by sales of both print and electronic information as well as by related information businesses.)

Reed Elsevier
The parent company of such information resources as *ScienceDirect*, *Embase*, and *LexisNexis*, *Reed Elsevier* employs over 37,000 people worldwide and, in 2001, reported net profits of approximately $929,048,000 with total revenues of approximately $6,609,246,000.

EBSCO Information Services
EBSCO is the parent company for a number of information businesses, including the *EBSCOhost* electronic databases. *Forbes Magazine* ranks *EBSCO* among the top 200 privately held companies. *EBSCO's* annual sales began topping the $1 billion mark in 1997.

Wolters Kluwer
With 20,000 employees worldwide, *Wolters Kluwer* is the parent company of such online information providers as *Ovid Technologies* and *Lippincott, Williams & Wilkins*. In 2001 *Wolters Kluwer* reported a net income of approximately $12,300,000 on sales of $3,254,521,000.

Bertelsman Media Worldwide
Bertelsman Media Worldwide subsidiaries include *Random House* and *Bertelsman Springer* (publisher of over 400 electronic journals and 300 other electronic information products). In fiscal year 2000–2001, *Bertelsman Media Worldwide* had a net income of approximately $853,212,000 and employed some 82,000 persons worldwide.

Yet another way to demonstrate the size of the electronic-publishing business is to divulge to students the cost of some of the electronic information resources to which your institution subscribes. Often, the most accurate and up-to-date source for such figures will be your library's acquisitions department.

ETHICS

Wherever there are economic considerations, there will be ethical considerations as well. While the ever-changing world of electronic information makes the border between what is ethical and unethical difficult to map, instructors need to instill at least a sense of ethical boundaries in users of electronic information. In a nutshell, the ethics of electronic information can be summed up by the three *C*'s: cheating, copyright, and crime.

CHEATING

Since the late 1990s, the academic world has been in a tizzy about online cheating. It seems as if every other issue of the *Chronicle of Higher Education* has a feature or opinion piece with something to say about students plagiarizing from the Web, and searches in library science and education databases turn up a spate of recent articles on the topic. Though the majority opinion among academics is that online cheating is a scourge, there are a few voices suggesting that in a Net-dominated, postmodern world, the very definition of plagiarism is due for serious revision. Outside of academia, the popular media have picked up the story, often emphasizing its "what's-wrong-with-kids-today/end-of-Western-civilization-as-we-know-it" elements. While online cheating is a problem, it is important to put it into perspective.

For starters, students have always cheated. Long before there was a Web, students cajoled friends or paid strangers to "help" them with their papers. Popular magazines like *Rolling Stone* and *National Lampoon* regularly carried classified ads for "research services" that were no more than term-paper mills. Campus residence houses kept files of previously turned-in papers from which house members routinely plagiarized. Out of ignorance or desperation, students inserted into their own papers unattributed quotations and paraphrases taken from printed books or articles.

Given that cheating has long been an established fact of student life, why the rising concern about the role of the Internet in plagiarism?

Speed: A student who wanted to use the services of a mail-order term-paper mill had to plan at least a few weeks in advance in order to receive the paper on time. This was a serious limiting factor on the success of traditional term-paper mills as the ability to plan in advance has never been a defining characteristic of the typical student who cheats. By resorting to the Web, however, students with credit cards can purchase papers and have them downloaded to their personal computers in a matter of minutes.

Scope: Only a handful of mail-order term-paper mills ever ran classified ads in popular magazines; on the other hand, scores of such services thrive on the Web. There are even term-paper sites that do not charge for the use of their papers, usually because they work on a quasi-*Napster* model in which visitors have to submit a paper of their own before they can access papers submitted by others. In the same vein, students seeking "help" with a paper in the days before the Web were largely limited to friends and acquaintances located on their own campuses; today, students can employ e-mail, online chat rooms, instant messaging, Usenet groups, and the like to seek "help" from people located thousands of miles away.

Cut and Paste: Prior to the spread of electronic information, plagiarizers at least had to go to the trouble of transcribing the words that they copied into their papers. On the Web, the same result can be produced with a couple of clicks of the mouse.

ONLINE PLAGIARISM: THE ROLE OF THE INFORMATION LITERACY PROFESSIONAL

What can information literacy professionals do to combat online plagiarism? One thing they cannot do is fight the battle alone. If classroom instructors are not able and willing to stop online plagiarism, it is not going to stop. However, information literacy professionals can contribute in a number of important ways:

Explain the Concept of Plagiarism

Too often, students are sternly admonished not to plagiarize even though they have little idea of what constitutes plagiarism. Providing students with a clear definition of plagiarism (legal dictionaries are one good source) will help students grasp the concept while reinforcing the point that plagiarism is wrong. Contrasting intentional plagiarism with unintentional plagiarism is also a useful exercise because students often do not know that it is possible to plagiarize unintentionally. Similarly, many students are under the impression that so long as the words on the page are their own, it is not plagiarism; for this reason, it is important that they are taught the concept of paraphrasing and understand that an unattributed paraphrase is just as much plagiarism as an unattributed quotation. On a different tack, presenting examples of what is *not* plagiarism (i.e., the student's original ideas and words, information that falls under the rubric of common knowledge) not only clarifies the concept, but also reduces anxiety by showing students that they do not need to cite every independent clause in their papers in order to avoid plagiarism.

Teach How to Cite Sources

Even if students know when they should cite sources, they sometimes plagiarize because they do not know how to cite. Making students aware of the various style guides (*APA, MLA, Chicago*, etc.) is essential. Citing electronic sources is a special challenge to many students, so conducting real-life exercises in which students locate a variety of online sources and then practice citing them is particularly helpful. A few useful Web sites with information on how to cite sources include:

Purdue University OWL (Online Writing Lab)
Research and Documenting Sources
owl.english.purdue.edu/handouts/research/

University of Illinois Urbana Champaign Library
Guide to Style Manuals: Citing Print & Electronic
Resources
www.library.uiuc.edu/rex/instruction/styleguide.htm

University of North Carolina Chapel Hill
The Writing Center
www.unc.edu/depts/wcweb/

Describe the Penalties
If your institution has a specific policy on plagiarism, be sure to provide a copy of it to students. Policy or not, students should understand that, depending on the circumstances, plagiarism can get you an F, kicked out of school, fired, sued in civil court, or even charged with a crime.

Explain How Easy It Is to Get Caught
Students may think that plagiarism is hard to detect. They may even have successfully passed off plagiarism as their own work in the past. But they do need to understand that no plagiarist gets away with it forever. There are a number of tip-offs indicating that a work may be plagiarized:

- The quality of the work is markedly better than what the student has turned in previously.
- The understanding of the topic evidenced in the work is much deeper than what the student has demonstrated in class or on previous assignments.
- There are no recent sources cited in the work, suggesting that the work was created at some time in the past rather than specifically for the assignment at hand.
- The topic of the paper varies (a little or a lot) from what was covered in the course or from the topic the student proposed to write about prior to the paper coming due.
- The style of some sentences or paragraphs in the work is markedly different from the rest of the work.

None Dare Call It Cheating—Or Would They?

How is the Web changing the way we think about academic honesty? Here is a hypothetical example:

A student is assigned to write a research paper on the Civil War battle of Shiloh. He goes to *amazon.com* and searches the word *shiloh*. One of the hits—James L. McDonough's *Shiloh: In Hell Before Night*—invites you to "Look Inside." With one click, the student is able to access 18 full-text pages from the book, including a lengthy excerpt. The student finds a suitable quotation among the excerpt pages, incorporates it into his paper, and cites the quotation as if it had been taken from the printed version of the book. Is this cheating?

Professor A: The student didn't actually read the printed book, but his citation would lead you to believe he had. If that's not cheating, at least it is dishonest.

Professor B: But if the online version is exactly the same as the print version, what difference does it make?

Professor A: The difference is the student didn't read the entire book. Reading a few sample pages selected by the sales department at *amazon.com* is no different than reading *Cliff Notes*.

Professor B: Come on, scholars cite information from books all the time without reading the entire book.

Professor A: It is different if you have the entire contents book at your disposal. Then, at least, there is the *possibility* of reading the entire work.

Professor B: So would you be satisfied if, for form's sake, the student had dropped by the library and flipped through the printed copy before he turned in his paper?

Professor A: Of course not. You know I'm never satisfied with anything.

One effective way to demonstrate how easy plagiarism is to detect is to show how an instructor can paste a line or two of suspected text into an Internet search engine and, with luck, pull up the source of the text. Students also need to know that their instructors are aware of such Web sites as www.schoolsucks.com and www.cheathouse.com. Visiting a few such sites during an instruction session and discussing their downsides (in-

Intellectual Property
Increasingly, the phrase *intellectual property* is used in connection with copyright, and this usage can be confusing. The idea of intellectual property encompasses not only copyright, but also ideas, inventions, trade secrets, processes, computer programs, data, formulas, patents, and trademarks. While the law varies, much of what applies to copyright generally applies to intellectual property. For example, mounting a trademarked image on your Web site would expose you to much the same legal liability you would face if you mounted a copyrighted image.

cluding that fact that the quality of many of the papers available from such sites is too low to earn a decent grade) could do a lot to discourage the cheater who thinks that online term-paper mills are closely guarded secrets known only to students. Similarly, visits to anti-plagiarism sites such as www.turnitin.com may also serve as a deterrent.

COPYRIGHT

Copyright is one of the most contentious issues of the Information Age. On the one hand, a large segment of the population buys into the idea that freely distributing electronic files (which may contain copyrighted music, text, artwork, etc.) is sharing, not theft. On the other hand, industries that rely on intellectual property as their main source of profit have successfully lobbied the U.S. federal government into passing copyright laws that increasingly favor the interests of the creators of intellectual property over the interests of the general public. Whether you are a die-hard *Napster* junkie or a recording industry executive, an understanding of copyright law is an essential part of electronic information literacy.

WHAT DO ELECTRONIC INFORMATION LITERATES NEED TO KNOW ABOUT COPYRIGHT?

DEFINITION AND PURPOSE OF COPYRIGHT

A legal dictionary is a good source for a general definition of copyright. The purpose of copyright is harder to pin down than a definition. Article I, Section 8, Clause 8 of the United States Constitution gets at the purpose of copyright by stating that Congress shall have the power "to promote the Progress of Science and useful Arts, by securing for limited times to Authors and Inventors the exclusive Right to their respective Writings and Discoveries." To put this idea in more contemporary terms, what the Constitution says is that the purpose of copyright is to balance the rights of the creator of intellectual property with society's need to progress. On the one hand, if copyright law does not give creators sufficient protection, then it takes away the incentive to create. Why would musicians, for example, want to write songs and record albums if the copyright law is so weak that they cannot make any money from their creative output? On the other hand, copyright law must not so favor the creators of information that the resulting monopolistic control of information and ideas stifles further creativity. Imagine, for example, a copyright law so restrictive that facts—such as the score of a baseball game or the price of a stock—were protected by copyright and could not be disseminated without the permission of their owners.

HISTORY AND CONTROVERSIES

Understanding the history of copyright is necessary to appreciate the full complexity of the subject. The Association of Research Libraries' Web page *Timeline: A History of Copyright in the U.S.* (arl.cni.org/info/frn/copy/timeline.html) gives a good overview of the history of copyright; in addition, you can turn to any of the many published books that treat the history of copyright.

Examining copyright controversies—especially current ones—is an excellent way to increase understanding and awareness of copyright. The *Napster* controversy of 2000–2001 stands out because it received so much news coverage and impacted the lives of many high-school and college students. A good source on the Web for copyright controversies is the *copyright website* (www.benedict.com).

<hr>

Recommended Reading
For the lay reader, one of the best recent books on copyright in the electronic environment is Gretchen McCord Hoffmann's *Copyright in Cyberspace: Questions & Answers for Librarians* (New York: Neal-Schuman, 2001).

WHAT IS PROTECTED BY COPYRIGHT?

Before getting down to specifics, it is worth noting that creators do not have to register their intellectual property for it to be copyrighted. Registration of copyright comes in to play only if the copyright is violated and the owner wishes to seek punitive damages, as opposed to just actual damages, in civil court. Without oversimplifying, it is safe to say that the following types of intellectual property are protected by copyright law:

- Literary works.
- Music (including lyrics).
- Dramatic works.
- Dance and pantomime.
- Visual works (pictures, graphics, and sculptures).
- Audiovisual works (including motion pictures and sound recordings).
- Architectural works.
- Computer software.

PUBLIC DOMAIN

Students need to understand that works in the public domain are not protected by copyright. When copyrights (and patents) expire, intellectual property enters the public domain where it may be used freely by all. One trend of recent copyright legislation is to lengthen the amount of time that intellectual property remains under copyright. The article "New Rules for Using Public Domain Materials" (copylaw.com/new_articles/PublicDomain.html) does a good job of explaining the complicated process of determining whether or not a work is in the public domain. Also useful for leaning about public domain issues is the Web site of The *Center for the Public Domain* (www.centerforthepublicdomain.org).

Besides works on which copyright has expired, works created by the United States government go into the public domain with no waiting period.

Elvis and Nixon

On the Web, one of the most commonly seen photographs of Elvis Presley shows him receiving an honorary Drug Enforcement Administration badge from President Richard Nixon. While this photograph has an ironic appeal, its popularity has more to do with copyright than with camp. Because the original photograph was created by the United States government, it is one of the few noncopyrighted photographs of Elvis. It is also one of the few images of Elvis that is not controlled by Elvis Presley Enterprises, the business arm of the Presley estate. (For a succinct account of how Elvis Presley Enterprises came to control the image of Elvis Presley, see Gwynne, S.C. "Love Me Legal Tender: If Elvis Revolutionized Pop, His Estate Revolutionized Celebrity Marketing." *Time*, August 4, 1997, 62–67.)

Which brings up an important point: Copyright is generally protected by the copyholder, not by any policing agency. Because Elvis Presley Enterprises is vigilant about protecting both its copyright and trademarks, the owner of a Web page that violates either is likely to get a cease-and-desist letter from company lawyers. In contrast, if a Web page contains copyrighted or trademarked material belonging to a person or group that does not make the effort to protect its intellectual property, the owner of the Web page might never be ordered to remove the offending material.

Copyright violations are almost always a civil matter and are normally resolved through litigation or the threat of litigation. However, recent legislation in the United States has made a felony of commercial copyright violations that total more than ten copies and have a value over $2,500. This means that if you made 300 CD copies of *Elvis: Aloha from Hawaii* and sold them for $10 each, you could face criminal as well as civil charges. For another example, the Digital Millennium Copyright Act makes it a crime to intentionally circumvent copyright-protection technology that controls access to a copyrighted work.

FAIR USE

As students learn about copyright laws, they often wonder if the work they do for school assignments might violate those laws. In all but exceptional cases, school assignments are protected by the fair-use exemptions to the copyright law. While the four factors listed below are used to determine what is or is not fair use, they represent a continuum rather than cut-and-dried rules. The truly contentious fair-use cases end up being decided in the courts.

1. Is copyrighted work being used for nonprofit educational purposes?
    Nonprofit, educational use is very likely to be considered fair use.
2. What is the nature of the copyrighted work?
    In general, the use of published, factual copyrighted works is more likely to be considered fair-use exemption than is the use of unpublished or imaginative works.
3. How much of the copyrighted work is being used in relation to the work as a whole?
    Excerpting one paragraph from a novel is more likely to be considered fair use than is excerpting several chapters. However, excerpting one line from a three-line poem might not be considered fair use.
4. Does the use harm the potential market for, or value of, the copyrighted work?
    This is a judgment call if there ever was one.

The United States Copyright Office's *Fair Use* (www.copyright.gov/fls/fairuse.html) is a good source of basic information on fair use, while University of Texas System's *Crash Course in Copyright* (www.utsystem.edu/OGC/IntellectualProperty/cprtindx.htm) provides a more in-depth treatment of the topic.

A Few Good Web Sites for Copyright Information

University of Illinois Urbana Champaign Library
Copyright
www.library.uiuc.edu/rex/erefs/copyright.htm

Stanford University Libraries
Copyright & Fair Use
fairuse.stanford.edu/

Library of Congress
United States Copyright Office
www.loc.gov/copyright/

World Intellectual Property Organization
www.wipo.org/

CRIME

The information literate individual understands that the accessing and/or distributing of electronic information can go beyond the moral sphere and into the criminal. The major online crimes include:

- Committing fraud or theft.
- Violating copyright for commercial purposes (more than ten copies worth more than $2,500).
- Distributing or receiving child pornography.
- Threatening or harassing someone.
- Releasing viruses or worms.
- Gaining illegal access to computer systems (hacking).
- Using computers to circumvent local laws. (Online gambling is a leading example of this type of crime.)

As with most crimes, claiming ignorance of the law is not an excuse. Nor is one likely to be let off by claiming "I was just kidding around" or "I'm only a student" or "I didn't mean to do any harm." When it comes to computer crime, even something done in fun can end up bringing serious consequences.

UNETHICAL BEHAVIOR IS WRONG

As a final word on ethics, it does not hurt to remind students that some behavior is just wrong. The following examples illustrate why ethics are important in the realm of information and research, regardless of whether or not the information is obtained offline or in print, and regardless of whether or not the action is actually against the law:

A securities analyst owns shares in an Internet startup company called WhatBusinessPlan.com. The analyst's research indicates that this company is heading straight for bankruptcy, but he goes ahead and gives WhatBusinessPlan.com a high rating so that the value of the shares he owns will rise. Based on the analyst's recommendation, individual investors, mutual funds, and pension funds purchase stock in WhatBusinessPlan.com.

An architect is designing a skyscraper to be built in the Los Angeles area. Two of the sources he consults indicate that his design will survive a serious earthquake, but a number of other equally reliable sources indicate that it might not. The architect decides to ignore the bad news and present his design as seismically safe.

A medical doctor is considering the best course of treatment for a patient with a life-threatening illness. A review of the research indicates that Drug A is probably the best treatment, with Drug B running a close second. However, the doctor chooses to prescribe Drug B because its manufacturer is paying her way to a medical conference in Hawaii.

4 TEACHING STUDENTS THE ESSENTIALS OF ELECTRONIC SEARCHING AND INFORMATION RETRIEVAL

ELECTRONIC SEARCHING: A HARD SELL

On any given day, the majority of automobile drivers manage to get from Point A to Point B without incident. Even so, many drivers would agree with the following statement: "There are a lot of drivers on the road who could use more driver's education."

However, most drivers would *not* agree with the statement, "I am among those drivers who need more education." Most drivers are, in fact, so convinced that they know how to drive well that the only thing that can prompt them to take more driver's education is a court order.

In most states and provinces, librarians cannot threaten people with fines and jail time for refusing to attend sessions on electronic searching. Yet most people who do electronic searching could use some instruction on the subject. This means that instructors must not only provide instruction, they must also sell the need for it. Even when students are required to attend an instruction session that covers electronic searching—the educational equivalent of being forced to take defensive driving to clear up a traffic ticket—the instruction will not be effective if the students firmly believe that such instruction is a waste of their time.

WHY EFFECTIVE ELECTRONIC SEARCHING IS NOT AS EASY AS IT SEEMS

One way to sell instruction is to demonstrate to students that there is a significant difference between quick-and-dirty electronic searching (which just about anyone can do) and effective electronic searching (which requires knowledge and practice). Once again, real examples are most convincing.

THE QUICK-AND-DIRTY SEARCH

First of all, it is only fair to admit to students that quick-and-dirty electronic searching works fine in some situations. Example:

1. You need the phone number for Movies 12, a cinema in Columbus, Ohio.
2. In either a Web search engine or the address/location bar of your Web browser you type:
   movies 12 columbus ohio
3. The search results appear, you click a link or two, and the phone number is yours.

The above search is quick-and-dirty, but because it quickly retrieves the needed information, it is effective.

On the other hand, as information needs become more complex, quick-and-dirty searches become less effective. The reason for this is that the computers that power search engines are simply high-speed matching machines that do not understand meaning. Perhaps advances in artificial intelligence will change this, but for the time being the average searcher is stuck with using computers that do not think. If, for instance, in the Movies 12 example given above the searcher had been a little more sloppy and simply typed:

movies columbus

the search would have retrieved hundreds of hits on Web pages dealing with (among other subjects):

- Various movies about the explorer Christopher Columbus.
- The 1969 film *Goodbye, Columbus*.

- Chris Columbus (director of *Harry Potter*, *Mrs. Doubtfire*, *Home Alone*, etc.).
- Movie theaters in Columbus (Ohio, Georgia, etc.).

The number of hits retrieved by searching **movies columbus** is so high that the chances of quickly finding the desired phone number would be greatly reduced. All of which should bring up the question, "Why is it so hard for computers to understanding meaning?" There are a number of reasons:

Words Have More Than One Meaning

The word *columbus* signifies the explorer; the movie director; any number of less famous people with the name "Columbus"; and various cities, counties, parks, and streets bearing the name "Columbus." To a computer, however, there is no distinction between any of the above; all are equally *columbus*.

Meanings Have More Than One Word

A place where movies are shown might be called a *cinema*, a *theater*, a *drive-in*, a *multiplex*, or even a *revival house*. Searching one term does not automatically retrieve all the synonyms associated with it, which of course means that a quick-and-dirty search using only one of these terms might not retrieve all useful information.

Besides causing a searcher to miss out on useful information, the synonym used can influence the type of information retrieved. Movies are variously called *movies*, *films*, *flicks*, *motion pictures*, *the cinema*, and *moving pictures*. Searching the phrase *film reviews* instead of *movie reviews* tends to retrieve a more scholarly/intellectual set of hits because film scholars and serious reviewers are more likely to use the word *film* rather than *movie*. Similarly, searching the somewhat archaic term *moving pictures* is likely to retrieve hits dealing with older films and cinema history rather than reviews of the latest Hollywood blockbuster.

As a general strategy, using precise specialist jargon (i.e., *neoplasm* rather than *cancer*, *arbitrage* rather than *takeover*, *rana catesbeiana* rather than *bullfrog*) in searches will retrieve hits that are more scholarly than those retrieved by searching lay language.

Words Have More Than One Spelling

So is it *theater* or *theatre*? Or perhaps it should be *theaters* or *theatres*? While some search engines automatically account for standard variations in spelling and plural/singular forms, searchers should not take this for granted. A related concern is the fact that capitalization (or lack thereof) makes a difference with some search engines. Finally, misspelling a word—let's say *colombus* instead of *Columbus*—may retrieve no hits, irrelevant hits, or hits on information compiled by "experts" who do not know how to spell the subject of their alleged expertise.

The World Is a Complicated Place

In the quick-and-dirty search example given above—**movies 12 columbus ohio**—it is true that after doing the search you could find the desired phone number in just a few clicks. However, the fact is that there are *two* Movies 12 in Columbus, Ohio—one at the Market at Mill Run and the other at Carriage Place. If you did not know that there were two Movies 12 in Columbus, or if you did not pay close attention to the search results, there is a fifty-fifty chance that the quick-and-dirty search would have led you to the wrong phone number.

Figure 4–1: Information Roadblocks

The following text describes common roadblocks encountered by anyone searching for information.

Cost
Cost is a barrier to information whenever the person seeking the information is unwilling or unable to pay the asking price. It is also a barrier when institutions (such as libraries or schools) are unable to afford the cost of providing access to the communities they serve.

Litigation
Lawsuits or court orders can make information disappear. In 2001, the U.S. Department of the Interior's entire Web site went offline for several weeks because of a court order issued during a lawsuit filed against the Department.

Gray Literature
Articles published in mainstream periodicals and books published by established publishing houses are easy to find because they show up in indexes, catalogs, and full-text information databases. Gray literature, on the other hand, is harder to locate because it is out of the scope of the standard tools for locating information. Some examples of gray literature include:

- Unpublished reports produced by governments or private companies.
- Unpublished manuscripts, letters, memoranda, etc.
- Informal electronic documents (including preprints, e-mails, etc.).
- Ephemera (vanity-press publications, photocopy-press publications, posters, flyers, etc.).

Lack of Subject Knowledge
Searchers may be unable to identify information because they do not know the subject in question well enough to be aware of key terms, concepts, and names associated with the subject. Not knowing how to spell key terms or names can be a major information roadblock when searching electronically.

Sometimes a searcher with little subject knowledge might fail to recognize that a piece of information is, in fact, information. For example, a student writing a paper on World War II might not realize that the bundle of V-mail his great uncle sent home from the Pacific is, in fact, a treasure trove of firsthand information on the war.

Date of Creation
Old information can be hard to find because it has not been included in electronic indexes or full-text databases. An article originally published in 1945 is unlikely to turn up (as either a citation or full text) in any electronic information resource, though a citation to it could be found in a printed periodical index from the period.

By the same token, very recently published information can also be hard too find. A journal article published last week almost certainly will not be available via most second-party full-text

---

Figure 4–1: *(continued)*

---

information resources (e.g., *Infotrac*, *Journals@Ovid*, etc.). Increasingly, however, recently published articles are immediately available on the Web site of the journal in which the article was published—available to subscribers, at any rate.

Physical Location
The sole source of the information needed may be a book on the other side of the country. Or the other side of the Atlantic.

Rarity
Even if a researcher crosses the Atlantic to Ireland, it is not likely he or she would be allowed to handle the original *Book of Kells* due to its rarity and consequent value.

Lost Information
When information is gone it is gone. Most of the information from the 1890 census was lost in a fire and nothing will ever bring it back.

Uncollected Information
How many African American students attended the University of Idaho in 1955? How many left-handed hitters played in the American Association baseball league in 1883? How many Uzbek widows under the age of 45 are HIV positive? No matter how desirable a piece of information might be, it cannot be accessed if nobody collected and recorded it.

Historical Distance
A twenty-first-century American might not be able to make sense of the information contained in the diary of an eighteenth-century English clergyman because the events, customs, and places described are unfamiliar. And if that diary were in the form of the original manuscript or a facsimile, the archaic handwriting could be an additional barrier.

Changes in Terminology
For years, the city now known as "Beijing" was commonly referred to as "Peking." The Indian tribe once known as the "Papago" is now more properly referred to (at least by professional historians and anthropologists) as the "Tohono O'odham." Early twentieth-century periodical indexes put citations to articles about people with disabilities under such subject headings as "Spastics" and "Cripples." These and other changes in terminology can make it difficult for present-day researchers to find older information.

False Drops
False drops are irrelevant hits retrieved by a search. For example, a searcher does a Boolean AND search using the words *date* and *rape* hoping to find information on the sex crime of date rape. However, the search results include several false drops that deal with agriculture. Why? Because *date* and *rape*(seed) are both agricultural crops.

Sometimes the sheer number of false drops can overwhelm a search. Trying to search the open

---

Figure 4–1: (continued)

Web for scholarly information on sex is nearly impossible because any Web search that includes the word *sex* will retrieve thousands of hits on pornographic Web sites.

Copyright
Copyright issues can make information inaccessible. In some cases, copyright holders choose to protect their copyright by never allowing their work to appear in electronic format. Sometimes information that was once in electronic format simply disappears. The landmark case of *New York Times Company v Tasini*, which dealt with the right of freelance writers to collect royalties when articles they had originally written for print publication went online, caused thousands of newspaper articles to disappear from the full-text databases that once carried them.

Synonyms
Airplane or *aircraft*? *Sports* or *athletics*? *Handicapped* or *disabled* or *persons with disabilities*? Failing to take into account all possible synonyms can cause a searcher to miss relevant information.

Homonyms
Homonyms such as *Indian* (Native American *or* native of the Indian subcontinent) and *cancer* (the disease *or* the astrological symbol) cause false drops that hinder access to information.

Variant Spellings
Labour or labor? Theater or theatre? As with synonyms, failing to take variant spellings into account can cause a searcher to miss relevant information.

Format
Information on a CD-ROM disc is useless without a CD player. Information on microfilm is useless without a microfilm reader.

Technology
Technology is a barrier both when it is lacking (you cannot use the Web if you do not have the necessary technology) and when those who wish to access information do not know how to use the technology that could give them access.

Language Barriers
Obviously, an article written in Croatian is no use to someone who does not read Croatian or lacks the resources to have the article translated into a familiar language. Also, information is harder to find if it is published in a language different from the language in which the search is conducted. For example, searching the English term *AIDS* is unlikely to retrieve Spanish-language articles about *SIDA*. Other language barriers include:

- Archaic language.
- Jargon, slang, or nicknames.

Figure 4–1: *(continued)*

- Expert or insider language.
- Unfamiliar acronyms or abbreviations.

Accessibility Barriers

Some information may be unusable to persons with disabilities. For example, the information contained in a graphic image may be unusable by a blind person; an audio file may be unusable by a deaf person; and so on.

Lack of Fixed Vocabulary

Properly applied and properly searched, fixed vocabularies enhance both precision and recall. The lack of a fixed vocabulary requires searchers to construct searches that take into account such barriers as variant spellings, synonyms, homonyms, archaic language, foreign language, abbreviations, and so on.

Problems with Fixed Vocabularies

While fixed vocabularies can be a boon to searchers, they also have their limits:

- The searcher does not understand how fixed vocabularies work or does not know how to limit a search to the fixed vocabulary.
- The indexer assigned the wrong fixed-vocabulary term or did not assign enough fixed-vocabulary terms to fully describe the information in question.
- The fixed vocabulary is dated (i.e., old periodical indexes using the fixed-vocabulary term *cripples* instead of *disabled*).
- The fixed vocabulary does not reflect real usage and/or does not provide sufficient cross references to direct the searcher to the correct fixed-vocabulary term. For example, a database might use the fixed-vocabulary term *motion pictures* but fail to provide cross references to it from such common terms as *movies* or *films*.

Secrecy

Chances are good that the formula for Coca-Cola, the private phone number of the President of the United States, or the names of CIA agents currently working in South America will not turn up in any publicly available information resource.

Privacy

Personal health and financial records are leading examples of types of information that are not generally available (and rightly so) thanks to privacy laws.

Private Ownership

Privately owned information may not only be hard to find, the owner of the information may not allow access to it. Even when privately owned information (such as the private papers of a well-known individual) is donated to an archive, there may be restrictions on who may access the information or on when it may be accessed (e.g., no access until 25 years after the death of the individual to whom the papers belonged).

Figure 4–1: *(continued)*

Criminal Statutes
Some types of information are illegal to possess or distribute. Examples include pornographic images of children, plans for building weapons of mass destruction, and (in some countries) writings and images that would be protected as free speech in other countries.

Satire or Parody
Satire or parody can make information hard to find because they disguise the true nature of what is being presented. For a hypothetical example, a political liberal might create a Web site called *www.loveconservatives.com* and employ parody to attack conservative ideology. Someone searching the Web for examples of liberal political activism would be unlikely to locate this site via any type of electronic search. For a list of such sites, see *"Bogus and Questionable Websites"* at www.podbaydoor.com/bogus.htm.

Intentional Deception
The prime example of intentional deception occurs when Web site developers use metadata and other techniques to make their sites turn up as hits in searches on topics that have nothing to do with the sites' real content. This technique is common among pornographic Web sites. Somewhat similar is the practice of Web sites paying fees to Web search engines and directories so that their sites will always rank high following searches using certain keywords even though other sites might offer more relevant information.

Intentional Interference
Information can become unavailable when individuals or groups bring down Web sites, unleash viruses, and otherwise disrupt the flow information across networks.

Censorship
Censorship can hide information. For example, some libraries and computer labs use filtering software to prevent access to objectionable materials. While the intent of filters is to prevent access to pornography, they can unintentionally filter absolutely unobjectionable sites (as when filters prevented Web surfers from accessing information about Super Bowl XXX because anything with *XXX* was automatically filtered). More significantly, some filtering software programs intentionally filter nonpornographic Web sites because the ideas and opinions they express are considered objectionable.

Fads
As topics go in and out of fashion, the amount of information on them increases and decreases. Take for example, the creation of an all-volunteer military for the United States. Because this was an extremely controversial topic in the early-to-mid 1970s, searching databases that cover those years is likely to retrieve more information than would searching databases that cover earlier or later periods.

HOW TO CONDUCT AN EFFECTIVE ELECTRONIC SEARCH

Back in the days when the only electronic-searching game in town was the *DIALOG*-type database that charged for both connection time and (in many cases) the number of hits downloaded, expert searchers would spend a good deal of advance time carefully formulating complex, fully developed searches that they hoped would let them instantly retrieve the information needed and get out of the database fast. Most electronic searchers today have never searched under such limitations and probably never will. Almost without exception, electronic searchers can take all the time they want to conduct a search, a fact which has turned electronic searching from a preplanned, lightning-strike affair into a supremely iterative process.

This does not mean, however, that learning as much as possible about a topic before conducting a search is not an important element of effective searching. For anyone searching an unfamiliar topic, spending a little time with a general or (better yet) subject encyclopedia is well worth the effort. If nothing else, such preliminary study familiarizes searchers with key terms, concepts, and names associated with the topic in question. Simply knowing how to spell key terms and names is a big plus when conducting an electronic search.

THE ITERATIVE SEARCH

If there is one point about doing an electronic search that instructors should hammer home with students it is the point that electronic searching is an iterative process that conforms to the following general pattern:

- Enter a search.
- Get feedback (number and/or relevance of hits).
- Revise the search based on the feedback.
- Enter the revised search.
- Get more feedback.

And on and on the process goes until you find the information you need or quit searching. Given the size and complexity of online information resources, there is no way to know in advance exactly what information a resource might contain; only the iterative search process can reveal that. Even experienced electronic searchers whose years of practice give them a reasonable idea of what to expect from a particular resource do not know for certain what they will find until they have gone through the cycle of search, feedback, and revision.

Figure 4–2: Precision Versus Recall

When searching an electronic information resource, the goal is to strike a balance between precision and recall. Precision means finding the exact information needed with no false drops; terms such as *focusing* and *narrowing* are often used in connection with the concept of precision. Recall means retrieving everything that is relevant to an information need; terms such as *broadening* and *widening* are often used in connection with the concept of recall. Balance between precision and recall is crucial because there are pitfalls inherent in going too far in one direction or the other.

The Precision Pitfall occurs when a search is so exact that it excludes relevant information. For example, imagine constructing a search so precise that it returns only those results which *support* the theory of global warming and excludes all information expressing opposite points of view. While such a loaded search might help a writer churn out an argumentative thesis, this is not honest research.

The Recall Pitfall is something every electronic searcher has experienced. If a search has too little precision and too much recall, it will retrieve an overwhelming number of irrelevant hits. If, for example, a searcher needs scholarly information on the U.S. Civil War battle of Fredericksburg, it does not much matter that a search managed to retrieve 500 scholarly hits on the subject if those hits are buried under 15,000 irrelevant, nonscholarly hits on everything from a list of the best hotels near the battlefield site to the minutes of a meeting of a Civil War reenactment society to e-mails between players of an online game based on the battle.

Trying to strike the balance between precision and recall is, of course, what the iterative search process is all about. Based on the feedback received from searches—number of hits and/or relevance of the hits retrieved—searchers make decisions about whether they have 1) struck the right balance, or 2) need more precision, or 3) need greater recall, or 4) need to conduct the search in a different information resource.

To achieve more precision searchers can add additional terms to their searches or use more precise terms (e.g., search "burglary" instead of "crime").

To achieve greater recall searchers can remove terms from their searches or use more general terms (e.g. search "natural disasters" instead of "tornados").

SAMPLE ITERATIVE SEARCH

Research Question: What are the penalties for insider trading in the United States?
Sample Search in: *AltaVista*

Figure 4–3: Sample Iterative Search		
Action	*Feedback*	*Response*
Search: **insider trading**	@ 120,000 hits	Narrow search by adding additional term(s).
Revised search: **insider trading penalties**	@ 2,300 hits	Click Help link and read instructions on how to search *AltaVista*.
Revised search: **+"insider trading" +penalties**	@ 1,600 hits	A few good hits turned up, but many deal with other countries. Limit search to United States.
Revised search: **+"insider trading" +penalties +"united staets"**	0 hits	Misspelled word Check spelling and redo search.
Revised search: **+"insider trading" +penalties +"united states"**	@ 740 hits	Some good hits appear at the top of the list, including what prove to be valuable pages from the U.S. Securities & Exchange Commission.
Revised search: **+"securities fraud" +"prison sentences" +"united states"**	@ 40 hits	Continue searching and revising.

WHEN TO QUIT?

One element of the iterative search process that sometimes gets short shrift is knowing when to quit. The search-feedback loop can be described by a curve that indicates diminishing returns the more times a search is revised, with revision becoming fruitless at some point on the curve. It is time to quit searching when you have:

- Concluded that you have all the information you need.
- Concluded that the information you need does not exist.
- Decided to continue your search in a different information resource.
  * In the insider-trading example given above, you might choose to continue the search you began in the Web search engine *AltaVista* in the business database *ABI/Inform*.
- Decided to consult with someone (instructor, librarian, classmate) or some thing (a book, an article, etc.) to get ideas and information that will allow you to conduct a more productive search and/or conduct your search in a more appropriate information resource—possibly a resource you did not know existed or had not considered.

GENERIC THINGS THAT ELECTRONIC SEARCHERS SHOULD KNOW ABOUT

Knowledge of the following techniques and concepts will help anyone become a better electronic searcher.

Database

Because every searchable electronic information resource is built on a database, all searches of electronic information resources are, in fact, database searches. The size of the underlying database, the quality of its content, and the quality of its indexing directly influence the usefulness of any electronic information resource. It never hurts to have a least some knowledge of how databases (especially relational databases) are constructed and how they work.

Records

In the jargon of database design, a record is a collection of fields (e.g., title, author, abstract, subject heading, etc.) that together represent one *thing*. In a bibliographic database, a record is typically a citation to a book or article or other publication. In a full-text database, a record is typically the full text of an article, book chapter, or other publication. While it is common to think of Web search engines as full-text databases, the records produced by Web search engines do not contain the full text of Web pages but rather *links* to Web pages.

Help Menus

The lengths to which people will go to avoid reading the manual is legendary; nonetheless, reading help menus is essential for conducting an effective search in an unfamiliar resource or in a resource which has recently changed its search syntax. Besides telling users how to search a resource, help menus often provide important information about the scope of the information resource.

Scope

Before searching an information resource, it is important to learn as much as possible about its scope. Scope includes such elements as:

- Subjects covered:
  * Business? History? Anything and everything?
- Intended audience for information:
  * Scholars/experts? Lay people? Children?
- Types of information included or excluded:
  * Full-text documents? Citations? Images? Mix of types?
- Information formats included or excluded:
  * Journal articles? Dissertations? Mix of formats?
- Time period covered:
  * Information published/created starting with Year XXXX and going to the present?
  * Information about events that occurred between Year YYYY and Year ZZZZ?
- Currency:
  * How often is the resource updated?
- Other limitations:
  * Geographic area (e.g., U.S. only).
  * Language (e.g., English-language publications only).
  * Provenance (e.g., only those items found in the collection of a particular library).

Defaults

Electronic information resources typically have default settings that impact both how searches are performed and how search results are displayed. For example, some Web search engines default to a Boolean OR search unless the user specifies otherwise. Some information resources have a default display in which the results of a search are displayed from most relevant to least relevant; others default to a most-recent-to-oldest display order. Because defaults vary from resource to resource, it is important to check a resource's help menu to find out what the defaults are and how to override them if need be.

Keyword Searching

Most electronic information resources allow some form of searching in which one or more keywords (as typed in by the searcher) are matched against words in the database. All matches are then displayed. Keyword searching typically works on simple matching without regard for meaning or context. It is worth knowing exactly what is or is not being searched in a keyword search. For example, does a keyword search in a full-text resource actually search every word of every document, or does it search only words found in titles, abstracts, and subject headings?

Boolean Logic

Electronic information resources typically allow searchers to narrow or broaden searches by applying one of the Boolean operators:

- AND
- OR
- NOT

Searchers need to understand not only how Boolean operators work, they must also know how to apply operators in whatever database they are searching. For example, in some resources searchers must type a Boolean operator in all capital letters to indicate that it is being used as an operator (as opposed to a search term). Or searchers may need to use a resource's advanced search interface to apply Boolean operators. (See the attached PowerPoint presentation "Boolean Logic" for ideas on teaching the concept of Boolean operators.)

Proximity Operators

Some electronic information resources allow the use of proximity operators to specify that search words or phrases must be within a certain number of words in order to produce a hit. A commonly used proximity operator is NEAR, but other operators are used as well. Resources that allow proximity searching have a default distance for NEAR searches; for example, the default for NEAR might be that the search words/phrases are within ten words of each other. Searchers may have the option of selecting a proximity other than the default: within three words, fifty words, in the same paragraph, on the same page, and so on. It may also be possible to specify word/phrase order; for example, **Phrase A** must be within 10 words of **Word B** and **Phrase A** must precede **Word B**.

Fixed Vocabulary

Fixed vocabularies serve to overcome some of the problems caused by the inability of computers to understand meaning and context. Although the term *fixed vocabulary* implies more than just subject headings, for the average searcher the terms *fixed vocabulary* and *subject headings* are interchangeable.

Example: A periodical database that uses a fixed vocabulary applies the subject heading *airplane* to articles having to do with fixed-wing flight. Therefore, searching the fixed-vocabulary term *airplane* will retrieve every relevant article in the database regardless of whether the terminology used in the original article was *airplane* or *aircraft* or *plane* or *biplane* or *jet* or *avion* or *Flugzeug* or whatever. At the same time, this search will exclude irrelevant articles that happen to use the word *airplane*, such as reviews of the 1980 comedy film *Airplane* or histories of the 1960s rock band *Jefferson Airplane*.

As a rule, fixed-vocabulary searches are not default, so searchers need to learn how to limit a search to fixed vocabulary if that is their wish. Some electronic information resources provide cross references that direct searchers to the correct fixed-vocabulary term (e.g., a search on the term *Lou Gehrig's disease* is redirected to the fixed-vocabulary term *amyotrophic lateral sclerosis*) or which suggests broader or narrower search terms.

Finally, searchers must understand that not all electronic information resources employ fixed vocabularies.

Subject Categories

Subject categories are often used by Web directories, the classic example being the *Yahoo!* directory. Searchers navigate subject categories by starting with a general category such as "Education" or "Social Science" and working down to more specific categories. The process is often compared to peeling an onion. While subject categories are useful, such categories lack the precision and consistency found in well-managed fixed vocabularies.

Metadata

In its broadest definition, metadata is simply data about data. Perhaps the most familiar form of metadata is the subject heading. Objects found on the Web (Web pages, images, documents, etc.) may include metadata that provides information about the object: who created it, when it was created, where it was created, what it is about, and on and on. Metadata is not typically displayed in a Web browser but can be seen as part of the mark-up language that underlies the Web object. Metadata is usually intended as an aid to electronic searching, but it can also be used deceptively, as when pornographic Web sites load themselves with metadata in the hope that their pages will turn up in just about any search. Note that some Web search engines pay attention to metadata while others simply ignore it.

Hits and False Drops

In the jargon of electronic searching, *hits* refers to the number of items retrieved by a search. The term *false drops* refers to irrelevant hits retrieved by a search. (See "Information Roadblocks," above.)

Web Conventions

Because most electronic information resources are now found on the Web, it is crucial that searchers understand basic conventions used on the Web. For example, searchers must understand that to type in a search term they must first click their mouse inside the search box. *Mouserobics*, an online tutorial that is described in Chapter 1 of this book, is a good resource for those who need to learn Web conventions.

Limits

Many electronic information resources allow searchers to limit searches as a way of narrowing their results. Although the specifics of setting limits varies from resource to resource, some of the more common limits include:

- Field Limits
  * Limit search to a particular field, such as author field, title field, subject-heading field, abstract field, and so on.
- Language
  * Limit search results to English. Or exclude a particular language.
- Date of publication
  * Limit results to a particular date or date range.
- Format
  * Retrieve only full-text documents. Or only images. Or only audio files.
- Phrase
  * Search *nuclear fusion* as a phrase rather than as separate keywords. In many (but not all) search interfaces, putting quotation marks around two or more words indicates the words should be searched as a phrase.
- Proximity
  * Search *obstetrics* but only when it appears within *n* words of *liability*.

Basic and Advanced Searching

Electronic information resources commonly offer both basic and advanced search interfaces. Typically, the default is to the basic search with the searcher having the option of choosing the advanced search (sometimes called the "power search"). The advanced search interface allows searches that are more exact than those that can be created using the basic search interface. Even within the same resource, the syntax for constructing advanced searches can differ greatly from the syntax for basic searches. Reading the help menu is essential.

Truncation

Truncation allows a searcher to retrieve hits on various forms of a word. Truncating the word *costume* to *costum** (an example of end or root truncation) would retrieve hits containing any of the following words: *costume, costumes, costumed, costuming, costumer, costumers*. Truncating the word *woman* to wom*n (an example of internal or wildcard truncation) would retrieve hits containing either the word *woman* or *women* (but not the neologism *wymyn*).

Although the asterisk is widely used as a truncation

symbol, its use is not universal. Once again, read the help menu to find out for sure.

Display Order and Format
Searchers may be able to specify the order in which results are displayed.

- Most recent oldest.
- Oldest to most recent.
- Alphabetically by author.
- Alphabetically by journal title.
- By relevance (as determined by the search engine).

Searchers may also be able to specify the format in which results are displayed.

- Brief citation.
- Citation plus abstract.
- Full text.

Search History and Save Search
A search-history feature (which may go by other names) allows searchers to look at the searches they have already conducted and, if they wish, combine these searches with each other or with additional search terms. Often previous searches can be combined by typing the line number assigned to the search rather than by retyping the entire search.

A save-search feature allows searchers to permanently save frequently used searches. Such a feature is most useful for serious scholars who periodically rerun a complex search as part of a personal current-awareness program.

Stopwords
Stopwords are simply words that a database will not search. Usually, stopwords are common words such as *of*, *the*, *an*, *a*, *to*, *from*, and so on. The words *and*, *or*, and *not* may be treated as stopwords unless the searcher follows the resource's syntax for specifying that the word should be used as a Boolean operator.

Vague or Common Words
Vague words are almost useless in electronic searching. For example, students who are assigned to research a topic such as "The impact of Martin Luther King, Jr.'s,

'I Have a Dream' speech on the Civil Rights Movement" will dutifully include the word *impact* as part of their electronic search. But *impact* is (at least in the sense used here) such a vague word that including it in a search is likely to do nothing more than exclude relevant hits. Other examples of popular vague words include *aspect*, *effect*, *extent*, *role*, *ramifications*, and *results*.

A related example occurs when a searcher does a keyword search on an extremely common word. For example, it does no good to search the word *education* in the *ERIC* database or the word *agriculture* in the *Agricola* database because virtually every record in *ERIC* includes the word *education* and every record in *Agricola* includes the word *agriculture*.

Natural-Language Searching

The intent of natural-language searching is to allow searchers to construct searches in regular language without the need to worry about Boolean operators, limits, and the like. The results produced by readily available electronic information resources that allow natural-language searching are, so far, not impressive. Whether or not search engines will eventually be able to act more like thinking machines than matching machines remains to be seen. The *Ask Jeeves* Web search engine (www.askjeeves.com) is one well-known example of a natural-language search interface.

CHOOSING THE BEST RESOURCES TO SEARCH

As with conducting a search, choosing which resources to search is an iterative process. If a search of Resource A produces no relevant hits, then try the search in Resource B. If Resource B provides only popular information when scholarly information is needed, move on to Resource C. One of the great things about the Web is that searchers have many resources from which to choose. Of course this also means that making the right or wrong choices about which resources to search has a huge impact on the amount and quality of information retrieved. For this reason, choosing which information resources to search is as important a part of electronic searching as constructing an effective search.

THERE IS NO UNIVERSAL SEARCH INTERFACE

Probably the most important thing for students to accept is the fact that—despite what the last half-century of science fiction has taught us—there is no universal search interface. The persistent belief that there must be, somewhere, "The Computer" that puts all the world's information at one's fingertips is close cousin to such immortal information legends as: "*Lexis-Nexis* has the full text of everything" and "The Library of Congress has at least one copy of every book ever published."

WHY USE ANYTHING OTHER THAN A WEB SEARCH ENGINE?

Many searchers automatically choose Web search engines when they need information. Why? Because Web search engines retrieve information that is (for the most part) full text and free. This does not mean, however, that a Web search engine is always the best choice, and it is the job of instructors to convince students that there is more to life than full text and free.

> **Full Text.** Just about everyone prefers the convenience of electronic full-text information delivered right to their desktop. So why use an electronic information resource that does not provide full text? The answer is simple: lots of information is not available via electronic full text. Using bibliographic electronic information resources greatly expands the amount of information from which searchers may choose.

> **Free.** Why should I (or my library) pay for information when the Web has so much free information? Just as there is plenty of full-text information that is not available in electronic full text, there is plenty of information that is not available for free. Proprietary information resources not only provide access to otherwise unavailable information, they also offer value-added features such as fixed vocabulary, consistent updates, powerful search interfaces, and so on.

> Because proprietary (as well as many open-access) information resources cannot be searched via Web search engines, it is necessary to give up the "If it's not on *Google*, it doesn't exist" mindset and take advantage of proprietary databases—especially those made available free of charge to end users through libraries or other institutions.

Figure 4–4: Web Search Engines (and Their Limitations)

Web search engines are awfully alluring. You type in a few keywords, click a button, and links to a world of information materialize under your mouse pointer. No trip to the library. No books to crack. No sweat.

Of course anyone who has seriously searched for information using a Web search engine can testify that, while Web search engines are powerful tools, using them is not all that simple. The more searchers understand about Web search engines, and their limitations, the more likely they will be able to use them effectively.

The Brief History of Web Search Engines

One of the limitations of the early Web was that there was no way to search it. You either had to know the URL of the Web site you wanted to visit or follow links from one page to the next, hoping to find what you were looking for. That was not a big problem when (circa 1992) there were only 50 sites on the entire Web, but as the Web grew the need for a way to search it became apparent. The first Web search engine, *WebCrawler*, debuted in April 1994. Since then, a number of Web search engines have come and gone. As the Web has grown, the size of Web search engines has grown as well. Today, a number of search engines index more than 200 million Web pages, with the largest engines topping out at over 600 million pages.

How Web Search Engines Work

If you are going to use Web search engines, it helps to know a little bit about how they work. For starters, it is important to understand that a search engine is a big, fast computer connected to the Web. Most search engines share the following characteristics:

- **Spiders**
  Search engines have spiders—computer programs that "crawl" the Web and bring back to the search engine information about the Web pages they find. Spiders are sometimes called "Web crawlers." The information spiders retrieve about an individual Web page might include the page's URL, its title, all the words found on the page, and any metadata attached to the page.

- **Database**
  When information from spiders is returned to the search engine, it is compiled in a database. As with other electronic information resources, the quality of a Web search engine is dependent on the size of the underlying database and the quality of the database's indexing.

- **Indexing**
  Of course a database is not much use if it is not indexed in such a way that useful information can be retrieved from it. For example, a search-engine database might be indexed so that it is possible to limit a search to retrieve only those Web pages in which the keyword *elvis* is part of the page's title (as opposed to retrieving all Web pages on which the keyword *elvis* appears anywhere). Or it might be possible to limit a search to retrieve only JPEG images for which the keyword *elvis* is part of the file name. A large-but-poorly-indexed database is not very useful.

Figure 4–4: *(continued)*

- **Syntax**
  A search engine's syntax is the set of rules for how a search should be constructed. For example, a search engine's syntax might specify that putting quotation marks around two or more words means that those words will be searched as a phrase. A search engine's help menu should explain its syntax.

- **User Interface**
  The user interface is where users enter search terms into a Web search engine and view retrieved results. Very often, Web search engines have basic and advanced interfaces; they may also have special interfaces for searching only audio, image, video, or other types of files.

Freshness

Freshness refers to how frequently the information in a Web search engine's database is updated. Although most searchers believe that when they use a search engine they are searching the entire Web as it exists at that moment, they are actually searching the search engine's compiled database of Web pages. If that database has not been updated for two months, users are actually searching the Web as it was two months previously. It is sometimes hard to tell how fresh a Web search engine really is because some parts of the search engine's database (its "Current News" section, for example) may be updated many times in a single day while other parts of the database may go for weeks without an update.

Web Directories Versus Web Search Engines

At one time, Web directories and Web search engines were distinct entities. Searchers clicked down through directories' subject categories or they entered keywords into search engines. Today, many Web search engines also offer subject categories and Web directories offer search engines. (A Web directory's search engine usually defaults to a search of the Web directory only, but it may also be used to search the open Web.)

As a rule of thumb, taking a directory approach is most useful when the topic at hand is loosely defined: "I'd like to find out *something* about the Women's Suffrage Movement, but I'm not sure what." On the other hand, using a search engine is most effective when the topic at hand is specific: "I'm interested in finding out about Elizabeth Cady Stanton's role in the 1848 First Women's-Rights Convention."

General-Purpose Versus Focused Web Search Engines

General-purpose Web search engines (*AltaVista, Lycos, Google*, et al.) retrieve hits on just about any topic because their databases are compiled from information gleaned from large sections of the open Web. However, the Web also hosts many focused Web search engines that may search only a single Web site or single area of interest. For example, searching *FirstGov* will retrieve only hits on government information, while searching *NewsIndex* will retrieve only hits on current news items. Using a focused Web search engine can improve search results by cutting out the false drops generated during searches of the open Web.

Figure 4–4: *(continued)*

The Invisible Web

Even the biggest general-purpose Web search engine falls far short of searching the entire Web. The reason for this is that large sections of the Web are invisible to Web search engines. For example, Web search engines cannot search proprietary Web-based information resources such as *Compendex* or *Ethnic News Watch* or *ABI/Inform*. Similarly, many open-access resources such as *PubMed* cannot be searched via a general-purpose Web search engine. The important point here is that no search engine of any type can claim to search the entire Web.

Pay for Positioning and Advertising

In pay-for-positioning schemes, owners of Web sites pay the owners of Web search engines so that their Web sites are featured at the top of the list of hits retrieved for certain types of searches. For example, *Widgets Unlimited* might pay a search engine so that the *WidgetsUnlimited.com* page will be featured at the top of the list for any search involving the word *widget*. The downside for searchers is that *WidgetsUnlimited.com* may not be the most relevant site for their search.

Web search engines also accept advertising, which is why, for example, an ad for sinus medicine appears at the top of the results page following a search on the phrase "runny nose."

Pay-for-positioning and advertising may be necessary for economic survival, but both practices compromise the objectivity of Web search engines.

Search Engines Change

Web search engines have been known to change their user interfaces fairly often. This means that the syntax used for SearchEngine-X a month ago may not apply today; when this kind of change happens, a visit to the search engine's help menu is in order. Also, the very database that underlies a search engine may change, as was the case in 2002 when *WebCrawler* began searching the *Excite* database even though www.webcrawler.com continued to exist as a URL and continued to wear the *WebCrawler* livery. (Notess, Greg R. 2002. "Dead Search Engines." *Online* 26, no.3:63–64.)

Metasearch Engines

Metasearch engines are Web search engines that search a number of other Web search engines and retrieve the compiled results. For example, searching the phrase "Apollo 13" in the metasearch engine *metacrawler* retrieves approximately 70 hits from eight different Web search engines. While metasearch engines can be useful, it is important to remember that the results they retrieve are selective. Searching the phrase "Apollo 13" in any one of the eight Web search engines searched by *metacrawler* retrieves more than 70 hits.

Further Reading

Anyone who is interested in learning more about how Web search engines work or who would like to keep up on changes in the world of Web search engines should visit Gregg R. Notess' *Search Engine Showdown*: *The Users' Guide to Web Searching* at searchengineshowdown.com.

5 TEACHING STUDENTS HOW TO EVALUATE ELECTRONIC INFORMATION

It would be great if all information could be neatly sorted into piles labeled "Good Information" and "Bad Information," but the fact is that evaluating information is more a business of shades of gray than a business of black and white. There are many things to consider when evaluating a piece of information and answers are rarely clear-cut. That said, the ability to do the hard job of evaluating information is a vital skill for anyone living in the Information Age.

JUNK SCIENCE AND THE PROBLEM OF EVALUATING INFORMATION

The debate over junk science provides a vivid example of how hard it can be to evaluate information.

Properly used, the term *junk science* describes any scientific or social-science research that employs faulty methodologies. Say, for example, a team of researchers conducts a survey to determine the average income of Americans but, in so doing, surveys only professional athletes. Obviously, such a study will produce inflated numbers having little to do with the reality of the average American income. This would be junk science at its finest.

The problem with the term *junk science* is that it is rarely used properly; instead, it is used by politicians, lobbyists, lawyers, activists, and others to characterize any research that goes against their worldview. A politician who favors the aggressive extraction and use of fossil fuels might label any research that supports the theory of global warming as junk science, while a Green Party politician might dismiss as junk science any research that indicates global warming is not occurring.

Junk-science charges and counter charges can leave an honest information seeker's head spinning. Consider the Web sites *Cen-*

ter for Science in the Public Interest (www.cspinet.org) and *American Council on Science and Health* (www.acsh.org). Both sites claim to be science-based and objective, yet the information these sites present on food safety and nutrition is frequently contradictory.

For another example, the Web site *Junkscience.com* (www.junkscience.com) sports the motto "All the Junk That's Fit to Debunk," yet virtually all the debunking on this site is of science that supports the liberal agenda. This is not to say that liberals never engage in junk science; rather, it is hard to believe that a Web site that claims to be against all junk science cannot seem to find examples from both the liberal and conservative sides.

Not only does the junk-science problem make it hard to evaluate information, it also can contribute to "information cynicism" among those trying to get at the truth. Faced with so much contradictory information, it is tempting to throw up one's hands and say, "I give up. I'll believe what I want to believe, information be damned. If I like to smoke, I'll believe the tiny handful who say the dangers of smoking are overrated and ignore the hundreds of studies that indicate otherwise. If I don't like to wear a seat belt, I'll accept as valid the few studies that say seat belts don't save lives and ignore the overwhelming evidence to the contrary. After all, it's all just opinion, and one opinion is as good as the other, right?"

Perhaps the reason cynics say, "It's all just opinion," is that science appears to fall short of the perfection that many nonscientists expect of it. Nonscientists often think that science should be an unchanging monolith built of irrefutable facts, while the truth is that science is as mutable as any other human endeavor. Because they are human beings, scientists bring their feelings, biases, and values to the laboratory bench. They disagree with each other and sometimes engage in professional and personal rivalries. Scientists can be wrong. A few scientists are outright dishonest. In spite of all this, science changes and progresses as new scientific hypotheses are proposed, tested, and shown to be valid or invalid. The fact that science changes is a reason to have faith in it, not a reason to turn one's back to it.

The following is just one example of how science can be wrong and how it can change. In the middle years of the twentieth century, medical science wrongly believed that schizophrenia was caused by environmental factors (for example, traumatic events suffered during childhood) and that this devastating form of mental illness could be cured through psychoanalytical techniques—the classic "talking cure." As scientists developed new methods for studying the brain, and as more and more scientists began to use these methods to experiment, observe, and draw conclusions about how the brain works, medical science came to accept the idea that schizophrenia results from organic conditions in the brain, not from environmental factors. Some scientists accepted the new ideas about schizophrenia more readily than others, but over time the emerging consensus won out, leading eventually to antipsychotic medications that have had success in treating the disease. There is still much to learn before science comes up with anything like a cure for schizophrenia, and no doubt before this happens scientific thinking about schizophrenia will change from what it is today.

In any field of learning—science, social science, engineering, humanities, the arts—absolute answers are not easy to find. Some argue they do not exist. Hardly an issue confronts humanity for which there are not multiple points of view and contradictory sets of information. There are limits to how far information can lead us and times when we have to make decisions based on our values as much as on the information available to us. Still, learning how to evaluate information so as to weed out the truly flawed information and base our thinking and action on the best information available can go a long way toward helping us decide what we truly value and help us stay clear of the slippery slope of cynicism and despair.

First Come, Best Served?

One of the temptations of electronic information is to do a quick search and grab onto the very first information that seems to meet your need (or which fits with your predrawn conclusion about what the answer should be). Of course one of the hallmarks of a careful information seeker is to not take as gospel the first bit of information that materializes and to compare, instead, information from a number of different sources. About the only exception to this rule is when the information seeker is very, very sure of the source. For example, an experienced chemist might accept as accurate a constant found in the *CRC Handbook of Basic Tables for Chemical Analysis* because the publications of the CRC Press have a long history of reliability.

What follows is a lesson in why jumping on the first answer that turns up is not always the best idea. This lesson can be used as a hands-on activity in the classroom with different questions substituted for the example used here.

Using the natural-language search engine *askjeeves.com*, I typed in the seemingly unambiguous question: "What is the distance from the Sun to Mars?"

The first couple of hits proved to be false drops—if the information was there, I could not find it. Then, on the Web site *SEDS: Students for the Exploration and Development of Space* (seds.lpl.arizona.edu), I found the figure of 227,940,000 kilometers from the Sun to Mars. I could have gone with this answer, but I checked the next hit retrieved by my search. This hit was on *dailypress.com*, and there it says that Mars is 206 million kilometers from the Sun at its closest, while it is 249 million kilometers from the Sun at its farthest.

Were the two sites providing conflicting information? Not really. The number given by the *SEDS* site is the *average* of the two numbers given at *dailypress.com*. The *SEDS* site simply assumes that its audience will understand that providing a single distance between two celestial objects implies the average distance. A nonastronomer, however, might not have realized that looking at the *SEDS* site alone.

The point here is even for a seemingly cut-and-dried question, the answer proved to be not all that simple—the distance from Mars to the Sun varies and so the question has more than one answer. Whether to use the *SEDS* answer, the *dailypress.com* answers, or research the question in even more depth depends on the information need. For someone writing an amateur astronomy article for the local paper, any of the numbers—average, closest, or farthest distance—would serve the purpose of giving readers some sense of how far Mars is from the Sun. If, however, a professional astronomer was working on creating an accurate map of the solar system, the numbers used would have to be much more precise than those found in either source turned up by a search of *askjeeves.com*.

WHY IS SCHOLARLY INFORMATION SO VALUED?

When teachers assign research-based projects, they often require that students use scholarly information; in particular, articles published in scholarly journals. To understand why scholarly information is so valued, it helps to understand both the difference between scholarly and nonscholarly information and the process through which scholarly information is created.

Figure 5–1: Scholarly Versus Nonscholarly Information

Scholarly Information	Nonscholarly Information
Author The authors of scholarly information are typically people who hold advanced degrees in the subjects on which they write; often, scholarly authors are faculty members at colleges or universities. Teams of scholars—in some cases very large teams—will often collaborate on a single manuscript (article, book chapter, etc.).	**Author** Nonscholarly information can be written by anyone—journalists, professional writers, or amateurs. Nonscholarly authors may have a lot of knowledge about the topics on which they write, or they may have almost none.
Research Scholarly information typically reports on original research; that is, the person or persons writing the article are the same people who conducted the basic research (i.e., laboratory experiment, clinical trial, field work, survey, etc.) that produced the data on which the article is based. Prior to conducting research, scholars conduct a literature review on the topic they propose to research; this is done both to increase the scholar's knowledge and to make sure that his or her research truly is original.	**Research** Research for nonscholarly information typically involves reviewing relevant materials on the subject in question as well as conducting interviews with people who possess special knowledge of the subject. Authors of nonscholarly information are not bound to any standards of research, so the quality of their research must be evaluated on a case-by-case basis.

Continued on following page

Figure 5–1: *(continued)*	
Scholarly Information	**Nonscholarly Information**
While conducting their actual research, scholars are bound to employ sound research methodologies in order to produce the most objective results possible.	

Peer Review

Scholarly information typically goes through a peer-review process prior to being accepted for publication. In its most rigorous form, peer review requires that a manuscript (minus the author's name) be sent to several experts in the field who then independently evaluate the manuscript and decide whether it should 1) not be published, 2) undergo revision prior to publication, or 3) be published as is. The peer-review process is also known as *refereeing* and scholarly journals are often called *refereed journals*.

Peer Review

Nonscholarly information rarely goes through a peer-review process. Decisions to publish or not publish are made by an editor or editorial board. Editors may not necessarily be experts on the subjects treated in the manuscripts they evaluate.

In the case of self-publication (in print or on the Web), the editor is left out of the equation and the author alone decides whether his or her work should be published.

Audience

The audience for scholarly information is other scholars in the field. Scholars assume a high level of knowledge among the members of their audience, a fact which can make some scholarly information unintelligible to anyone who is not a trained expert on the subject in question.

Audience

The audience for nonscholarly information can be just about anyone, though not necessarily everyone. A popular mass-circulation magazine like *Time* aims for broad audience, while a specialist publication such as *Fly Fishing & Fly Tying* aims for a narrow audience.

Formats

The bedrock format for scholarly information is the scholarly article. These are typically published in peer-reviewed scholarly journals. The other important format is the scholarly book, which may be written by a single author or consist of chapters contributed by a number of different authors

Formats

Formats for nonscholarly publications run the gamut from comic books to homegrown Web sites to high-quality books published by the finest publishing houses.

Continued on following page

Figure 5–1: *(continued)*	
Scholarly Information	**Nonscholarly Information**

under the auspices of a scholarly editor who takes overall responsibility for the book.

The Web is becoming an increasingly important format for scholarly publication. Most print-format scholarly journals also support (virtually) identical Web-based versions, and there are various efforts underway to develop methods for publishing peer-reviewed scholarly articles directly to the Web. (See *BioMed Central* (www. biomedcentral.com) and *e-Scholarship* (escholarship.cdlib.org) for two such examples.)

Scholarly Publishers

Scholarly information is most often published by scholarly publishers. Scholarly publishers are typically associated with learned societies or universities, operate on a nonprofit basis, and exist to further the spread of knowledge.

Scholarly information can also be published by for-profit publishers. For example, it is fairly common for journals that belong to learned societies to be published by for-profit publishers. The society takes responsibility for selecting and editing manuscripts, while the for-profit publisher takes responsibility for printing, marketing, and distributing the journal.

Nonscholarly Publishers

Nonscholarly publishers can be for-profit concerns. For such publishers the commercial potential of any manuscript is a major consideration—though not necessarily the only consideration—when deciding what manuscripts to publish or not publish.

It is also possible for a nonscholarly publisher to be a nonprofit concern. For example, a press belonging to a religious organization might be both nonscholarly and nonprofit.

Outlets for self-publishing, such as vanity-press books or personal Web sites, are another type of nonscholarly publisher.

Rewards

Scholars who publish are typically rewarded through academic tenure and promotion, the awarding of research grants, the respect of their peers, and the hope that

Rewards

Nonscholarly publishing can be financially rewarding. Writing a best-selling book or a successful screenplay can make an author wealthy, though most authors never reap

Continued on following page

Figure 5–1: *(continued)*	
Scholarly Information	**Nonscholarly Information**
their work has furthered knowledge within their field of expertise. Scholarly publishing rarely results in direct financial rewards to the author.	such heady financial rewards. For many nonscholarly authors, personal satisfaction is a greater reward than any money they receive for their work.
Objectivity	**Objectivity**
Scholarly information is not perfectly objective. Scholars make mistakes. They sometimes cut corners or outright cheat. They disagree about what constitutes a sound research methodology. They have biases and blind spots. In short, they are human and the work they do is subject to the flaws that are part of being human. That said, scholarly information is, as a whole, the most accurate and objective information available.	The objectivity of any piece of nonscholarly information is a crap shoot. Nonscholarly authors can be as rigorously objective as the best scholars out there, or they can be the very antithesis of objective.

THE SCHOLARLY INFORMATION PROCESS

The following diagram illustrates the typical process through which a piece of scholarly information—in this case the classic article in a scholarly journal—is created. While the process outlined below is typical, it is important to remember that there can be many variations on this theme.

Figure 5–2: The Scholarly Information Process

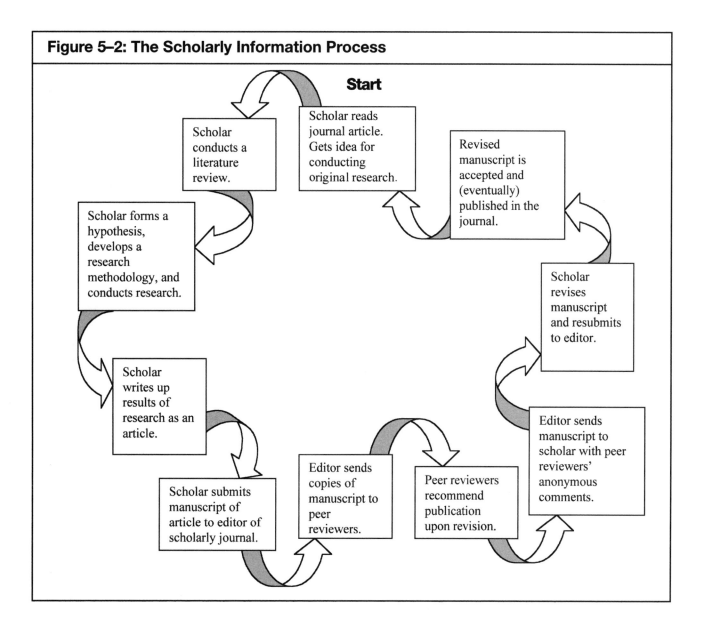

ECONOMICS OF SCHOLARLY PUBLISHING

Like any other endeavor, economics influences the creation of scholarly information. The following economic scenario is quite common in scholarly publishing:

1. A scientist receives a government grant to conduct research. The grant is paid for by taxpayers.
2. The scientist writes a journal article based on the results of the grant-funded research and submits it to a scholarly journal that belongs to a scholarly society.
3. Following peer-review and editorial work conducted by members and staff of the scholarly society, the final version of the article is sent to the for-profit publisher that actually prints the journal.
4. The author of the article pays the for-profit publisher "page charges"—a fee based on the number of pages in the published article. Often, page charges are paid for out of the author's research grant.
5. Libraries pay subscription fees to acquire copies of journal in which the article is published. Often these subscription fees are paid for by tax dollars.

Not surprisingly, scholars and librarians are quite concerned about scenarios such as the one described above. Because the United States funds so much scientific research, U.S. scholars and librarians are particularly concerned that U.S. taxpayers are being billed twice for information—once when they fund the research and once again when they buy back published articles through subscription charges. Many librarians and scholars are looking toward Web-based solutions that would keep in place the high standards of peer review while cutting out the for-profit publisher. Another potential advantage of direct-to-Web publication is that it could cut down on the often significant time lag between research and publication.

CHARACTERISTICS OF A SCHOLARLY JOURNAL

Because scholarly journals and popular magazines bear superficial resemblances, how does a researcher know if something is a scholarly journal? Here are some rules of thumb:

- Scholarly journals often have the word *journal* in the title. (Exception to the rule: *Ladies' Home Journal* is a magazine, not a scholarly journal.) Title phrases such as *proceedings of, transactions of, publication of,* and *bulletin of* are often tip-offs that a publication is scholarly.
- If the cover or title page of the publication indicates that it is published by a learned society or association, it is probably a scholarly journal. For example, when you look at the cover of the journal *Academic Medicine* it says below the title, "Journal of the Association of American Medical Colleges."
- Scholarly journals focus on a single, often very narrow, subject area in the sciences, social sciences, engineering, humanities, or the arts.
- Most scholarly journals do not contain advertisements. There are some notable exception to this rule: Many scholarly journals carry advertisements for scholarly books. Also, many scholarly medical journals carry advertisements—most notably for prescription drugs.
- As a rule, scholarly journals look very plain compared to popular magazines—lots of text, not a lot of images, not a lot of color. There are many exceptions to this rule. For example, scholarly art journals have many images and lots of color.
- The bulk of articles in scholarly journals explicitly cite the sources the authors consulted when researching their articles. Footnotes and/or bibliographies are the norm in scholarly articles.
- Most scholarly journals will have an "Instruction to Authors" section that spells out the procedure for submitting manuscripts to the journal. These instructions may appear in every issue or only in certain issues, such as the first issue of each year.

WHAT MAKES INFORMATION SUITABLE?

All the emphasis on scholarly information does not mean that nonscholarly information is without value. More important than whether information is scholarly or nonscholarly is whether or not information is suitable for the needs of the person using it. For example, a journal article describing a new form of quantum fluid with fractionally charged excitations is probably unsuitable for an 11-year-old who wants to do a cool science-fair project; that same article, however, would be entirely suitable for a graduate student in physics at Cal Tech. For someone who is writing exclusively for an audience that believes the King James version of the Bible presents the literal word of God and is, therefore, the source of all truth, the book of Genesis provides all the information needed on the creation of the world; on the other hand, Genesis is an unsuitable source for a student in a college geology class who needs scientific information on how the earth was formed.

**Is Print Information Always Better
Than Information Found on the Web?**

The short answer is "No." Here are some reasons why:

- The Web does not have a monopoly on bad information. There is plenty of it available in print format.
- Some information found on the Web is the equivalent of print information, as is the case when a print journal produces an equivalent Web-based version. Since both are virtually the same, one is no better than the other.
- There are Web sites that impose high standards on the information they provide by employing such quality controls as peer review, careful editing, and fact-checking. The information found on such Web sites is as good as anything found in print.

The Web's reputation as a source for bad information is based on the fact that much of the Web—the "open Web," if you will—imposes no standards at all. Anybody can say anything at any time. While there are plenty of such wide-open sites on the Web, they do not constitute the entire Web.

STRATEGIES FOR EVALUATING INFORMATION

The primary strategy for evaluating information in any format is to always question every bit of information you read, hear, or see no matter how credible the source may seem. Questioning information does not mean rejecting any information that falls short of absolute perfection—after all, nothing created by human beings, including scholarly information, can meet so lofty a standard—but rather to carefully consider all the strengths and weaknesses of any information you encounter and make sound decisions about how, or even whether, to apply that information to the fulfillment of your information need.

CURRENCY

Currency has to do with when information was created. Currency questions include:

Is Currency Important to My Information Need?

If you want to know what year George Washington died, the currency of the information source does not much matter as long as the source was published after Washington's death. A book published in 1830, an article published in 1928, or a Web page last updated yesterday could provide the information equally well. (Or equally badly if the information happens to be wrong.) On the other hand, if you are thinking of investing a large sum of money in a start-up company or want to know the latest drug therapies for pneumonia, accessing the most current information is crucial.

When Was the Information Created? When Was It Published?

While it is common to talk about "publication date" when considering the currency of information, it is really the date of creation that determines whether or not information is current. After all, there can be years of difference between when a piece of information is created and when it is published. Sir Isaac Newton wrote down his ideas about calculus around 1669, but they were not published until 1704. Such a gap between creation and publication may or may not be important, depending on one's information need.

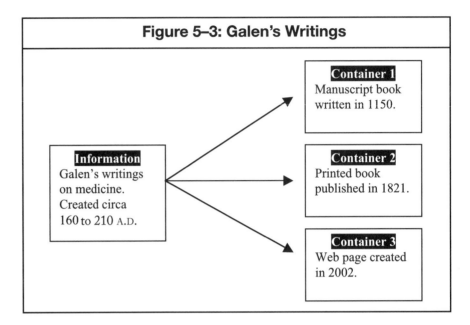

Figure 5–3: Galen's Writings

A related concept is knowing the difference between the date a piece of information was created and the date in which its container (book, journal, Web page, etc.) was created. For example, consider the writing of the Roman physician Galen who lived from 129A.D. to 210A.D.

Barring editorial errors, the information in all three of the above sources is the same even though the dates of the containers vary widely. If your information need is simply to read Galen's writings, then any of the three containers could supply your need (assuming you read Latin, of course). However, if you want current medical information, none of the containers will meet your need because the information itself remains almost 2,000 years old no matter how current the date of the container in which it is found.

When Was the Information Last Updated? Is It Updated Regularly?

Updating is important for time-sensitive information. Two-hour-old stock prices are not much help to a broker who needs to make a sell-or-hold decision *now*. With electronic information—which can be updated almost continuously—users of the information are dependent on the electronic information source itself to inform them when the information was last updated. Keep in mind that a Web site that says its information is updated daily (or hourly or every ten minutes) may not be updating *all* the information it presents that frequently.

AUTHORITY

Authority speaks to who created the information and who is, therefore, responsible for its accuracy. Authority is arguably the most important consideration when evaluating information.

Who Is the Author?

Authors can be individuals or corporate entities. Examples of corporate authors include businesses, universities, government agencies, organizations, and associations. Any legitimate information source will clearly identify the author of the information, and a red flag should go up for any information that is anonymous or which is attributed to a nom de plume.

Is the Author an Authority?

Whether the author is individual or corporate, it is important to ask what education, experience, or combination thereof qualifies the author to present information on the topic in question. Individuals will often try to disguise their lack of authority by describing themselves as "a noted researcher," "a leading expert," or "a frequent writer on the topic." These and other hedges may sound impressive, but they can be quite meaningless. Another ruse to look out for is an apparent corporate author who turns out to be, in fact, an individual—that grand sounding institute or corporation may be no more than a single person with a personal computer and a Web site. And information seekers always need to be aware of authors who flat-out lie about their credentials or claim expertise on the basis of a degree that has nothing to do with the topic at hand. An author may be a Ph.D. as claimed, but someone with a Ph.D. in American Literature is not automatically an expert in nutrition. All of which is not to say that one needs a graduate degree in a subject to be an authority—there are many self-taught experts who are well qualified to present information in their areas of expertise—but rather that users of information need to be alert to those whose claims to expertise exceed their grasp of the subject.

PUBLISHER

Another key to evaluating information is the publisher. The word *publisher* is related to the word *public*, and a publisher can be thought of as the person or group whose financial and other resources support the "making public" of a piece of information. In general, the reputation of a publisher—its selectivity, its objectivity, the expertise of its editors, and its experience publishing in a particular field or fields—serves as a measure of the quality of the information it publishes. Common types of publishers include commercial publishing houses, academic institutions, government agencies, and associations (e.g., learned societies, political associations, common-interest groups, nonprofits, etc.). Self-publishing occurs when an individual takes on the cost of publishing his or her own work.

With traditional print information sources, the publisher is usually obvious. For an article, it is the publisher of the magazine, newspaper, or journal in which the article appears; for a book, the publisher is named (usually) in the book's front matter. A red flag for print information is the "vanity-press" book whose publication was financed by its author.

The emergence of the Web profoundly changed the making public of information. Where self-publication in print was (and remains) an expensive, slow, and laborious undertaking, the Web makes it cheap and easy to become your own publisher. Millions have responded to this opportunity by creating Web sites devoted to just about every topic under the sun: families, pets, favorite film stars, political causes, hobbies, religion, poetry, and so on. On the typical self-published Web page, the author and the publisher are one and the same—a fact which makes knowing the author's qualifications for presenting information on the topic in question all the more important.

FUNDING

An old rule of investigative journalism is "Follow the money." Knowing who paid for the research behind, and/or publication of, a particular piece of information can alert an information seeker to possible conflicts of interest. Tobacco companies that fund research into the effects of smoking on health is a classic example of such a conflict of interest.

AFFILIATION

Knowing the affiliation of an individual author, corporate author, or publisher can be an aid to evaluating information. For example, knowing that the author of an article on weight loss is a professor at an accredited medical school lends credibility that would not be there if the author were, for example, vice-president of marketing for a company that sells weight-loss pills. (Of course the world is a complicated place, which is why researchers run into situations where an author is both a medical-school professor and the vice-president of a company that sells weight-loss pills.)

Of course simply being affiliated with an institution merely means that the author's expertise and authority has been formally recognized by the institution, not that the author is the absolute authority on a subject. Consider the fact that it is quite common for two similarly qualified experts affiliated with equally prestigious universities (or even with the same university) to hold very different opinions on a single question. In addition, affiliation does not mean that one's opinion reflects the official stance of the institution: Timothy Leary was a Harvard professor who endorsed the use of LSD, but Harvard University never, as an institution, endorsed LSD.

PRINT EQUIVALENT

If a piece of information found on the Web is the online equivalent of a print publication, then it is fairly safe to assume that any credibility attached to the print publication transfers to the Web information. If, for example, a scholarly journal appears in both a print and a Web version, then either version is equally credible. Information seekers should be aware, though, that there can be differences between "identical" print and online versions of the same piece of information. These differences can be intentional—as when the online version of a publication offers information, updates, or features (for example, video clips) that are not part of the print version. The differences can also be accidental—as when errors not found in the print version of a publication creep into the online version (and vice versa). Erroneous discrepancies between print and electronic versions of a publication are especially common when amateur editors post homemade electronic versions of public domain books and articles.

PURPOSE

It is always worthwhile to ask, "What is the purpose of this piece of information?" Some common purposes of information include:

- Direct sales (of everything from books to vitamins to farm tractors).
- Advertising of products or services.
- Public relations (for businesses, schools, government agencies, associations, etc.).
- Education.

- Entertainment.
- Advocating social, religious, or political agendas.
- Authorial ego gratification.
- Career advancement (including earning tenure).

While the list of purposes can go on, there are two important things to remember about the purpose of any piece of information:

1. All information has some purpose. In fact, it is hard to imagine that information could exist without a purpose.
2. A piece of information can have more than one purpose. For example, it is easy to imagine a piece of information that is all-at-once educational, entertaining, and profitable.

The important question that arises from the purposes associated with a piece of information is, "Do these purposes reveal any conflicts of interest?" For example, if a Web site called *Valerie's Vitamin Villa* is filled with articles extolling the benefits of taking vitamins while, at the same time, *Valerie's Vitamin Villa* also offers those same vitamins for sale to online customers, there is a clear conflict of interest. This conflict of interest is not necessarily fatal to the credibility of *Valerie's Vitamin Villa*, but it does mean that this site's information should undergo extra scrutiny before it is accepted as credible.

INTENDED AUDIENCE

Understanding the intended audience is useful in determining whether or not a piece of information is suitable for a particular information need. If your nutrition professor has required that everyone in the class use scholarly information sources for their final papers, then any nutrition information intended for nonscholarly audiences—children, the general public, owners of health-food stores, and so forth—is automatically unsuitable.

ACCURACY

In the fast-paced and often informal world of the Web, standards for grammar, spelling, and punctuation are more relaxed than in the traditional world of print. However, when a piece of information is riddled with basic errors, the careful information seeker starts questioning the credibility of the source. If a source presenting information on the artist Michelangelo cannot correctly spell the name of the artist or the names of the cities in which his artwork may be seen, it pays to wonder if other information presented by this source—dates, for just one example—may be similarly unreliable.

INDEPENDENT CONFIRMATION

A good way to evaluate the credibility of any source of information is to see if the information it presents can be independently confirmed. First off, it helps when authors cite the sources of information they used in their research. This means accurate, verifiable citations and not such generic citations as "leading experts agree," "it has been written," and other favorites of the hedger.

Figure 5–4: Reviewing Reviews

A review can help an information seeker by providing a third-party assessment of an information resource. Just as with any other type of information, it is necessary to evaluate the quality of a review before accepting or rejecting any conclusions it draws. When evaluating a review, it is necessary to ask many of the same questions asked of any other piece of information:

- Who wrote the review and is the reviewer qualified to make a knowledgeable and fair assessment of the thing he or she is reviewing?
- Where was the review published? Scholarly journal? Popular magazine? Personal Web page?
- Does the review reflect a careful reading of the thing being reviewed or does it seem to be a hasty opinion. (A one-sentence review that reads, "This book sucks," does not reflect careful reading.)

Also remember that a negative review can sometimes tell you that the thing being reviewed may very well fit your information need. Let's say the reviewer of a book on quantum mechanics criticizes it as being too basic for anyone who holds a degree in physics. That may be just the news you want to hear if you happen to be looking for a quantum physics book that a lay reader might understand.

Book Reviews

The most common type of review is the book review. An information seeker can track down book reviews by using specialized indexes of book reviews or by using periodical indexes. For example, to find a review of the business book *Less Is More: How Great Companies Use Productivity as a Competitive Tool in Business* an information seeker could search *ABI/Inform*, an index to business periodicals.

A quick way to find book reviews is to look up a book on a commercial bookstore Web site such as *amazon.com* or *www.barnesandnoble.com*. On such Web sites you may find:

- Excerpts from book reviews originally published in scholarly journals, popular magazines, trade publications, or newspapers.
- Blurbs written by the publisher of the book.

Figure 5–4: *(continued)*

- Online reviews submitted by visitors to the Web site.

Be aware that publishers have a vested interest in promoting sales of their books, so publishers' blurbs will never say anything critical of the book they are promoting. Also be aware that anyone, regardless of their lack knowledge or lack of objectivity, can submit a review to an online bookstore. Authors can even submit online reviews of their own books—sometimes under false names in order to give the impression of impartiality.

Review Articles

Specific articles from journals or magazines are rarely reviewed. Scholarly journals, however, publish special articles called "review articles" that analyze a number of recent articles on a very specific topic. Review articles are useful to information seekers because they often provide a convenient summary of the topic in question and also identify potentially useful articles on the topic.

The "systematic review" is a special type of review article that analyzes the findings of a number of recent articles on a specific topic and then synthesizes a consensus based on the findings of all the articles analyzed. For example, a systematic review might analyze the findings from all the recent articles on drug therapies for schizophrenia and then synthesize a consensus on the best way to treat schizophrenia with drugs. Reading a systematic review article is a good way to get a crash course in the latest thinking on a topic.

Reviews of Web Sites

The most common place to find reviews of Web sites is on the Web itself. Just be aware that reviews found on the open Web can be written by anyone and vary wildly in quality and objectivity.

The author of a Web site will sometimes make links to other sites that comment on his or her site, but such links almost never point to negative comments, only to positive ones. Some magazines and journals publish reviews of Web sites, and, just as with book reviews, such Web site reviews can be found through periodical indexes.

Evaluations of Web sites (as well as of printed books and articles) can sometimes be found in archives of listserv groups. For example, the archives of a listserv devoted to the history of the First World War might include threads evaluating various information resources relating to the War. As always, the quality and objectivity of such evaluations is entirely dependent on the knowledge and objectivity of those making the evaluations.

Information seekers can also go off on their own to see if information found in other sources supports what is found in the original source. The caveat here is to make sure that the other sources are themselves reliable. Especially on the Web, an information seeker might easily locate ten independent sources that all present the same wrong information. Ten (or 50 or 1,000) wrongs don't make a right.

Independent reviews can be helpful in determining credibility. See the box above, "Reviewing Reviews."

COVERAGE

How thoroughly a source covers its subject is yet another possible criterion for evaluation. One aspect of coverage to consider is what information is included and what is excluded. For example, an article on continent formation that fails to even mention plate tectonics would be suspect for such a glaring exclusion. Similarly, an article on planetary motion that seriously considered the possibility that the Earth is the center of the Universe would be suspect for including such long-discredited idea. Another aspect of coverage is depth. A Web page that attempted to cover the entire history of space exploration in two short paragraphs could not hope to offer the depth of a printed book that takes several hundred pages to do the same thing. Longer is not necessarily better, but it allows for the possibility of greater depth.

CITATION INDEXES

One method for evaluating scholarly journal articles is to consult the citation indexes published by the Institute for Scientific Information (ISI). These indexes allow information seekers to see the number of times that a particular article has been cited by authors of other articles in scholarly journals. The idea is that the more often an article has been cited, the greater its significance. The three ISI citation indexes are *Science Citation Index*, *Social Sciences Citation Index*, and *Arts & Humanities Citation Index*. Both the print and Web versions of these indexes are proprietary and require a paid subscription.

IMPACT FACTORS

Another method for evaluating scholarly journal articles is *ISI Journal Citation Reports*. This publication ranks scholarly journals based on the frequency with which the articles they publish are cited in other journals. The idea is that the more often a journal's articles are cited, the more important the journal is. By extension, articles published in high-impact journals are more prestigious than articles published in low-impact journals. As with the ISI citation indexes, *ISI Journal Citation Reports* is a proprietary, subscription-based resource.

LOGICAL FALLACIES

The appearance of any of the following logical fallacies is a red flag that the author of the information is either not playing by the rules or trying to trick the unwary reader. Though the most common logical fallacies are listed here, there are many others. Lists of logical fallacies and illustrative examples of fallacies may be found in college textbooks for both introductory philosophy courses and introductory writing courses.

Findings Based on a Single Authority

Experiments conducted by Dr. Blue show that eating strawberries cures breast cancer. His findings have been suppressed because the medical establishment is out to get him. As appealing as the idea of the lone, scorned, unrecognized genius may be, it is more the stuff of movies than of real life. The history of science shows that, much more often than not, genuine advances in scientific knowledge are warmly welcomed by the scientific community. Most "scorned geniuses" present findings that are not reproducible by other scientists, and reproducible results are part of the very definition of what is science.

Other authority-related fallacies include:

- Citing an anonymous authority or authorities. "All the leading experts agree. . . ."
- Citing an authority whose credentials do not qualify him or her as an expert on the subject in question. (It turns out Dr. Blue deserves the title of doctor only because he has a Ph.D. in art history.)
- Citing one authority as the final word on the subject without acknowledging that there is a significant amount of disagreement among equally qualified experts on the topic.

Findings Based on Anecdotal Evidence or Small Samples

A woman in Wisconsin ate strawberries and recovered from breast cancer. Even if the anecdote is true (many such stories are not), the sample (in this case, one person) is too small to be generalized to the population as a whole; that is, this one case does not prove that strawberries were the reason for the cure nor that strawberries will cure breast cancer in others.

Incomplete Information

A woman in Wisconsin ate strawberries and recovered from breast cancer. True. But the author failed to mention that she also underwent chemotherapy and radiation treatments at the same time she was eating all those strawberries.

Selective Bibliography

I can cite two studies that show strawberries cure cancer. But I am not going to cite the 75 studies that show strawberries have no effect at all.

Personal Attacks or Prejudicial Language

One of the biggest critics of strawberry therapy is Dr. Green, a so-called expert who has been censured for sexual harassment in the workplace. Dr. Green's personal behavior may be reprehensible, but it has nothing to do with whether or not strawberry therapy is a real cure or a fraud. Labeling Dr. Green as a "so-called expert" without any support for this accusation is an example of prejudicial language of the sort that honest scholars do not employ.

Statistical Shenanigans

If trends continue, every woman in the country will eventually fall victim to breast cancer. The preceding sentence is an example of a flat-line projection, a pseudo statistic that can be used to prove just about anything. Under the illogic of the flat-line projection, if it is raining when you wake up, it would be possible to say, "If trends continue, it will never stop raining." A flat-line projection is just one of many ways in which statistics (or pseudo-statistics) can be used to draw false conclusions. Sorting out the good statistics from the bad is not easy, and sometimes even the experts disagree. The best advice for those who are not trained in statistics is to follow this rule: The more astonishing the statistic, the more skeptical you should be.

No Areas of Uncertainty

Strawberries cure breast cancer 100% of the time in 100% of patients. Nothing is that certain.

False Dilemma

Either eat strawberries or die of breast cancer. False dilemmas present only a few options (usually two) when there may be many. You might not eat strawberries and still never get breast cancer. If you do get breast cancer, you might be cured and so not die of it. You might eat strawberries and die of breast cancer anyway. Or you might get run over by an ice-cream truck.

Arguments from Ignorance

Since science cannot prove that strawberries do not cure breast cancer, that proves they must cure it. Just because something has not been proven to be false does not mean that it is true. Failing to prove that UFOs do not exist is not proof that they do.

Faulty If/Then Reasoning

If you don't eat strawberries, your body will lack nutrients. If you lack proper nutrients, your immune system will be suppressed. If your immune system is suppressed, then you are more susceptible to illness. If you are susceptible to illness, then you are more likely to die of breast cancer. Putting together a slippery slope of if/then arguments seems convincing at first, but if you cut out the middle statements you see that the path from the first if/then to the final result is dubious at best.

Casual Fallacies

Statistics show that as strawberry consumption has declined, breast-cancer rates have increased. This may be quite true, but it does not prove that the decline in strawberry consumption is the *cause* of the rise in breast-cancer rates. The fact that one thing happened first does not prove that it caused something that happened later.

Casual fallacies take several forms, including the "complex-cause fallacy" that occurs when someone asserts that a single thing is the cause of something when, in fact, there are multiple causes. Asserting that "Poor diet causes cancer" is a complex-cause fallacy because even though diet is known to play a role in some types of cancer, cancer is a complex cluster of diseases and there are many other causes (smoking, pollutants, exposure to X-rays, genetic predisposition, etc.).

Another common casual fallacy is the "wrong-direction fallacy," which occurs when cause and effect are reversed. An example would be if someone contended that "Crime went up in the Erie Street Neighborhood because gun ownership went up," when, in truth, gun ownership did not go up until after crime went up.

Unrelated Points
If you believe that a proper diet is important to good health, then you must accept the fact that strawberries cure breast cancer. This type of fallacy makes it seem as if you must accept both points or reject both points, but the truth is you can accept one and still reject the other because the two points are not directly related to each other.

FINAL THOUGHTS ON EVALUATING INFORMATION

If an information seeker cannot remember anything else about evaluating information, then at least remember:

1. Maintain a healthy skepticism about *all* information.
2. Question the purpose behind every piece of information.
3. Don't be fooled by cool. Great graphics, polished presentation, and glib language do not in themselves guarantee that the information being presented is good information.

PART II
12 READY-TO-GO POWERPOINT
PRESENTATIONS FOR TEACHING
ELECTRONIC INFORMATION LITERACY

1. BOOLEAN LOGIC

Boolean Logic

- George Boole
- 1854–Boolean Algebra
- Applications for computers

Boolean Operators

- AND
  - Narrows
- OR
  - Broadens
- NOT
  - Narrows

Boolean AND

A AND B

Boolean OR

A OR B

Boolean NOT

A NOT B

Boolean Logic

animal **AND** mammal

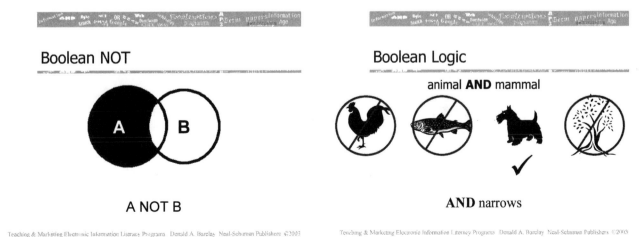

AND narrows

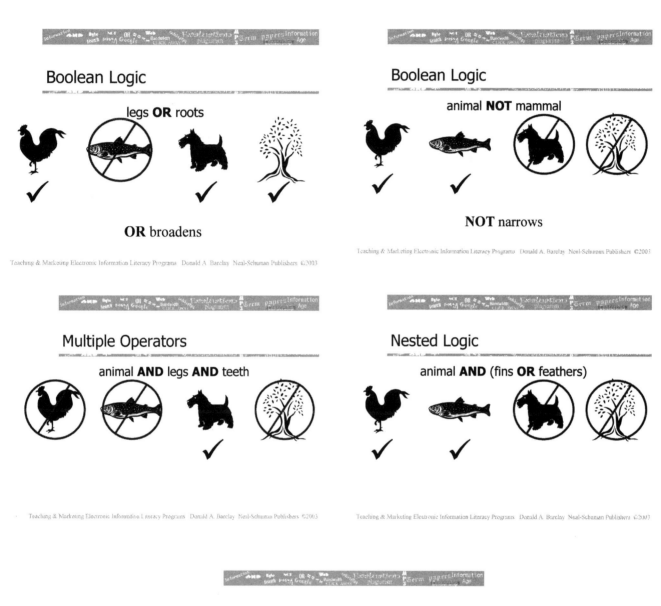

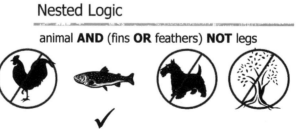

television **AND** violence

Calabro, Karen, Thomas A. Mackey, and Steven Williams. 2003. "Evaluation of training designed to prevent and manage patient violence." *Abstracts in Social Gerontology* 46, no. 1: 5-147

Nabi, R.L., and J.L. Sullivan. 2002. "Does television viewing relate to engagement in protective action against crime? A cultivation analysis from a theory of reasoned action perspective." *Violence & Abuse Abstracts* 8, no. 3 179-248.

Yan, M. Z. 2003. "Market structure and local signal carriage decisions in the cable television industry: results from count analysis." *Communication Abstracts* 26, no. 1: 3-151

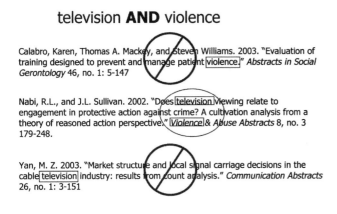

television **OR** violence

Calabro, Karen, Thomas A. Mackey, and Steven Williams. 2003. "Evaluation of training designed to prevent and manage patient violence." *Abstracts in Social Gerontology* 46, no. 1: 5-147

Nabi, R.L., and J.L. Sullivan. 2002. "Does television viewing relate to engagement in protective action against crime? A cultivation analysis from a theory of reasoned action perspective." *Violence & Abuse Abstracts* 8, no. 3 179-248.

Yan, M. Z. 2003. "Market structure and local signal carriage decisions in the cable television industry: results from count analysis." *Communication Abstracts* 26, no. 1: 3-151

television **NOT** violence

Calabro, Karen, Thomas A. Mackey, and Steven Williams. 2003. "Evaluation of training designed to prevent and manage patient violence." *Abstracts in Social Gerontology* 46, no. 1: 5-147

Nabi, R.L., and J.L. Sullivan. 2002. "Does television viewing relate to engagement in protective action against crime? A cultivation analysis from a theory of reasoned action perspective." *Violence & Abuse Abstracts* 8, no. 3 179-248.

Yan, M. Z. 2003. "Market structure and local signal carriage decisions in the cable television industry: results from count analysis." *Communication Abstracts* 26, no. 1: 3-151

television **AND** violence

Calabro, Karen, Thomas A. Mackey, and Steven Williams. 2003. "Evaluation of training designed to prevent and manage patient violence." *Abstracts in Social Gerontology* 46, no. 1: 5-147

Nabi, R.L., and J.L. Sullivan. 2002. "Does television viewing relate to engagement in protective action against crime? A cultivation analysis from a theory of reasoned action perspective." *Abstracts* 8, no. 3 179-248.

Yan, M. Z. 2003. "Market structure and local signal carriage decisions in the cable television industry: results from count analysis." *Communication Abstracts* 26, no. 1: 3-151

AND Narrows

television **OR** violence

Calabro, Karen, Thomas A. Mackey, and Steven Williams. 2003. "Evaluation of training designed to prevent and manage patient violence." *Abstracts in Social Gerontology* 46, no. 1: 5-147

Nabi, R.L., and J.L. Sullivan. 2002. "Does television viewing relate to engagement in protective action against crime? A cultivation analysis from a theory of reasoned action perspective." *Abstracts* 8, no. 3 179-248.

Yan, M. Z. 2003. "Market structure and local signal carriage decisions in the cable television industry: results from count analysis." *Communication Abstracts* 26, no. 1: 3-151

OR Broadens

television **NOT** violence

Calabro, Karen, Thomas A. Mackey, and Steven Williams. 2003. "Evaluation of training designed to prevent and manage patient violence." *Abstracts in Social Gerontology* 46, no. 1: 5-147

Nabi, R.L., and J.L. Sullivan. 2002. "Does television viewing relate to engagement in protective action against crime? A cultivation analysis from a theory of reasoned action perspective." *Violence & Abuse Abstracts* 8, no. 3 179-248.

Yan, M. Z. 2003. "Market structure and local signal carriage decisions in the cable television industry: results from count analysis." *Communication Abstracts* 26, no. 1: 3-151

NOT Narrows

2. ECONOMICS OF ELECTRONIC INFORMATION

Economics of Electronic Information

Information can be open access . . .

. . . but no information is free.

Open-Access Information

Open-access information is freely available to anyone, but the costs associated with its creation and accessibility must still be paid by *someone*:

- A government agency
  - PubMed
- An organization
  - Project Gutenberg
- A business
  - Ford Motor Company
- An individual
  - Personal Web pages

Proprietary Information Resources

- Full-text books & periodicals.
- Bibliographic databases.
- Fee-based information services
- Proprietary information resources require some form of payment for access to the information they contain.

Access to Proprietary Information Can Be Controlled By . . .

- Password
- IP Address
- Digital Certificates

Proprietary Information Payment Schemes

- Individual pays per-use or by subscription.
- School, library, or other entity pays subscription on behalf of its students, faculty, employees, etc.
- Access to information paid for by advertisers.
  - This last scheme has largely failed and was in-part responsible for the dot-com bust.

Proprietary Information Is Big Business

- Reed Elsevier
  - 2001 total revenues @ $6,609,246,000.
- †EBSCO Information Services
  - Annual sales began topping the $1 billion mark in 1997.
- †Wolters Kluwer
  - 2001 sales @ $3,254,521,000.
- †Bertelsman Media Worldwide
  - FY 2000-2001 net income @ $853,212,000.

3. ELECTRONIC SEARCHING ESSENTIALS

Electronic Searching Essentials

Teaching & Marketing Electronic Information Literacy Programs   Donald A. Barclay   Neal-Schuman Publishers ©2003

Electronic Searching Is Not Perfect . . .

- Most electronic searching simply matches identical terms.
- It does not take into account meaning or context.

Teaching & Marketing Electronic Information Literacy Programs   Donald A. Barclay   Neal-Schuman Publishers ©2003

Electronic Searching Is Not Perfect . . .

- Example: Searching *Columbus* retrieves hits on:
  - Christopher Columbus (15th Century explorer).
  - Chris Columbus (film director, b. 1958).
  - "Goodbye Columbus" (short story, 1959).
  - *Goodbye Columbus* (film, 1969).
  - Columbus, Ohio; Columbus, New Mexico; Columbus, Georgia . . . .

Teaching & Marketing Electronic Information Literacy Programs   Donald A. Barclay   Neal-Schuman Publishers ©2003

Hit

- A *hit* is anything retrieved by a search.
  - Searching *cancer* in *PubMed* database retrieves @ 1.5 million hits.
- Retrieving overwhelming numbers of hits is one of the biggest obstacles to searching large information resources, including the Web.

Teaching & Marketing Electronic Information Literacy Programs   Donald A. Barclay   Neal-Schuman Publishers ©2003

False Drop

- A *false drop* is anything retrieved by a search that is not relevant to what the searcher intended to find.
  - Example: Searching *Ronald Reagan* in hopes of finding information on the former President might retrieve false drops relating to *Ronald Reagan National Airport*.
  - Example: Searching *bonds* in hopes of finding investment information might retrieve false drops relating to baseball player *Barry Bonds*.

Teaching & Marketing Electronic Information Literacy Programs   Donald A. Barclay   Neal-Schuman Publishers ©2003

It Pays to Prepare in Advance When Searching an Unfamiliar Topic

- Read a relevant article or two from a general or subject encyclopedia.
- Get familiar with key terms and names associated with the topic.
  - Knowing how to spell key terms and names is essential when conducting an electronic search.

Teaching & Marketing Electronic Information Literacy Programs   Donald A. Barclay   Neal-Schuman Publishers ©2003

Techniques And Concepts

That every electronic searcher should know.

Databases

- All searchable electronic information resources are built on some type of database.
- Most are built on relational databases.
- Size of database, quality of content, and quality of indexing are key to the usefulness of any electronic-information resource.

Record

A record is a collection of fields (title, author, abstract, subject heading, etc.) that represents one *thing*.

Sample Database Record

ARTICLE RECORD

NAL CALL NO	41.8 V641
Author	Barlow, R.M.
Article Title	Dietary transmission of bovine spongiform encephalopathy to mice.
Source Info	The Veterinary record : journal of the British Veterinary Association.Feb 3, 1990. v. 126 (5) (ABBREV TITLE = Vet Rec J Br Vet Assoc)
Pages	p. 111-112. ill.
Note	Includes references.
CAB Subject	cattle diseases.
CAB Subject	encephalopathy.
CAB Subject	disease transmission.
CAB Subject	mice.
CAB Subject	brain.
CAB Subject	cerebrospinal fluid.
CAB Subject	scrapie agent.
Other Author	Middleton, D.J.

Record (cont.)

- In a bibliographic database, a record is typically a *citation* to a book, article or other publication.
- In a full-text database, a record is typically the *full text* of an article, book chapter, or other publication.
- In Web search engines, records contain *links* to Web pages, not actual Web pages.

Help Menu

- Reading help menus leads to more effective searches.
- Reading help menus is essential when using unfamiliar resources.
- Help menus often provide important information about the scope of an information resource.

Elements of Scope

- Subjects covered.
  - Business? History? Anything and everything?
- Intended audience.
  - Scholars/experts? Laypersons? Children?
- Types of information included or excluded:
  - Full-text documents? Citations? Images?
- Information formats included or excluded:
  - Journal articles? Dissertations? Book chapters?

Elements of Scope (cont.)

- Time period covered.
  - Example: If a database contains citations to articles published from 1979 to the present, a searcher cannot use it to look up an article published in 1973.
- Currency.
  - How often resource is updated?
- Other possible limitations:
  - Place of publication, language of publication, provenance.

Defaults

- Electronic-information resources typically have default settings.
  - Example: Some Web search engines default to a Boolean **OR** search.
- Defaults vary from resource to resource.
- Check help menus to learn:
  - What the defaults are.
  - How to override them if need be.

Keyword Searching

- User types in keyword(s), information resource displays matches.
- Keyword matching occurs without regard for meaning or context.
  - *Indian* (Native American) equivalent to *Indian* (native of Asian subcontinent).
- Keyword searching may search full text or only bibliographic information (title, subject, abstract, etc.), depending on information resource.

4. ELECTRONIC SEARCHING ESSENTIALS 2

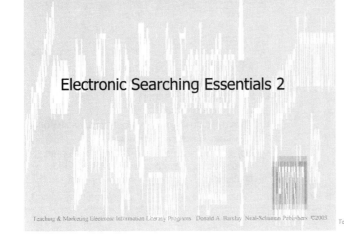

Electronic Searching Essentials 2

Proximity Operators

- Search words/phrases must be within a certain number of words to produce a hit.
- Most commonly used proximity operator is NEAR.
- Usually a default distance for NEAR searches.
    - Within 10 words, in same paragraph, etc.
- Searcher may have option to select a proximity other than the default or to specify the order in which search words/phrases appear be considered.

Sample Proximity Operator Search

europe **NEAR** disease **NEAR** cattle

produces a hit on the following article:

Since 1996, evidence has been increasing for a causal relationship between ongoing outbreaks in Europe of a disease in cattle called bovine spongiform encephalopathy (BSE, or "mad cow disease") and a disease in humans called new variant Cruetzfeldt-Jakob disease (nvCJD). Both disorders are invariably fatal brain diseases with unusually long incubation periods measured in years, and are caused by an unconventional transmissible agent (a prion). Although there is strong evidence that . . .

Sample Proximity Operator Search

europe **NEAR** disease **NEAR** cattle

Since 1996, evidence has been increasing for a causal relationship between ongoing outbreaks in **Europe** of a **disease** in **cattle** called bovine spongiform encephalopathy (BSE, or "mad cow disease") and a disease in humans called new variant Cruetzfeldt-Jakob disease (nvCJD). Both disorders are invariably fatal brain diseases with unusually long incubation periods measured in years, and are caused by an unconventional transmissible agent (a prion). Although there is strong evidence that . . .

Fixed Vocabularies

- Fixed vocabularies try to compensate for the inability of computers to understand meaning and context.
- Not all information resources use fixed vocabularies.
    - The average Web search engine does not use fixed vocabularies.
- Fixed-vocabulary searches are usually not default.
    - Searchers must intentionally limit a search to fixed vocabulary. Limit procedure varies from resource to resource.

Subject Headings

- Subject headings are a product of fixed vocabularies.
- Subject headings are assigned by indexers in order to improve both precision and recall.
- Cross references may redirect searchers to broader, narrower, alternative, or preferred subject headings.

Search of the subject heading **airplane** in a typical online library catalog . . .

- Would retrieve *Esos Intrépidos Hombres del Aire: Antología de Anécdotas Y Cuentos de Aviación.*
  - Even though the word *airplane* appears nowhere in the book.
- Would **not** retrieve *Airplane!* (screenplay of the 1980 movie).
  - Even though the word *airplane* is in the title.

Subject Categories

- Often used by Web directories.
  - Yahoo! is classic example.
- Start with broad category.
  - Example: **Education**.
- "Peel the onion" down to more specific categories.
  - Example: **Elementary Schools**.
- Subject categories are useful but lack the precision and consistency found in well managed fixed vocabularies.

Metadata

- Data about data.
  - Subject headings are one type of metadata.
- A Web page may have metadata that provides information about the:
  - topic of page, who created it, when, where, etc.
- Metadata can aid electronic searching but can also be used deceptively.
- Some Web search engines ignore metadata.

Web Conventions

- Searchers must understand basic conventions used on the Web.
  - Example: Clicking on the down arrow on a box like this:

    `Search a State ▾`

    gives access to a drop-down menu.
- *Mousercise* is useful for those who need to learn Web conventions.

Limits

- Many electronic-information resources allow searchers to limit searches as a way of narrowing search results.
- Specifics of how to set limits vary from resource to resource.
  - Read help menus.

Typical Limits

- Field
  - Limit search to a particular field: author field, title field, subject-heading field, abstract field, and so on.
- Language
  - Limit search results to a single language.
  - Exclude a particular language.
- Date of publication
  - Limit results to a particular date or date range.

Typical Limits (cont.)

- Format
  - Retrieve only full-text documents, or only images, or only audio files.
- Phrase
  - Search *nuclear fusion* as a phrase rather than as separate keywords.
- Proximity
  - Search *obstetrics* but only when it appears within *n* words of *liability*.

Basic And Advanced Searching

- Electronic-information resources commonly offer both basic and advanced search interfaces.
  - Usually default to basic. Searcher must select advanced.
- Advanced search interfaces generally allow for more precise searching.
- Rules for constructing advanced searches can differ greatly from those for basic searches.
  - Read help menus.

Truncation

- Truncation retrieves hits on various forms of a search word.
  - Truncating *costume* to *costum** retrieves hits on: *costume, costumes, costumed, costuming, costumer,* or *costumers.*
  - Truncating *woman* to *wom*n* retrieves hits on either *woman* or *women.*
- Some information resources truncate automatically to allow for plurals, variants, etc.
- The asterisk is widely used as a truncation symbol but is not universal.

Display Order And Format

- Searchers may be able to specify the order in which results are displayed.
  - Most recent to oldest.
  - Oldest to most recent.
  - Alphabetically by author or title.
  - By relevance (as determined by the search engine).
- Searchers may be able to specify display format.
  - Brief citation.
  - Citation plus abstract.
  - Full text.

Search-History Feature

- Search-history feature displays searches already conducted during a search session.
  - Allows searchers to combine previous searches with each other or with additional search terms.
  - Searches may be combined using line numbers rather than retyping entire search.
- Save-search feature allows searchers to permanently save frequently used searches.

Stopwords

- Stopwords are common words that most information resources will not search.
  - Examples: *of, the, an, a, to, from,* etc.
- The words *and, or,* and *not* may be treated as stopwords unless the searcher follows the information resource's rules for specifying that the word is being used as a Boolean operator.
  - Example: **AND** is treated as a Boolean operator while **and** is treated as a stopword.

Vague Or Common Words

- Vague words are not useful in electronic searching.
  - Examples: *impact, aspect, effect, role, ramifications, results, influence,* etc.
- The same is true for words found throughout a database.
  - Example: Keyword searching the word *education* in the *ERIC* (education) database is not helpful—virtually every record in *ERIC* includes the word *education* somewhere.

Natural-Language Searching

- Intent is to let searchers construct searches without the need for Boolean operators, limits, and the like.
- Technology of natural-language searching has a long way to go.
- Ask Jeeves is one well known example of a natural-language search engine.
  - www.askjeeves.com

5. ETHICS OF ELECTRONIC INFORMATION

The Ethics of Electronic Information

The Three *C*s

- Cheating.
- Copyright.
- Crime.

Cheating Is Not New

- Friends have always "helped" friends with papers.
- Term-paper mills advertised in popular magazines.
- Residence houses maintained files of papers.
- Students intentionally or unintentionally put unattributed quotations and paraphrases into their papers.

Online Cheating

- Makes cheating quicker and easier:
  - Credit-card payment.
  - Cut & paste.
- Extends the cheater's reach worldwide.
- Has brought more term-paper mills into the market.
- Is, in some ways, easier to detect than old-fashioned plagiarism.

Your Instructors Know

- About *Cheathouse.com*, *schoolsucks.com*, and so on.
- How to type a suspect phrase into a search engine.
- The hallmarks of a plagiarized paper.

Hallmarks of Plagiarized Papers

- Quality of the work or comprehension of topic is unexpectedly high (or low).
- Few or no recent sources are cited.
- Topic varies (a little or a lot) from proposed topic.
- Style of some sentences or paragraphs markedly different from the rest of the work.

Possible Penalties for Plagiarism

- Failing grade.
- Expulsion.
- Firing.
- Civil suit.
- Criminal charges.

What Is Plagiarism?

Presenting the words or ideas of someone else as if they were your own.

What Is Not Plagiarism?

- Your original words.
- Your original ideas.
- Common knowledge.

What Is Common Knowledge?

Generally agreed upon facts that do not change in any essential way and which are referenced in multiple sources:

- Babe Ruth hit 714 career home runs.
- Tunis is a city located at 36° 47' North latitude and 10° 12' East longitude.
- John Wilkes Booth shot Abraham Lincoln in Ford's Theater on April 14, 1865.
- The formula for finding the area under a curve is:

$$A = \int_{x_1}^{x_2} y\,dx$$

How to Avoid Intentional Plagiarism

Don't do it.

How to Avoid Unintentional Plagiarism

- Learn what is or is not plagiarism.
- Learn how to cite sources.
- Remember to cite paraphrases as well as direct quotations.

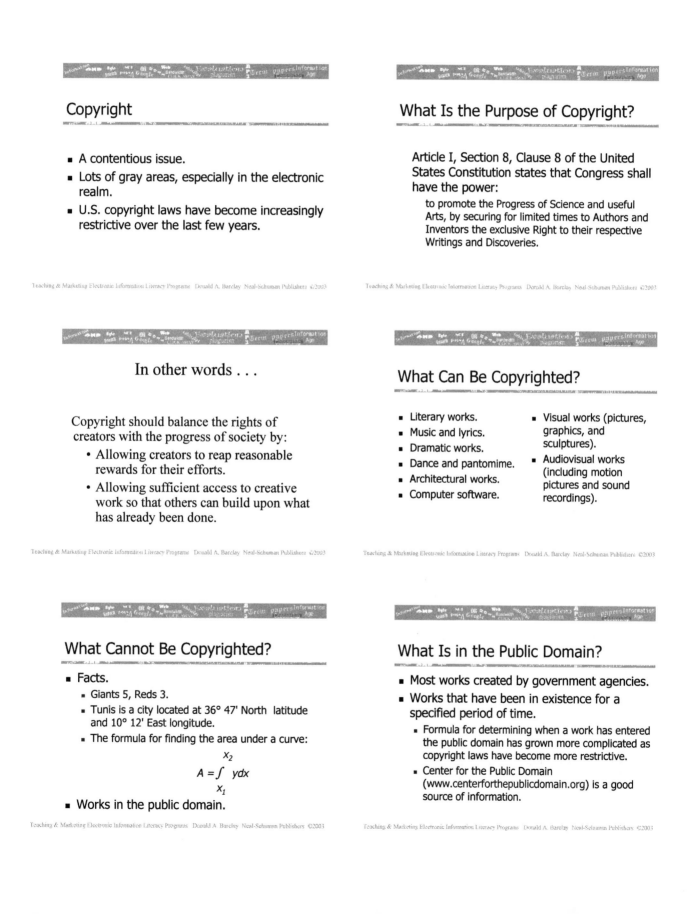

Copyright

- A contentious issue.
- Lots of gray areas, especially in the electronic realm.
- U.S. copyright laws have become increasingly restrictive over the last few years.

What Is the Purpose of Copyright?

Article I, Section 8, Clause 8 of the United States Constitution states that Congress shall have the power:

> to promote the Progress of Science and useful Arts, by securing for limited times to Authors and Inventors the exclusive Right to their respective Writings and Discoveries.

In other words . . .

Copyright should balance the rights of creators with the progress of society by:

- Allowing creators to reap reasonable rewards for their efforts.
- Allowing sufficient access to creative work so that others can build upon what has already been done.

What Can Be Copyrighted?

- Literary works.
- Music and lyrics.
- Dramatic works.
- Dance and pantomime.
- Architectural works.
- Computer software.
- Visual works (pictures, graphics, and sculptures).
- Audiovisual works (including motion pictures and sound recordings).

What Cannot Be Copyrighted?

- Facts.
  - Giants 5, Reds 3.
  - Tunis is a city located at 36° 47' North latitude and 10° 12' East longitude.
  - The formula for finding the area under a curve:
    $$A = \int_{x_1}^{x_2} y\,dx$$
- Works in the public domain.

What Is in the Public Domain?

- Most works created by government agencies.
- Works that have been in existence for a specified period of time.
  - Formula for determining when a work has entered the public domain has grown more complicated as copyright laws have become more restrictive.
  - Center for the Public Domain (www.centerforthepublicdomain.org) is a good source of information.

Intellectual Property

- The term *intellectual property* is broader than *copyright*.
- Encompasses everything covered by copyright plus: ideas, inventions, trade secrets, processes, data, formulas, patents, and trademarks.

If You Violate Copyright

- You might get a cease-and-desist letter.
- You might get sued in civil court.
- You might be charged with a crime if . . .
  - You make more than ten copies with a value of over $2,500.
  - You intentionally circumvent copyright-protection technology.

Fair Use

- The fair-use exemption allows educational use of copyrighted material.
- In most cases, student work done for classes is covered under fair use.
- There are four factors for determining fair use . . .

Four Fair-Use Factors

- Is work used for nonprofit educational purposes?
- What is the nature of the copyrighted work?
  - Use of factual works is more likely considered fair use than is the use of fictional/creative works.
- How much of work is being used?
- Does use harm potential market for/value of work?

Crime

Yes, misuse of electronic-information resources or misuse of computers can cross over into the criminal realm.

No, pleading, "But I'm only a student," will not lessen the penalties for any computer crimes you might commit.

Common Computer Crimes

- Using a computer to commit fraud or theft.
- Violating copyright for commercial purposes.
  - More than 10 copies worth more than $2,500.
- Distributing or receiving child pornography.
- Threatening or harassing someone via computer.
- Releasing viruses or worms.
- Gaining illegal access to computer systems (hacking).

6. EVALUATING INFORMATION

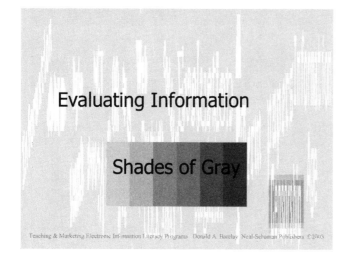

Evaluating Information

- The average person is bombarded with information, much of it unreliable.
- Evaluation requires both knowledge of information and critical-thinking abilities.
- Possibly the most important skill a citizen of the Information Age can possess.

Scholarly Information

- A highly credible type of information.
- Students often required to use scholarly information for research papers and projects.
- Knowing how to identify scholarly information is an important skill.

Scholarly	Non Scholarly
Author	**Author**
- Holds advanced degree in subject written about.	- May be journalist, professional writer, or amateur.
- Often professors.	- May have a lot of knowledge of subject written about—or next to none.
- Pairs or teams of researchers often collaborate to write a single article, chapter, book, etc.	

Scholarly	Non Scholarly
Research Methods	**Research Methods**
- Writings based on original research conducted by the author(s).	- Non-scholarly authors rarely conduct original research.
- Conduct a literature review prior to research.	- Research based on readings, interviews, etc.
- Ethically obligated to follow certain standards for impartial research.	- Quality and impartiality of research entirely dependent on the author

Scholarly	Non Scholarly
Peer Review	**Peer Review**
- Panel of scholars decides if information should be published.	- No peer review.
- Peer review may be blind.	- Decision to publish typically resides with editors.
- Also known as "refereeing" or "refereed journal."	- On Web, in particular, decision to publish may reside with author alone.

Scholarly | Non Scholarly

Objectivity
- By and large, the most objective type of information.
- However, scholars are human:
  - Mistakes.
  - Biases.
  - Personal rivalries.
  - Dishonesty.

Objectivity
- Objectivity is entirely dependent on the author.
- Can be objective, biased, or anywhere in between.

Scholarly | Non Scholarly

Audience
- Other scholars.
- Assumes readers have a high level of knowledge.
- Scholarly information may be unintelligible to the layperson.

Audience
- May be broad or specialized.
- *Time* magazine—seeks a broad audience.
- *Fly Fishing & Fly Tying*—seeks a specialized (but non-scholarly) audience.

Scholarly | Non Scholarly

Important Formats
- Articles published in peer-reviewed (aka "refereed") scholarly journals
- Scholarly books
  - Books by a single author.
  - Books with chapters by different scholars.

Important Formats
- Anything and everything
  - Magazines.
  - Newspapers.
  - Books.
  - Comic books.
  - Personal Web sites.
  - Videos.
  - Etc., etc.

Scholarly | Non Scholarly

Publishers
- Typically nonprofit, but can be for profit.
- Often associated with learned societies or universities.
- Market publications to scholars and academic libraries.

Publishers
- Typically for profit, but can be nonprofit.
- Commercial potential of a publication is often, though not always, the most important consideration.

Scholarly | Non Scholarly

Rewards
- Promotion and tenure.
- Respect of peers.
- Satisfaction of contributing new knowledge.
- Scholarly publications rarely earn much, if any, money for author.

Rewards
- Money.
- Prestige.
- Personal satisfaction.

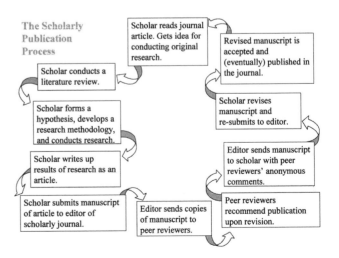

The Scholarly Publication Process

Scholar reads journal article. Gets idea for conducting original research.

Scholar conducts a literature review.

Scholar forms a hypothesis, develops a research methodology, and conducts research.

Scholar writes up results of research as an article.

Scholar submits manuscript of article to editor of scholarly journal.

Editor sends copies of manuscript to peer reviewers.

Peer reviewers recommend publication upon revision.

Editor sends manuscript to scholar with peer reviewers' anonymous comments.

Scholar revises manuscript and re-submits to editor.

Revised manuscript is accepted and (eventually) published in the journal.

Scholarly Journals Versus Popular Magazines

- Scholarly journals and popular magazines have superficial resemblances.
- Scholarly journals present research findings.
  - Intended audience is scholars.
- Magazines present news, information, opinion, and entertainment.
  - Intended audience is general public.

Identifying Scholarly Journals

- Scholarly journals often have the word *journal* in the title.
  - But *Ladies Home Journal* is a magazine.
- Other common title phrases for journals include:
  - *proceedings of*
  - *transactions of*
  - *publication of*
  - *bulletin of*

Identifying Scholarly Journals

- If cover or title page indicates affiliation with a learned society or association, it is probably a scholarly journal.

Athletic Physical Therapy

Publication of the Canadian Association of Sports Physical Therapists

Identifying Scholarly Journals

- Scholarly journals focus on a single, often very narrow subject area.
- Other than ads for scholarly books, most do not contain advertisements .
  - There are exceptions.
  - Example: Scholarly medical journals often carry advertisements for prescription drugs.

Identifying Scholarly Journals

- As a rule, scholarly journals look very plain compared to popular magazines
- Lots of text, not a lot of images, not a lot of color.
- There are exceptions to this rule.
  - Example: Scholarly art journals have many color images.

Identifying Scholarly Journals

- Most articles in scholarly journals have footnotes and/or bibliographies.
  - Scholarly authors *always* cite the sources they use in their research.
- Most scholarly journals will have an "Instruction to Authors" section.
  - These give authors the procedure for submitting manuscripts for publication.
  - Instructions may not appear in every issue.

Is print information always more credible than Web Information?

- No. You can find good and bad information in print just as you can on the Web.
- Some Web information is the exact equivalent of print information.
  - Example: A journal publishes an identical article both in print and on its Web site.
- Some Web sites impose exacting quality-control standards.
  - Peer review, careful editing, fact checking.

Logical Fallacies

- Arguments may sound reasonable but, on examination, are not.
- Used to mislead readers and listeners.
- Information sources that employ logical fallacies are worthy of suspicion.
- Examples of some of the more common logical fallacies include . . .

Authority Fallacies

- Findings based on a single authority.
- Citing anonymous authority or authorities. "All the leading experts agree . . ."
- Citing an authority who is not really an expert on the subject in question.
- Failing to acknowledge that there is a significant amount of disagreement among equally qualified experts on the topic.

Fallacy: Findings Based on Anecdotal Evidence or Small Samples

A woman in Wisconsin ate strawberries and recovered from breast cancer.

- If this is true, were strawberries the reason she recovered?
- Will strawberries have the same effect on others?

Fallacy: Incomplete Information

A woman in Wisconsin ate strawberries and recovered from breast cancer.

- True. But she also underwent chemotherapy and radiation treatments at the same time she was eating all those strawberries.

Fallacy: Selective Bibliography

I can cite two studies that show strawberries cure cancer.

- But I am not going to cite the seventy-five studies that show strawberries have no effect at all.

Fallacy: Personal Attacks or Prejudicial Language

One of the biggest critics of strawberry therapy is Dr. Green, a "so-called expert" who has been censured for sexual harassment in the workplace.

- Dr. Green's personal behavior, however bad, has nothing to do with his criticism of strawberry therapy.
- Labeling Dr. Green as a "so-called expert" without any support for this charge is prejudicial language.

Fallacy: Flat-Line Projections

If trends continue, every woman in the country will eventually fall victim to breast cancer.

- It is raining right now. If trends continue, it will never stop raining.
- Flat-line projections are just one of many ways to misrepresent statistical data.
- The more astounding the statistic, the more skeptical you should be.

Fallacy: No Areas of Uncertainty

Strawberries cure breast cancer 100% of the time in 100% of patients.

- Nothing is that certain.
- Even when the percentage is lowered to *99.something*, nothing is that certain.

Fallacy: False Dilemma

Either eat strawberries or die of cancer.

- False dilemmas present only two options when their may be many:
  - Eat strawberries and still die of cancer.
  - Don't eat strawberries, get cancer, and be cured by some other means.
  - Get run over by an ice-cream truck whether you eat strawberries or not.

Fallacy: Arguments from Ignorance

If science cannot prove that strawberries do not cure breast cancer, that proves they do.

- Failing to prove that Santa Claus does not exist does not prove that he does.
- Failing to prove that UFOs are not real does not prove that they are.

Fallacy: Faulty If/Then Reasoning

1. *If you don't eat strawberries, then your body will lack proper nutrients.*
2. *If you lack proper nutrients, then your immune system will be suppressed.*
3. *If your immune system is suppressed, then you are more susceptible to illness.*
4. *If you are susceptible to illness, then you are more likely to die of breast cancer.*

- Beware of slippery slopes created by chaining together if/then statements.

Casual Fallacies

As strawberry consumption has declined, breast-cancer rates have increased.

- Even if true, the fact that one thing happened first is not proof that it caused the later thing.
- Disco dancing became popular in the early 1970s, and so in 1978 the Yankees won their second consecutive World Series.

Other Casual Fallacies:

- Complex-cause fallacy: *Poor nutrition causes cancer.*
  - Nutrition is one of *many* things that are known to contribute to cancer. The causes of cancer are complex, not simple.
- Wrong-direction fallacy: *Crime went up on 12th Street as gun ownership went up.*
  - In the case of 12th Street, crime went up first. Gun ownership went up in *response* to crime.

Fallacy: Unrelated Points

If you believe that a proper diet is important to good health, then you must accept the fact that strawberries cure breast cancer.

- Such a statement makes it seem as if you must accept both points if you accept either. In fact, you can accept one while rejecting the other.

Primary Versus Secondary Sources of Information

Primary information is an account or record of events in which the author was an actual participant or firsthand observer.

Secondary information is an account or record of events created some time after the events took place, typically by an author who was not a direct participant or observer.

Primary/Secondary Example

Primary:
A group of cancer researchers at UCLA Medical Center keep detailed records of a clinical trial they are conducting on a promising new cancer medicine.

Secondary:
The Los Angeles Times runs a news article telling how a group of cancer researchers at UCLA Medical Center are conducting a clinical trial of a new cancer medicine.

Typical **primary sources** include:

- Letters.
- Diaries.
- A researcher's laboratory or field notes.
- Collections of data.
- Government records.
- Speeches.
- Photographs.

Typical **secondary sources** include:

- Most periodical articles and books about past events.
  - Based on primary sources and secondary sources.
- Textbooks and encyclopedias.
- Anything one step removed from the events it describes.

A Source May Be Both Primary And Secondary

- A *Los Angeles Times* article about the 9/11/01 World Trade Center attacks is a secondary source for most purposes.
- However, it is a primary source to a researcher studying media responses to the attacks.

Teaching & Marketing Electronic Information Literacy Programs Donald A. Barclay Neal-Schuman Publishers ©2003

7. INFORMATION ROADBLOCKS

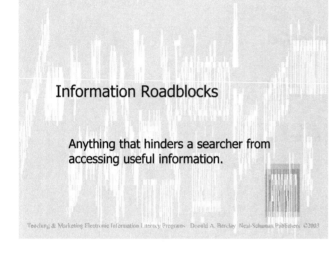

Information Roadblocks

Anything that hinders a searcher from accessing useful information.

Information Roadblocks

- Cost
  - Information cannot be accessed if individuals or institutions cannot afford to pay for access.
- Litigation
  - Lawsuits or court orders can make information disappear.
  - Example: In 2001, a lawsuit shut down the U.S. Department of the Interior's entire Web site for several weeks.

Information Roadblocks

- Gray Literature
  - Unpublished, undisseminated, informal, and/or ephemeral information is often hard to identify and access.
- Date of Creation
  - Information is usually harder to find if it is too old or too new to appear in electronic databases.

Information Roadblocks

- Lack of Subject Knowledge
  - Searchers may not know a subject well enough to be aware of (or even able to spell) key terms, concepts, and names associated with the subject.
  - Example: A student researching WW II may not know how to spell *Eisenhower* or not know that V-mail was a system that allowed U.S. soldiers serving overseas to send letters to the United States.

Information Roadblocks

- Inability to Recognize Information When It Comes In an Unfamiliar Format
  - Example: A student writing a paper on World War II might not realize that the pile of V-mail in his grandmother's attic is, in fact, a rich source of information on the war.

Information Roadblocks

- Physical Location
  - A unique information resource may be too distant for a searcher to easily access it.
- Rarity And Value
  - Extremely rare or valuable information resources are often not readily accessible.
  - Example: The average person cannot walk into Dublin's Trinity College Library and get access to the manuscript copy of *The Book of Kells*.

Information Roadblocks

- Lost Information
  - Most of the 1890 census was lost in a fire—the information it contained can never be recovered.
- Uncollected Information
  - If information was never collected and recorded, it cannot be accessed.
  - Example: Nobody knows how many African-American students (if any) attended the University of Idaho in 1935 because nobody collected or recorded that data.

Information Roadblocks

- Historical Distance
  - A 21st-Century American might not fully understand events or social customs mentioned in the diary of an 18th-century English clergyman.
  - Or be able to read 18th-century handwriting.
  - Or know that a town mentioned in the diary is now known by a different name.

Information Roadblocks

- False Drops
  - Retrieving overwhelming numbers of false drops (irrelevant hits) makes it difficult to find relevant information.
- Homonyms
  - Searching the word *Indian* (which can signify a Native American, or a native of the Indian subcontinent, or a brand of motorcycle) can result in false drops.
- Copyright
  - Copyright restrictions can render information inaccessible.

Information Roadblocks

- Synonyms
  - Failing to consider likely synonyms can cause searchers to miss information.
  - Example: Searching *airplane* does not automatically retrieve hits on synonyms *plane*, *aircraft*, etc.
- Variant Spellings
  - *Labor* vs. *labour*.
  - *Koran* vs. *Quran*.

Information Roadblocks

- Format
  - Information on a CD-ROM disc is useless without a CD player.
  - Information on microfilm is useless without a microfilm reader.
- Technology
  - Lack of access to technology or the inability to use technology can bar access.

Information Roadblocks

- Language barriers can arise when information contains:
  - Foreign language.
  - Archaic language.
  - Jargon, slang, or nicknames.
  - Expert or insider language.
  - Unfamiliar acronyms or abbreviations.

Information Roadblocks

- Accessibility issues.
  - Information in a graphic image may be inaccessible to a blind person.
  - Information in a sound file may be inaccessible to a deaf person.

Information Roadblocks

- Lack of Fixed Vocabulary
  - Fixed vocabularies (subject headings) can enhance both precision and recall.
  - The lack of a fixed vocabulary makes searching more difficult.

Possible Problems with Fixed Vocabularies

- Searchers do not understand fixed vocabularies and/or how to limit a search to a fixed vocabulary.
- Indexer assigns wrong or insufficient fixed-vocabulary terms.
- Fixed vocabulary is dated, doesn't reflect real usage, or doesn't provide sufficient cross references.

Information Roadblocks

- Secrecy
  - Formula for Coca-Cola, private phone number of the President of the U.S., names of active CIA agents–all are unlikely to turn up in publicly accessible information.
- Privacy
  - Health, financial, and other private records are protected by privacy laws.
- Private Ownership
  - Privately owned information may be both hard to find and unavailable for access.

Information Roadblocks

- Local or national criminal statutes make it illegal to access certain types of information, such as:
  - Pornographic images of children.
  - Plans for building weapons of mass destruction.
  - Banned political writings and images (in some countries).
- Intentional Interference
  - Viruses and denial-of-service attacks block access to electronic information.

Information Roadblocks

- Satire
  - Searchers can easily misinterpret the meaning or intent of information that is presented in a satirical way.
- Intentional Deception
  - Unscrupulous Websites use various techniques to deceive both search engines and online searchers as to a Web site's actual content.

Information Roadblocks

- Censorship
  - Government censorship, filtering software, computer-use policies, and the like can block access to information.
- Fads
  - As a topic goes out of fashion, the information about it ages and may actually decrease as information sources disappear over time.

8. ITERATIVE SEARCH PROCESS

The Iterative Search Process

- Enter search.
- Get feedback.
  - Number and/or relevance of hits.
- Alter the search based on feedback.
- Enter the altered search.
- Get more feedback.
- Alter search based on feedback. . . .

Enter Search

AGRICOLA

-Articles, etc.-

Advanced Keyword Search

Enter Search Expression:
→ cattle

Get Feedback

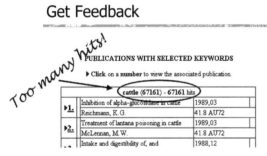

Too many hits!

PUBLICATIONS WITH SELECTED KEYWORDS

▶ Click on a **number** to view the associated publication.

	cattle (67161) - 67161 hits	
1.	Inhibition of alpha-glucosidase in cattle	1989,03
	Reichmann, K. G.	41.8 AU72
2.	Treatment of lantana poisoning in cattle	1989,03
	McLennan, M.W.	41.8 AU72
	Intake and digestibility of, and	1988,12

Revise Search

AGRICOLA

-Articles, etc.-

Advanced Keyword Search

Enter Search Expression:
→ cattle AND disease

Get More Feedback

Still too many hits!

PUBLICATIONS WITH SELECTED KEYWORDS

▶ Click on a **number** to view the associated publication.

	cattle and disease (4068) - 4068 hits	
1.	Inhibition of alpha glucosidase in cattle	1989,03
	Reichmann, K. G.	41.8 AU72
2.	Transmission of tuberculosis from	1989,0318
	Neill, S.D.	41.8 V641
3.	Cost of mastitis and its prevention in	1989,0515
	Ahl, A.S.	41.8 AM3

Revise Search Again

AGRICOLA

-Articles, etc.-

Advanced Keyword Search

Enter Search Expression:
→ cattle AND disease AND brain

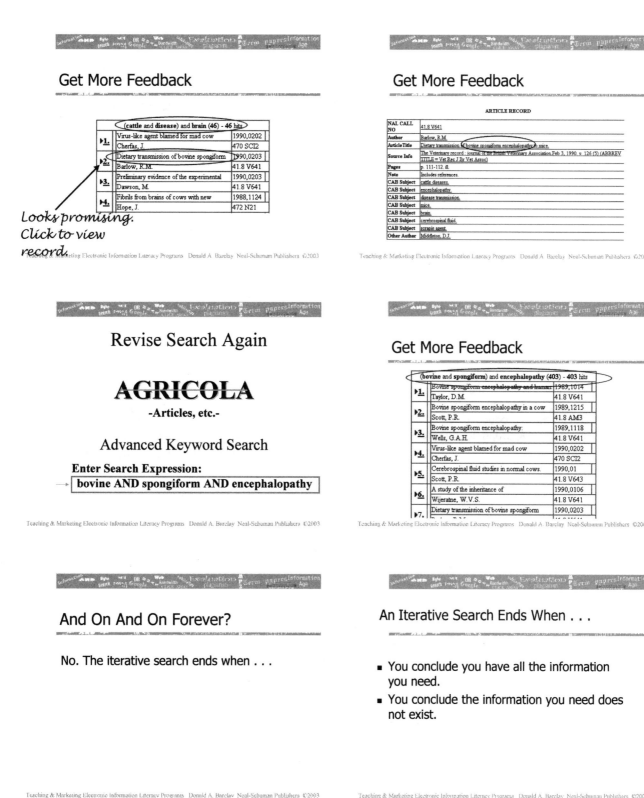

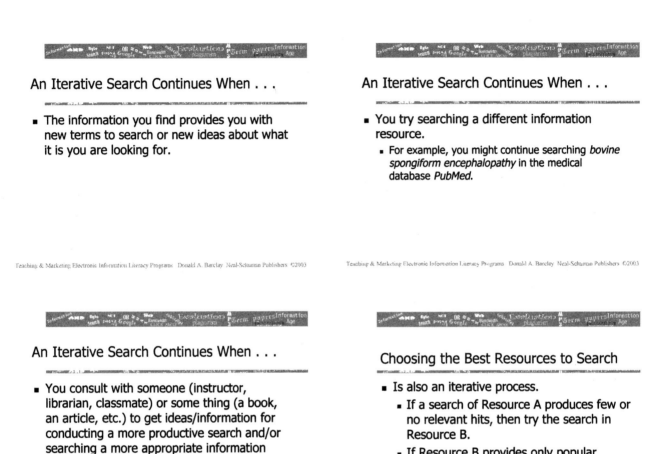

An Iterative Search Continues When . . .

- The information you find provides you with new terms to search or new ideas about what it is you are looking for.

An Iterative Search Continues When . . .

- You try searching a different information resource.
  - For example, you might continue searching *bovine spongiform encephalopathy* in the medical database *PubMed*.

An Iterative Search Continues When . . .

- You consult with someone (instructor, librarian, classmate) or some thing (a book, an article, etc.) to get ideas/information for conducting a more productive search and/or searching a more appropriate information resource.

Choosing the Best Resources to Search

- Is also an iterative process.
  - If a search of Resource A produces few or no relevant hits, then try the search in Resource B.
  - If Resource B provides only popular information when scholarly information is needed, move on to Resource C.

Choosing the Best Resources to Search

- Choices about which resources to search impact the amount and quality of information retrieved.
- There is no universal search interface that accesses all information.
  - "The Computer" exists only in science fiction.

9. PRECISION VERSUS RECALL

Precision Versus Recall

The goal of electronic searching is to strike a balance between precision and recall.

Precision

- Precision means finding the exact information needed with no false drops.
- Terms such as *focusing* and *narrowing* are associated with precision.

To Achieve More Precision

- Add additional terms to a search.
  - Search *cattle AND disease* instead of *cattle* alone.
- Use more precise search terms.
  - Search *bovine spongiform encephalitis* instead of *mad cow disease.*

Precision Pitfall

Being too precise can exclude potentially useful information.

Recall

- Recall means retrieving *everything* that is relevant to an information need.
- Terms such as *broadening* and *widening* are associated with recall.

To Achieve Greater Recall

- Remove terms from a search.
  - Search *brain disease* instead of *cattle AND brain disease.*
- Use more general search terms.
  - Search *brain disease* instead of *bovine spongiform encephalopathy.*

Recall Pitfall

Too much recall retrieves an overwhelming
number of hits, many of them irrelevant.

10. STRATEGIES FOR EVALUATION

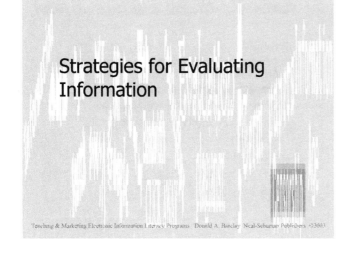

Strategies for Evaluating Information

Teaching & Marketing Electronic Information Literacy Programs   Donald A. Barclay   Neal-Schuman Publishers ©2003

The Basic Strategy for Evaluating Information

- Question all information regardless of its source.
- Be reasonable—no information can be absolutely perfect.

Teaching & Marketing Electronic Information Literacy Programs   Donald A. Barclay   Neal-Schuman Publishers ©2003

Currency

- Is the information up to date?
- If it is not, does this matter for your purpose?
  - Primary-source information may be old but still valuable.

Teaching & Marketing Electronic Information Literacy Programs   Donald A. Barclay   Neal-Schuman Publishers ©2003

Example Of Currency Not Being Important

What year did George Washington die? Any of the following sources could provide the correct (or incorrect) information:
- A book published in 1830.
- An article printed in 1928.
- A Web page created yesterday.

Teaching & Marketing Electronic Information Literacy Programs   Donald A. Barclay   Neal-Schuman Publishers ©2003

Example Of Currency Being Important

- I need information on a start-up company in which I might invest.
- I need to decide on the best therapy for my asthma.
- I need to know how many acres of rainforest remain in the Amazon Basin.
- I need the most recent information on federal expenditures on education.

Teaching & Marketing Electronic Information Literacy Programs   Donald A. Barclay   Neal-Schuman Publishers ©2003

Currency

- If information is online and currency is important, when was the information last updated?
- Be aware that date information was created may be different from date it was put in a particular "container."

Teaching & Marketing Electronic Information Literacy Programs   Donald A. Barclay   Neal-Schuman Publishers ©2003

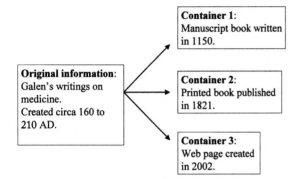

Original information: Galen's writings on medicine. Created circa 160 to 210 AD.	**Container 1**: Manuscript book written in 1150.
	Container 2: Printed book published in 1821.
	Container 3: Web page created in 2002.

Authority

- Arguably the most important thing to consider when evaluating information.
- *Authority* refers to who created the information and is responsible for its credibility.

Authority

- Personal Author
  - An individual of group of individuals acting as an author.
- Corporate Author
  - A business, agency, organization, or other body acting as an author.

Authority

- Who is the author?
  - Author should be clearly identified.
- Is the author an authority?
  - Does the author have the education, experience, or combination of the two to write authoritatively about the topic in question?

Authority

- Is the author affiliated with a reputable institution (university, agency, business, etc.)?
- Authors sometimes exaggerate, lie, or hedge about their qualifications.
  - What does it mean when an author claims to be "a leading researcher" or "a noted authority"?
  - Does a Ph.D. in music qualify an author as an expert on water pollution?

Publisher

- The publisher is the person or group who makes public a piece of information.
- Many types of publishers:
  - Commercial.
  - Academic.
  - Government agency.
  - Association.

Publisher

- As a rule, the more reputable the publisher, the more reliable the information.
- Self-published information is notoriously unreliable.
  - Most Web pages are self-published.

Funding

- Follow the money.
- Who put up the money to make the information public?
- Is there a conflict of interest?
  - Tobacco company pays for "research" into the effects of smoking on health.

Print Equivalent?

- Is a piece of electronic information the exact equivalent of printed information?
  - If so, then both are equally credible.
- Are there discrepancies—intentional or accidental—between "identical" electronic and print versions?

Purpose

All information has some purpose, such as:
- Direct sales.
- Advertising.
- Public relations.
- Education.
- Entertainment.
- Advocating social, religious, or political agendas.
- Authorial ego gratification.
- Career advancement (including earning tenure).

Purpose

- Information may have more than one purpose.
  - Example: A Web site could be both educational and entertaining.
- Does the purpose of the information reveal any conflicts of interest?

Conflict of Interest?

- *Valerie's Vitamin Villa* offers many articles extolling the benefits of taking vitamins.
- *Valerie's Vitamin Villa* also sells vitamins online.
- Because of this conflict of interest, information from articles found on *Valerie's Vitamin Villa* should undergo extra scrutiny before it is accepted as credible.

Intended Audience

- The intended audience can tell you if the information is appropriate for your purpose.
- Example: Sources of information on nutrition might be aimed at one of the following audiences:
  - Children.
  - General public.
  - Owners of health-food stores.
  - Scholarly researchers.

Accuracy

- Web standards for spelling and grammar are looser than for print.
- However, information riddled with errors of spelling, grammar, punctuation, or fact should raise questions.
  - If source cannot correctly spell Prozac, can you trust it to provide accurate dosage information?

Independent Confirmation

- Does author accurately cite the specific sources used?
- Can the same or similar information be verified by other sources?
  - Are these sources truly independent of each other?
- If the same bad information appears in 100 sources, that does not make it good information.

Coverage

- In what depth does the source cover its topic?
- Does it include extraneous information?
- Does it exclude information that should be included?

Final Thoughts on Evaluating Information

1. Maintain a healthy skepticism about all information.
2. Question the purpose behind every piece of information.
3. Don't be fooled by cool. Great graphics, polished presentation, and glib language do not in themselves guarantee that the information being presented is good information.

11. WEB SEARCH ENGINES

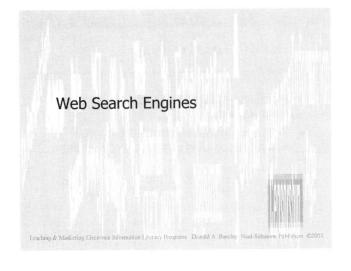

Web Search Engines

Hundreds of Web Search Engines

- *AltaVista*
- *Lycos*
- *Google*
- *Dogpile*
- *Ask Jeeves*
- *And on and on...*

Advantages of Web Search Engines

- Most provide full-text information.
  - I get everything I need right on my desktop, and I get it instantly.
- Most are free.
  - I don't pay anything. I don't need a password. I can access them from anywhere.
- Why would I use anything else to search for information?

Why Use Anything Else?

- Web search engines are fantastic tools, but they are not the only tools.
- Everything is not available in full-text electronic format.
  - Using bibliographic databases expands your universe of information.
- Lots of information on the Web cannot be accessed via Web search engines.
  - The "Invisible Web."

The Invisible Web

- Large sections of the Web are invisible to Web search engines.
  - All proprietary Web-based information resources–*Compendex, Ethnic News Watch, ABI/Inform*, etc.–cannot be searched via Web search engines.
  - Many open-access resources, such as *PubMed*, cannot be searched via Web Search engines.
- No search engine of any type can claim to search the entire Web.

Brief History: Web Search Engines

- First Web search engine, *WebCrawler*, debuted in April 1994.
- Web search engines have constantly come and gone since 1994.
- As of 2003, there are hundreds of general and specialized Web search engines.
  - A few dozen large players dominate.

How Web Search Engines Work

- Search-engine **spiders** (computer programs) "crawl" the Web and retrieve information about pages they find.
  - Spiders retrieve such information as the title of the page, text and images found on the page, metadata attached to the page, and the page's URL.
- No single spider can crawl the entire Web.
- Significant areas of the Web are off limits to spiders (the Invisible Web).

How Web Search Engines Work

- Information collected by spiders is complied in a **database**.
- When you use a Web search engine, you search the compiled database, not the actual Web.
- The quality of a Web search engine depends on the size of its database and the quality of indexing.

How Web Search Engines Work

- **Syntax** is a search engine's set of rules for how a search should be constructed.
  - Example: A search engine's syntax might specify that putting quotation marks around two or more words means that those words will be searched as a phrase.
- A search engine's help menu should spell out its rules for constructing searches (syntax).

How Web Search Engines Work

- The **user interface** allows searchers to enter search terms and view search results.
- Many Web search engines offer basic and advanced interfaces.
  - An advanced interface may go by "Power Search," "Advanced Search," or some other name.
- May also offer special interfaces for searching a single type of file: audio, image, video, etc.

How Web Search Engines Work

- **Freshness** refers to how frequently the information in the database is updated.
  - If database has not been updated for two months, users are actually searching the Web as it was two months previously.
- It is sometimes hard to tell how fresh a database really is.
  - Some prominent parts of a database may be updated more often than the bulk of the database.

Web Directories Versus Search Engines

- Searchers click down through a directory's subject categories instead of entering keywords.
  - Many directories offer search engines (and vice versa).
  - A directory's search engine may offer the choice of searching only the directory or searching the open Web.

Web Directories Versus Search Engines

- Directories often work best when a topic is loosely defined.
  - "I need information about the early women's suffrage movement, but I'm not sure what I need."

Web Directories Versus Search Engines

- Search engines often work best when a topic is specific.
  - "I need to know about Elizabeth Cady Stanton's role in the 1848 First Women's-Rights Convention."

General-Purpose Versus Specialized Web Search Engines

- General-purpose Web search engines (*AltaVista, Lycos, Google,* et al.) retrieve hits on just about any topic from anywhere on the open Web.
- Specialized Web search engines may search only a single Web site or single area of interest.
  - FirstGov retrieves only U.S. government information
  - NewsIndex retrieves only current news items.
- Specialized Web search engine may be more precise than engines that search the open Web.

Pay for Positioning And Advertising

- Owners of Web sites may pay owners of Web search engines or directories for prominent positioning.
  - Widgets Unlimited might pay *bigbadsearch.com* so that *WidgetsUnlimited.com* is at the top of the list for *any* search involving the word *widget*.

Pay for Positioning And Advertising

- Web search engines and directories accept advertising.
  - An ad for sinus medicine appears at the top of the results page following a search on the phrase "runny nose."
- Pay-for-positioning and advertising compromise objectivity of Web search engines and directories.
  - Is this the best information available, or simply the best financed information?

Search Engines Change

- Web search engines change user interfaces fairly often.
  - The search rules that applied six months ago may not apply today. (Use help menus.)
- The database underlying a search engine may change.
  - In 2002 *WebCrawler* began searching the Excite database while keeping www.webcrawler.com URL and *WebCrawler* livery.

Metasearch Engines

- Metasearch engines search a number of other Web search engines and retrieve the complied results.
  - Searching "Apollo 13" in the metasearch engine metacrawler retrieves approximately 70 hits from eight different Web search engines.

Metasearch Engines

- Results obtained from metasearch engines are selective.
  - Searching the phrase "Apollo 13" in any one of the eight Web search engines searched by *metacrawler* retrieves more than 70 hits.

12. WHY IT'S ALL NOT "JUST A CLICK AWAY"

It's All "Just A Click Away"

And other myth-information

What the Myth Implies

- All information is easily findable and instantly available on the Web.
- All information is freely available to everybody.
- No mental or physical effort required.
- No need to evaluate or think about how you will apply information need.

Sources of the Myth

- Wishful thinking.
- Hype.
- Hubris.
- Appearance of thoroughness.

- Convenience.
- It's all on the Web for free.
- Don't know any other way to find information.

But I Get Good Grades Using the Web to Do Research

- Information that is good enough for the grade may not be good enough for real life.
- Would you drive across a bridge constructed entirely on the basis of information obtained by searching Google?
- Would you want a doctor to operate on you using instructions somebody found on Yahoo!?

Librarians Are Not Anti-Net

- Librarians developed some of the earliest Web sites.
- "Surfing the Net" was coined by a librarian.
- Many "free" electronic-information resources are paid for by libraries.
- Librarians contribute useful content to the Web.
- Librarians oppose Net censorship and restrictive copyright laws.
- Many librarians are really good at finding information on the Net.

Demythologizing the Net

- Not All Information Is Free
  - www.lexis-nexis.com
- Some Information Is Secret
  - Can you find the formula for Coca-Cola™ on the Web?
  - Can you find the names of CIA agents operating in Latin America on the Web?
- Not All Information Is Good Information
  - Can you find Web sites that maintain the Earth is flat?

PART III
BECOMING A MASTER ELECTRONIC
INFORMATION LITERACY INSTRUCTOR

6 MASTERING THE "ONE-SHOT" 50-MINUTE CLASS

Scarlet Smith, Coordinator of Instruction at Normal State University Library, returns to her darkened office after her usual three-hour Wednesday evening stint at the reference desk. The message light on her telephone is blinking, casting its red glow on the pile of approval slips Scarlet has been meaning to get to for the last three weeks. With a sigh, she punches up the waiting message:

> Scarlet, this is Terry Brown over in Psychology. I'm really sorry to spring this on you at the last minute, but I just discovered today that my sophomore honors class knows *nothing* about using the library's online resources. I've given them an assignment to locate three journal articles on a psychology topic of their own choosing and write up a comparison of the research methodologies. I'd like them to use *PsycLit* and at least try to use the online journal collection. If Friday at 1:00 is all right, I can give you the whole class period. Call me back at extension 1856. Thanks. Oh, there are 20 students in the class.

For Scarlet, or anyone else who has been in the library-instruction business for long, requests like this are routine. Because the scope of the assignment is rather limited, fulfilling Professor Brown's request will not be nearly so impossible as teaching—in 50 minutes—a class of freshman composition students everything there is to know about locating, evaluating, and using print and electronic information. And thank goodness for professors like Terry who care enough about information literacy to give the library a whole class period; a lot of faculty are unwilling to shoehorn so much as a minute of information literacy instruction into their jam-packed syllabi.

As far from ideal as the one-shot instruction session is, one shot is often all that the information literacy instructor has. The challenge, therefore, is to make sure that your one shot hits home.

LESSON PLANNING

Lesson plans can be great aids to an instructor who has to cover a lot of ground in a short time, but Scarlet never forgets that knowledge of her subject—the art and science of identifying, accessing, evaluating, and using information—is more important than any plan. A great lesson plan without subject knowledge is like a great battle plan without an army. Useless.

That said, Scarlet's all-purpose lesson plan is quite simple:

- Tell them what I am going to teach.
- Teach it.
- Recap what I just taught them.

Some instructors may think that such an abbreviated lesson plan would suit them just fine; others may think it outright disrespectful of the art of teaching. Both opinions are tenable. The fact is that for any lesson plan to be successful, it must fit the instructor's teaching style. If your teaching style is as loose and flexible as Scarlet's—and you really know your subject well—you can jot the lesson plan for a 50-minute class on a Post-it. If your teaching style is highly organized, then your lesson plan might fill several sheets of paper. And there may be times when you need to vary both your style and your plan. When teaching a class for the first time, teaching an unfamiliar topic, or teaching in an unusual setting, even the loosest instructor may need to draft a detailed lesson plan. And there may be times when an organized teacher has to loosen up and improvise instead of following the score as written.

THE THREE-TO-FOUR-POINT RULE

Whether her lesson plan is sketchy or detailed, Scarlet knows that in a 50-minute class even the best instructor can effectively teach at most three to four main points. Three or four main points is not many when you think of everything you really *should* cover. Boiling down a class that *could* contain ten times as many main points to three or four is not easy, but it is necessary because 1) no student is going to be able to absorb more in 50 minutes, and 2) the process of boiling down helps the instructor decide what is really core to the class she is planning to teach.

To prepare for Professor Brown's psychology class, Scarlet follows her usual method. First, she writes down the objective or objectives. In a 50-minute class there often is only one objective. Then she draws a line down the middle of a sheet of paper. On the left she lists every point she knows in her heart she *should* cover. When that is done, she chooses from her list the three or four main points she really will cover and lists them on the right. In making her list, Scarlet keeps in mind the importance of making the instruction relevant to the course and the students' assignment. She knows that if she comes at these students with a generic library song and dance, she will lose them in the first five minutes. Besides, 50 minutes will not permit her the luxury of indulging in any irrelevancies. Scarlet's list follows:

Figure 6–1: The Three-to-Four-Point Rule

Objective
Students will able to locate copies of at least three scholarly articles on a psychology topic of their own choosing.

Main points that I *should* cover	Main points I will actually cover
circulation policies and procedures	identifying scholarly journals
online catalog—author, title, subject, and call-number searching—basic & advanced	using *PsycLit* to find articles on psychology topics
L.C. call-number system	accessing the articles identified in *PsycLit*
L.C. subject headings	
important locations in the library	
using the *PsycLit* database	
Boolean logic	
other social-science databases	
scholarly publishing in the social sciences	
Interlibrary loan	
identifying scholarly journals	
accessing unbound, bound, and online periodicals	
locating and using microfilm/fiche	
navigating library Web site	
library services for students—term-paper assistance	
evaluating information	
copyright and plagiarism	

Scarlet knows from experience that some of the points in the left-hand column might also end up getting covered, however briefly, if the students' questions or comments lead to a deviation from the plan. Scarlet checks herself. Student questions are *not* deviations. They are typically the most important part of any class and she always allows time for them as part of her lesson planning. Though Scarlet finds it easy to remember to frequently ask students if there are any questions, she has to remind herself to pause long enough to allow students enough time to formulate and give voice to their questions. Every time she asks if there are questions, she allows at least 30 seconds to pass on the clock in the back of the classroom before moving along to the next item. Thirty seconds is a long time when you are standing in front of a silent classroom, but Scarlet finds that such pauses really do generate questions that otherwise would never be asked.

As for the main points, Scarlet is such a pro at this kind of instruction that she does not need to write out what she is going to do for each main point or note how much time she will spend on each. This is all in her head. If she were to write out a more formal lesson plan, it would look something like the following:

Figure 6–2: Formal Lesson Plan	
Activity	**Time Allotted**
Getting settled/introductions Give handouts to students Quick icebreaker—tell joke about the penguin who walks into the psychologist's office. Recap students' assignment and tell them what I am going to teach them.	Five minutes (but usually takes longer)
1st Main Point: **Identify Scholarly Journals** Students will find copies of print scholarly journals and popular magazines I've set out at their workstations. Ask students to sort them into categories (group activity—each row a group) and report. Should lead to discussion of differences.	15 minutes
2nd Main Point: **Using *PsycLit*.** Each student will access *PsycLit* at their workstation. Challenge them to find an article on	20 minutes

Figure 6–2: *(continued)*	
Activity	**Time Allotted**
medication for treating schizophrenia published in year they were born (so young, so young). A little demo, lots of running around room, lots of questions. Healthy chaos.	
3rd Main Point: **Accessing articles found in *PsycLit*.** Demo online catalog. Find at least one print and one online article. Each student will access one online article to discover the joy of full text.	10 minutes (Not enough time but what are you going to do?)
Remind students what they've learned as they stampede out the door.	30 seconds (follow the herd out into the library if necessary).

HANDOUTS

Once she settles on the main points, Scarlet can create a one-page class outline to photocopy and give to the students. In between the main points listed on the outline she leaves as much white space as possible so students can use the outline to take notes. Whenever she uses this type of handout, Scarlet includes the date, the name/number of the course, and the professor's name as a way of showing students that they are not about to be fed a bowl of canned library soup. She also puts her own name on such handouts in the hope that it will help prevent her from remaining an anonymous "library lady" in the minds of the students. A faint hope, perhaps, but better than nothing. Scarlet will also give each of Professor Brown's students the library's general fact sheet and the detailed guide to using *PsycLit* that the social-sciences librarian prepared last year. Scarlet likes handouts because they give students something to refer to afterwards while also taking care of those time-consuming details that are deadly dull to go over in class. (Who enjoys listening to someone recite the library phone number and hours?) Scarlet makes it her habit to never overload students with too many handouts, knowing that two or, at most, three carefully chosen items are more likely to be read than is a thick sheaf. The outline handout that Scarlet eventually prepares for Professor Brown's class follows:

Figure 6–3: Sample Outline Handout

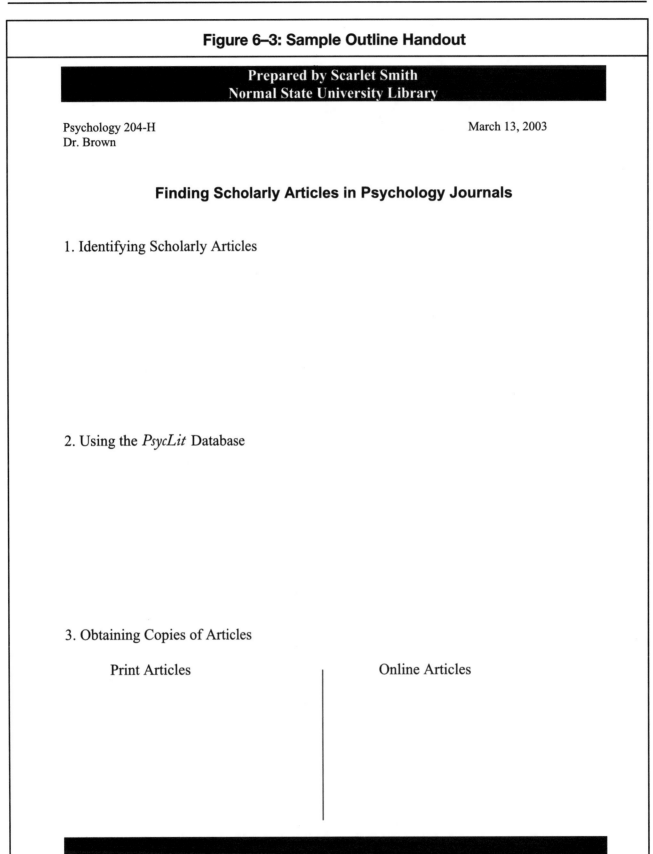

Prepared by Scarlet Smith
Normal State University Library

Psychology 204-H   March 13, 2003
Dr. Brown

Finding Scholarly Articles in Psychology Journals

1. Identifying Scholarly Articles

2. Using the *PsycLit* Database

3. Obtaining Copies of Articles

    Print Articles   Online Articles

501.555.5152

SLIDE PRESENTATIONS

Scarlet is pretty handy with PowerPoint and often uses slides as part of her teaching arsenal. In the case of Professor Brown's class, she decides to pass on using slides because she feels that the time will be better spent doing hands-on work in *PsycLit*. When Scarlet uses slides, she has some basic rules of thumb that she follows:

1. No more than 50 words per slide.
   - Any more than 50 words per slide is hard to read and antithetical to the highly visual nature of the slide medium. Anything that takes more than 50 words to say should be chopped up into multiple slides, handed out in paper form, or expressed in a more visual format such as a graph or an image.
2. No type smaller than 24 point.
   - Do not give your audience eyestrain. If you know a slide show will be presented in a very large hall, on a poor-quality projector, or under unfavorable lighting conditions, then set an even higher minimum type size. Also, the minimum size must be set higher (often much higher) for fancy scripts, such as fonts that mimic handwriting.
3. Do not overdo fancy fonts, wild colors, animations, or sound effects.
   - Overdoing any of the above takes away from the over-all impact of a presentation. One swiveling photograph, drumroll, or unexpected burst of color in the middle of a presentation can be a real attention getter, but twenty such occurrences are just an annoyance. Fancy fonts can be exceptionally hard to read, so use them sparingly.
4. Do not read every word on every slide.
   - Unless you have reason to believe that your audience cannot read the slides, do not stand there and read them word for word. Nothing is deadlier to an audience. Slides are supposed to provide emphasis, not serve as the speaker's big-screen teleprompter.
5. Do not make too many slides.
   - Most slide shows go on way too long and present way too many slides. A few well-chosen and interesting slides will make the most memorable impact.
6. Proofread carefully.
   - Think of all the times you have sat in an audience and spotted errors in the speaker's slide presentation. Now

go back and proofread you own presentation one more time.

WHAT CAN BE DONE AHEAD OF TIME?

In the case of Professor Brown's class there is not enough lead time, but given her choice and a cooperative faculty member, Scarlet likes to make the most of one-shot instruction sessions by having the students do some work ahead of time. Some of her favorite ahead-of-time activities include:

- **Evaluation Instrument.** Students complete an instrument that evaluates their information literacy skills. Getting such an evaluation back prior to a one-shot session allows Scarlet to adjust content to the students' level and avoid covering things the students already know. (See Chapter 1.)
- **Information-Seeking Activity.** Students complete an exercise or tutorial (print or online) that gets them into the library and/or accessing electronic information. Scarlet has had the most success by using structured activities that directly relate to the students' coursework. When students have completed an activity prior to an instruction session, precious instruction time can focus on questions students bring, problems they encountered, or information literacy concepts that go beyond the basics covered by the activity.
- **Assigned Reading.** Students receive a brief reading assignment that serves as grist for the upcoming instruction session. Examples include:
  * An article that discusses the proliferation of unreliable information on the Web.
  * Two articles—one scholarly, one popular—that discuss the same topic.
  * A library pathfinder or other in-house publication that applies to an assignment on which the students are working.
  * Anything provocative—an anti-library screed from the campus newspaper, a pseudo-scientific article from a popular magazine, an advertisement for a term-paper mill—that can serve as a springboard for in-class discussion.

LIKE WATCHING PAINT DRY

If there was one thing Scarlet dreaded about one-shot instruction sessions, it was looking out onto a sea of bored, nonresponsive faces. Often, students come to instruction sessions harboring one or more of the following expectations:

- Libraries and librarians are boring.
- This will be a rehash of a library tour I've already had.
- This will not teach me anything that will help me get a better grade.
- I can find everything I need on the Net.

Scarlet's job, then, is to keep the instruction session from being boring while still making sure that the students actually learn something. Here is how she does it:

ENERGY LEVEL

If the instructor comes in looking and sounding like she's ready for a nap, the students are going to tune out. You have to give off energy to get energy back, so before stepping into the classroom Scarlet often shuts the door to her office and practices yoga for five minutes. But of course there are many other ways to get energized. Scarlet knows instructors who drink coffee, go outside and walk around the library building three times, put on the Walkman and listen to Warren Zevon's "I'll Sleep When I'm Dead"—whatever it takes to get fired up for teaching.

POWER, PACING, AND PITCH

Nothing will put students into a coma faster than a monotone voice, so Scarlet uses the concepts of power, pacing, and pitch to keep her voice out of the dead zone. **Power** involves varying the loudness of the voice for emphasis—while it seems obvious that suddenly shifting up to a LOUD VOICE will catch the attention of listeners, it is perhaps surprising to learn that dropping down to a soft *stage whisper* can achieve the same end. **Pacing** means occasionally speeding up or slowing down the rate of speech. Most instructors tend to talk fast all of the time—especially when they feel rushed to cover everything in their lesson plan. Varying the pace of speech makes it harder to tune out what is being said and can be used to add emphasis to important points. **Pitch** involves shifting the voice up or down the scale—sometimes within a single word—to provide emphasis. Formal voice training is probably the best way to gain control over power, pacing, and pitch, but practicing with a tape recorder is a reasonable substitute for those who do not have time for formal training. For good examples of how effective power, pacing, and pitch can be, simply listen to how they are employed by the more polished voices you hear on radio. Whether you think he is great or pure corn, radio personality Paul Harvey is a master of the three *p*'s and you can learn a lot by listening to the way he uses his voice to keep his audience interested in what he is saying.

DRAMA QUEEN

If you want to be an effective instructor, it does not hurt to be a ham. The building blocks of drama—body movement, gestures, facial expressions, vocal control (see above), costumes, settings, and props—can all be used effectively by an instructor. If actual acting lessons are out of the question, consider videotaping yourself teaching to an empty room. Review the tape (no one else has to see it), noting what you would like to change about the way you move, talk, gesture, and so forth. By viewing a videotape of yourself as a teacher you might discover that you constantly bob your head in a most annoying way. Or stand with your hands stiffly at your side most of the time. Or turn your back to your audience far too frequently. Or you might discover that you have a nice smile that you should use more often. Or that the way you move your hands when speaking is quite effective and is a strength you can exploit. Try your revised "act" in front of the camera again (and again and again), reviewing and refining your performance each time. Even after you feel comfortable with your dramatic persona, it does not hurt to retape yourself from time to time in order to reevaluate your performance.

Many elements of stagecraft can be successfully incorporated into an instruction session: magic, ventriloquism, rope tricks, dance, song, juggling, puppetry—anything goes just so long as it can be somehow tied into the educational purpose of the class. Let's face it, it is better to be known among the student population as "that crazy librarian who juggles four Ginzu knives" than as "Sominex in human form." Not all stagecraft requires a lifetime of practice to master. Scarlet purchased a deck of trick cards, quickly learned a trick or two, and then worked her "magic act" into instruction sessions.

Costumes and props are other pieces of stagecraft that instructors can employ. Everyone has heard stories about history teachers who dress up as Abraham Lincoln and the like, and while dressing up as Melvyl Dewey might be both too extreme and too obtuse, pieces of costume such as hats, T-shirts, and so on can be effective for engaging the attention of students or emphasizing points. After all, Matthew Lesko, the frantic free-government-money guy, has made a career out of wearing a suit covered with question marks. In the area of props, just about any common objects can be turned into teaching tools. Scarlet likes to use a tray and some old plastic bowls and plates to demonstrate the principle of the "Boolean Café," where soup **OR** salad gives the diner more food, while soup **AND** salad gives the diner less. Even bringing in a prop as simple as a bound journal so that students can see what one actually looks like is an effective teaching tool. (There is a lesson in library jargon for you. If you have never heard the phrase "bound journal," what would you think it was? A magazine tied up with string or perhaps chained to a book-shelf? The diary of a slave or prisoner? A journal that was on its way (bound) to some particular location?)

Finally, since the classroom is the instructor's stage, it does not hurt to improve the scenery as much as possible. Anything from changes in lighting to (framed) posters on the walls can improve the stage setting. Before Scarlet went to work on redecorating the library's instruction room—a windowless cubicle with cement-block walls, harsh fluorescent lights, and a drab tile floor—it looked like a place where the Secret Police might torture political prisoners; now, at least, it looks like a place where students might actually learn something without electrodes being attached to their bodies.

ANECDOTES, FACETIAE, AND SATIRE

No, you do not have to be Robin Williams to use humor in the classroom. No, you should not concentrate so hard on being funny that the educational content of the class ends up lost in laughter. However, a well-told joke or anecdote that makes a point relevant to what is being taught can be a powerful teaching tool. While Scarlet is always on the lookout for good jokes of the "A penguin walks into a psychologist's office. . . ." variety, she prefers to use anecdotes when she can. While some of the anecdotes she uses come from things she reads or hears, her favorites tend to come from personal experiences, such as the following:

> One Saturday afternoon an older gentleman came up to the reference desk where I was working. He was wearing camouflage pants, an olive-drab T-shirt, and white sneakers with holes in the toes. And *no* socks. A few thin white hairs just peaked out from under his "Don't Tread on Me" baseball cap.
>
> For a minute he just stood there, looking me up and down like he was having a hard time deciding if a woman

wearing a Guatemalan vest and Birkenstocks could be trusted. Finally, he said in a booming voice, "I need all the info you can find on black U.N. helicopters shooting American citizens up in Washington State."

His voice practically echoed, it was so loud. People all around the reference area were craning their necks to get a good look at this character. "I'll see what I can find," I said, trying to smile.

So I went to work. This was back in the days when the Web was barely a glimmer, so I started out by trying a couple of periodical and newspaper indexes. Nothing. I searched *Nexis* and came up empty no matter what combination of key words I used. After a good 20 minutes, I turned to the man and said, "I'm sorry, sir, but I can't find anything about black helicopters shooting people in Washington State."

He looked at me with blazing eyes, "Well of course you can't," he shouted, his already loud voice rising with each word, "THE GOVERNMENT IS COVERING IT ALL UP!"

It's a funny story, but it has a serious point. Today, because of the Web, I'm sure that same gentleman could find (without going to a library) all the information he wanted "proving" that black helicopters were gunning down Americans. Not only that, he could set up his *own* Web site to spread the word about black helicopters attacking Americans from Vancouver to Olympia and Spokane to Seattle.

Scarlet is able to use anecdotes like this one effectively because she practices. She usually starts by telling the anecdote to herself, out loud, several times. Practicing anecdotes out loud is a favorite drive-time activity for Scarlet, albeit one that gets her occasional stares from other drivers. Practicing allows her to hone her plots, choose her words, and work out the voices of the different characters. Once she gets an anecdote honed, she tries telling it to a variety of friends and colleagues to see how it goes over. Does it make listeners laugh, leave them aghast, or just plain bore them? Do listeners get the anecdote as told, or is more exposition necessary? Only after trying out an anecdote on several listeners will Scarlet use it in the classroom, and even then she continues to rework it based on reactions from students.

Like all good anecdotes, Scarlet's stories contain just enough concrete details to set the stage and sketch the characters involved. For example, briefly describing the clothes worn by the two principal characters in the anecdote tells listeners a lot about the dynamic between Scarlet and her unusual patron. As it should, the anecdote works up to a climax, an "ah-ha moment" that can be either humorous or serious. Finally, the point drawn from the anecdote is related to what Scarlet is trying to teach—the easy availability of unsubstantiated information on the Web.

ANALOGIES

An analogy compares two seemingly different things. Analogies can be effective teaching tools when the instructor compares something familiar to something unfamiliar in order to help students understand the unfamiliar thing. Here is a sample analogy:

> An analogy is like a three-legged stool. A three-legged stool needs three solid legs to stand. If any leg is missing or weak, the whole stool topples over. In an analogy, one leg is the familiar thing, one leg is the unfamiliar thing, and the remaining leg is the connection that draws the two things together. If any of these legs is missing or weak, the analogy, like a stool, topples over.

An analogy should always begin by stating the two things being compared: "**Thing A** is like **Thing B**," with **Thing A** being the unfamiliar thing and **Thing B** being the familiar thing:

"The Web is like a town hall meeting."

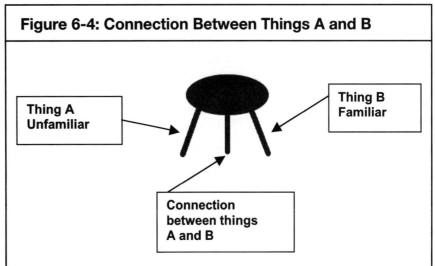

Figure 6-4: Connection Between Things A and B

The analogy should describe the familiar thing first and then describe the unfamiliar thing in such a way as to make a clear connection between the unfamiliar and the familiar:

The Web is like a town hall meeting. When you go to a town hall meeting, everyone is allowed to speak their mind. Some speakers are well informed, some are uninformed, and some are crackpots. Town hall meetings attract leaders who can sway many people to follow them; unfortunately, such leaders are not necessarily the best-informed people at the meeting.

Just as at a town hall meeting, everyone gets to speak on the Web regardless of how well informed or how crackpot their ideas. Popular Web sites are like town hall leaders who manage to sway lots of people, and, like popular leaders, popular Web sites do not necessarily have the best information.

The above analogy follows the standard format. Would it really work? It would so long as the audience understands, or immediately grasps, the essence of what a town hall meeting is. The one caveat of any analogy is that analogies work best when the familiar thing really is familiar to listeners (or at least quick and easy to grasp); if it is not, the whole analogy falls apart. This is why an instructor at Diné College in Tsaile, Arizona, might avoid drawing an analogy between a database search and a New England clambake. Or why an instructor at a high school in Dade County, Florida, might avoid drawing an analogy between citing references and building a snow man.

VIDEO CLIPS

Scarlet sometimes uses short (from 30 seconds to a few minutes long) video clips as a way to break the ice and engage students' interest. She has gleaned useful clips relating to information issues from television commercials, news segments, films, and television programs. The use of video clips is always fraught with potential copyright issues, so Scarlet makes it a point to keep up on the law and keep her use of video clips within the boundaries of fair use.

ACTIVE LEARNING

No law says that a 50-minute class has to consist entirely of an active instructor lecturing to passive students; in fact, 50 minutes of straight lecture is a poor way to teach just about anything. By far the best way Scarlet has found to avoid excessive lecturing and get students involved is to use active-learning techniques.

The most basic active-learning technique in the realm of information literacy is to get students' hands onto computers. Through a lot of lobbying on Scarlet's part, the N.S.U. Library has a classroom with 25 networked computers, an instructor's workstation, and a ceiling-mounted projector. She would prefer that the computers not be lined up in five immovable rows and that the monitors not block the view of any student below median height, but she is not complaining. Trying to teach electronic information literacy without a networked workstation for each student is like trying to teach downhill skiing without skis or snow and only a distant mountain at which the instructor can point from time to time. With workstations at their disposal, students can actively try their hands at what is being taught and perhaps walk out of an instruction session with information they can use to complete their assignments.

One downside of putting a live computer in front of each student is that students invariably surf the Web, check their e-mail, do instant messaging, play Minesweeper, and otherwise fail to stick with the program. This bothers some instructors more than others, and those who are bothered can try various ways to control it, such as not giving students the login password until it is time to use the computers, installing heavy-duty filtering software on workstations, and employing classroom-control systems that give an instructor control over what is displayed on student workstations. For those who are interested, the ACRL Instruction Section maintains a Web page that lists classroom-control systems at www.ala.org/acrl/is//projects/control.html. An alternative approach is to consider recreational computing a cost of doing business and take it as a challenge to your ability to keep students interested in what you are teaching.

In Need of Active Learning Ideas?

See Jane Birks and Fiona Hunt's *Hands-On Information Literacy Activities* (New York: Neal-Schuman, 2003).

Of course active-learning techniques do not always require computers. A student-generated brainstorming session is a type of active learning, as is any kind of group work in which students break out and report back to the rest of the class. One example of an active-learning technique is Scarlet's practice of teaching the concept (and inadequacies) of fixed vocabularies by supplying students with telephone yellow pages and a list of types of business to locate—a store that sells washing machines, a pizza parlor, a shop that fixes transmissions, a movie theater, and so on. By the time the students report back on the various headings under which they looked and their successes and failures, they know more about fixed vocabularies than they could have learned from a week of lectures.

Scarlet is always on the lookout for new active-learning techniques and often finds good ones by talking to colleagues, searching *ERIC*, and exploring the American Library Association Web site, home to a number of useful *ALA/ACRL* (Association of College and Research Libraries) Web pages relating to active learning.

CODA

Before turning out the light and heading home, Scarlet picks up her phone and dials extension 1856. She gets voice mail, which is just what she expected. Librarians and university police officers are the only university employees working on campus at this time of night. "Terry, this is Scarlet Smith returning your call. I'll be able to do your class on Friday. We were lucky that the classroom wasn't already booked. See you at 1:00. You can thank me profusely then. Bye."

7 TACKLING THE EXTENDED ELECTRONIC INFORMATION LITERACY COURSE

The idea of teaching an extended information literacy course has powerful appeal. Instead of a frenzied 50 minutes to teach students how to fill some narrow and immediate information need, you have an entire quarter or semester to cover the field of information in depth and breadth. Instead of being an anonymous "library dude" teaching equally anonymous students, you become a teacher with a name. In turn, you get to know students by their names and have the opportunity to develop lasting, frequently rewarding, teacher-student relationships. Your students (most of them, anyway) are more motivated than the students you typically encounter in a one-shot session—if for no other reason than the fact that they want a passing grade at the end of the course. You have the opportunity to employ teaching methods and assignments that would never work in a one-shot instruction session, and you get ongoing feedback from students that, if you are open to it, will help you to improve as an instructor.

On the other hand, teaching an extended class represents a serious commitment of time and resources. And as eager as you may be to reap the considerable rewards of teaching an extended course, it is important to ask yourself whether or not you have the necessary time and resources to take on such a task. For this reason, anyone who wants to develop and teach an extended course needs to be sure that there is administrative support for it. If the administrators above you are not willing to support the proposed course both financially and politically, it is best not to pursue this option.

WHAT KIND OF COURSE?

Before you can get administrative support, you must be able to show administrators just what it is you are planning to do. This means that, early on, you will have to make some fundamental decisions about the kind of course you are planning to teach.

One fundamental decision is whether the course will be a general information literacy course or whether it will be tied in some way to an existing course or subject area. A general course takes a broad approach to the field of information and strives to make all comers information literate. The advantage of this approach is that a general course can appeal to a wide spectrum of students from a variety of majors. However, some argue that a general information literacy course is not an effective approach on the grounds that information literacy cannot be separated from subject content. An information literacy course that is tied to an existing course or subject area avoids the disconnect between information and subject. For example, the library might collaborate with the history department to offer "Information Literacy for Historians" that is taught as a one-credit lab taken in conjunction with a capstone course for history majors.

A second fundamental decision about an extended course concerns striking the right balance between the practical and the theoretical. The practical extreme is embodied by the old-fashioned, largely extinct library-skills class, while the theoretical extreme would look something like a graduate seminar in information science. Where on the continuum a course ends up depends in part on the preferences of the instructor and in part on the culture of the institution at which the course is taught. The only rule is that pushing too far towards one extreme or the other is likely to result in a class that nobody wants to take.

GETTING A COURSE APPROVED

In most academic institutions, getting a new course approved ranges from difficult to impossible. There are always plenty of reasons to object to a proposed course. Some of these objections spring from genuine academic concerns: "The course as proposed is not rigorous enough." Some objections spring from bureaucratic inertia: "The university has never had a library course, so how are we supposed to give this course a number when we don't even have a prefix for library courses?" And some objections (usually the unspoken ones) spring from the basest sort of campus politics: "We don't want the library getting its hands on any student-fee dollars."

Assuming the library administration already supports the proposed course, a good first step before setting out to tilt at the course-approval windmills is to line up as many nonlibrary supporters as you can. Pitch your proposed course to those outside the library—teaching faculty, deans, vice presidents, and so on—who might be supportive of an information literacy course. On many campuses, the grapevine is sensitive enough to pick up any murmurs of support from on high, and it is not dirty pool to get a few of those murmurs started through your own initiative.

The second step toward approval is to learn everything you can about how courses get approved at your institution. What is the process and how long does it normally take? What documentation is required? What committees make the decision and who sits on those committees? What is the role of the faculty senate? Talking to a faculty member who has recently seen a new course through the approval process is a good strategy. So, too, is familiarizing yourself with all relevant sections of your institution's policy manual. The course-approval process can be incredibly complex, so be prepared to spend some time mastering all its ins and outs.

Two documents that will most likely be required as part of the course-approval process are a syllabus (see the section later in this chapter) and a course description of the sort appropriate for inclusion in a course catalog. Such course descriptions are, by necessity, brief, but they are nonetheless important. Put some time and care into writing up course descriptions; for inspiration, peruse course descriptions found in your institution's course catalog as well as in the catalogs of other institutions. A course description might read something like the following:

> **LIB 301: Information Literacy. 3 Credits.**
> Students will attend lectures, do hands-on assignments, and complete written research projects to obtain the technological skills and critical-thinking abilities needed to use printed and electronic information resources. The course focuses on how to locate, critically evaluate, and apply information for academic, professional, and personal purposes. Prerequisite: English 100 or equivalent.

One possible strategy is to start by getting a proposed course approved as a temporary course. On most campuses it is much easier to get a new course approved as a temporary course than as a permanent course. You will likely be permitted to teach the course two or more times under the "temporary" banner, giving you a chance to try out the course and, ideally, build support for it. Successful temporary courses stand a better chance of becoming permanent courses than do untried and unproven courses.

GETTING STUDENTS TO TAKE THE COURSE

The surest way to get students to take a course is to have it adopted as a required course within the institution's core/general-education curriculum. The chance of this happening is probably zero, as the competition to have courses adopted as core/general-education requirements is fierce on most campuses. Getting an information literacy class adopted as a requirement for one or more majors is only slightly less difficult. More possible is getting a course adopted as an elective in the core/general-education curriculum or as an elective for one or more majors.

When a course is offered as a pure elective that does not help students fulfill their graduation requirements, it is very difficult to get students to enroll. Even those students who recognize the value of an information literacy course may choose not to enroll because they do not have the time or financial resources to take on an extra course.

In any case, it is important to advertise a course, especially a new one. Flyers, announcements on Web sites, and plugs made during one-shot instruction sessions are good ways to spread the word. If the budget allows, consider paying for a well-timed advertisement in the campus newspaper. Do not forget to make advisors aware of the course so that they can recommend it to their advisees. In the end, though, the best way to popularize a course is to provide such an interesting and useful course that students who take it recommend it to their friends.

THE SYLLABUS

The course syllabus has three important roles: calendar, planning document, and contract.

In its role as a calendar, the syllabus spells out specific days on which a class will meet, the holidays when it will not meet, and such important dates as dead week, finals, and so on.

In its role as a planning document, the syllabus allows the instructor to map out what topics will be covered during the course, the order in which they will be covered, the due dates for assignments, and so on. When students receive the syllabus, they can use it to plan how and when they will fulfill the requirements of the course.

In its role as a contract between the instructor and students, the syllabus spells out the requirements for the course, the way grades will be determined, and other policy matters.

No single document is more important to the success of an extended course than the syllabus, so it is crucial that an instructor put a lot of time and thought into writing it. Once the syllabus has been distributed to students (every student in the class must receive a copy) and everyone has agreed to its terms, the instructor should not alter any part of the syllabus without discussing those changes with the students. Some instructors make it a practice not to make any major changes to the syllabus without the unanimous consent of the class.

A hypothetical syllabus for an extended information literacy course follows. While this syllabus is not presented as a document to be slavishly followed, it does include all the major parts of a syllabus and suggests how a syllabus might be structured. Essential points that should be covered on any syllabus are:

- Course name, number, and section.
- Course meeting time, days, and location.
- Instructor's name, contact information, and office hours.
- Textbooks (if any are required).
- Course description. This could consist of either the verbatim catalog description or a fuller description. It might also include a statement of the instructor's approach, philosophy, goals, and so forth.
- Grading policy. Be very specific about how the grade is determined, as this part of the syllabus can be interpreted as a contract. This section could also include statements about attendance policy and academic honesty.
- Statement on accommodation for anyone with a disability. Very often institutions will provide instructors with boilerplate for this section of the syllabus.
- Course schedule. The level of detail in the course schedule will vary from instructor to instructor, but it should at least give due dates for assignments (including reading assignments).

Figure 7–1: Sample Syllabus

Course Syllabus for LIB 301 (1) Information Literacy
Spring 2004
Tuesdays & Thursdays, 1:00 p.m.–2:30 p.m.
Room 123
Normal State University Library

Instructor

Scarlet Smith   Office: 245 NSU Library
Coordinator of Information Literacy   Office Phone: 208.555.7120
Normal State University Library   E-mail: *ssmith@library.nsu.edu*

Office Hours
Mondays & Wednesdays: 1:00 p.m.–2:00 p.m.
Tuesdays & Thursdays: 11:00 a.m.–Noon
And by appointment

Textbook
Peacock, M. T. *Cracking the Information Nut: Information Literacy for the 21st Century*. New York: Ritz Brothers Publishing, 2002.

Official Course Description (As printed in the Normal State University 2003–2004 Catalog)

> **LIB 301: Information Literacy. 3 Credits.**
> Students will attend lectures, do hands-on assignments, and complete written research projects to obtain the technological skills and critical-thinking abilities needed to use the printed- and electronic information resources. The course focuses on how to locate, critically evaluate, and apply information for academic, professional, and personal purposes. Prerequisite: English 100 or equivalent.

Grading
Each student's course grade will be based on the following:

> **Attendance (30%)**
> Everyone gets two free absences. Use them wisely.

> **Weekly Assignments (25%)**
> There will be 14 assignments in total. You will receive explicit written instructions for each assignment.

> **In-Class Presentation (15%)**
> You will receive a written list of possible topics along with a description of what is required of an in-class presentation. You may also suggest a topic not on the list, but all topics are subject to instructor approval. Once topics have been assigned, you will be given a date for your presentation.

Continued on following page

Figure 7–1: *(continued)*

Final Project (30%)

For a final project, each student will prepare an annotated bibliography on a topic of his or her own choosing (subject to the approval of the instructor). You will receive a written description of what is required of your final project. There is no final exam in this class; however, during the time set aside for taking the final each student will give a short presentation on his or her final project.

ADA Compliance

Anyone with a disability who will require accommodation under the terms of federal regulations must present a written accommodation request to the instructor within 11 days after the first class session. Copies of the Normal State University ADA Compliance Policy, ADA Policy on Auxiliary Aids and Reasonable Accommodation, and the ADA Grievance Procedures are available through the office of the Dean of Students (Old Main, Room 205, Telephone 208.555.2445). It is also recommended that you register with the Office of Disability Accommodation (New Main, Room 118, Telephone 208.555.4323).

Course Schedule

Tuesdays	*Thursdays*
January 13 • Introduction to the Course. • A Short History of Information.	January 15 • How Libraries Have Always Worked—And How They Are Changing. • Peacock, Chapter 1.
January 20 • Videotape: James Burke's *Connections*, "Faith in Numbers." • Assignment #1 Due.	January 22 • Information Myths: Why It All Is Not Just a Click Away. • Peacock, Chapter 1. • In-class Presentation #1.
January 27 • Economics of Information. • Assignment #2 Due.	January 29 • Copyright in the Digital Age. • Peacock, Chapter 2. • In-class Presentations #2 & #3.
February 3 • Database Structures. • Assignment #3 Due.	February 5 • Electronic Searching Part 1. • Peacock, Chapter 3. • In-class Presentations #4 & #5.

Continued on following page

Figure 7–1: *(continued)*

Tuesdays	Thursdays
February 10 • Electronic Searching Part 2. • Assignment #4 Due.	**February 12** • Web Search Engines: How They Work And How They Don't. • Peacock, Chapter 4. • In-class Presentations #6 & #7.
February 17 • Censorship. • Assignment #5 Due.	**February 19** • Privacy in the Information Age. • Peacock, Chapter 5. • In-class Presentations #8 & #9.
February 24 • Writing the Classic Research Paper: From Hitting the Reference Books to Citing Sources. • Assignment #6 Due.	**February 26** • Guest Lecture: "Computers, Information, and the Law," David Brown, CIO, NSU Division of Information Technology. • Peacock, Chapter 6. • In-class Presentations #10 & #11.
March 2 • Scholarly Information. • Assignment #7 Due.	**March 4** • Government Information. • Peacock, Chapter 7. • In-class Presentations #12 & #13.
March 9 • Evaluating Information Part 1. • Assignment #8 Due.	**March 11** • Evaluating Information Part 2. • Peacock, Chapter 8. • In-class Presentations #14 & #15.
March 16 • Spring Break.	**March 18** • Spring Break.
March 23 • Use and Misuse of Statistics. • Assignment #9 Due.	**March 25** • Presentation of Proposed Topics for Final Projects. • Peacock, Chapter 9. • In-class Presentations #16 & #17.

Continued on following page

Figure 7–1: *(continued)*

Tuesdays	*Thursdays*
March 30 • Academic Honesty in the Age of the Web. • Assignment #10 Due.	April 1 • Media Literacy. • Peacock, Chapter 10. • In-class Presentations #18 & #19.
April 6 • Using Microsoft PowerPoint. • Assignment #11 Due.	April 8 • Mock Court: The Napster Case. • Peacock, Chapter 11. • In-class Presentations #20 & #21.
April 13 • Catch-up Day. • Assignment #12 Due.	April 15 • Peer Evaluation of Final Projects: Group Work. • Peacock, Chapter 12. • In-Class Presentations #22 & #23.
April 20 • Futurism: Where Is Information Headed? • Assignment #13 Due.	April 22 • What Does It Mean to Be Educated in the 21st Century? • Peacock, Chapter 13. • In-class Presentations #24 & #25.
April 27 • Dead Week. • Assignment #14 Due.	April 29 • Dead Week.

Finals Week
Monday, May 3, 9:30 a.m. to Noon.
Presentation of Final Projects.
Course Evaluations.

ASSIGNMENTS

Coming up with good assignments is one of the most creative parts of teaching. A good assignment will do several things at once:

- Allow students to demonstrate their understanding or knowledge of a topic.

- Allow instructors to objectively assess students' performance and fairly assign grades on the basis of performance.
- Increase students' understanding or knowledge (i.e., students learn something as part of the process of completing the assignment).
- Engage students' interest and spark their enthusiasm for the subject.

Assignments for a typical extended course usually include one major project plus a number of smaller assignments. Of course there is no universal law that says course assignments have to be structured in this way. Nor does one particular type of assignment need to prevail. The different types of assignments that might be used in an information literacy course are as limitless as the instructor's imagination. Just a few types to consider include:

- Annotated bibliographies.
- Bibliographic essays.
- Hands-on information-seeking exercises (treasure hunts, etc.).
- Research journals or logs.
- Traditional research papers.
- Position/opinion/reaction papers.
- Case studies.
- Group projects.
- In-class presentations.
- In-class debates.
- Reviews (of books, Web sites, databases, search engines, etc.).

Just as the types of possible assignments are varied, so too are the formats in which assignments can be presented. Written and oral assignments are traditional, but assignments can also be presented in the form of Web pages, PowerPoint presentations, videos, and so on. Whatever the format, consider requiring that completed assignments be shared with the entire class instead of being treated as private communications between students and instructor. When assignments are shared with the entire class (perhaps via a course Web site), it tends to spur students to do better work, and the entire class benefits from the discoveries and insights of their fellow students. The one caveat for sharing assignments class wide is that doing so raises privacy issues; however, these issues can usually be worked out to everyone's satisfaction early on in the course.

Providing written instructions for every assignment is essential. By writing out instructions for each assignment the instructor can ensure, to the greatest degree possible, that students know exactly what work is expected, when it is due, and how the assignment will affect their grade. Receiving written instructions also gives students the best opportunity to ask for clarification on any aspect of an assignment they find puzzling. Only those instructors who really enjoy arguing at length with contentious students should give exclusively oral instructions for assignments. Consider the following campus urban legend:

> A student presents himself in his history professor's office a few hours after the final exam. The student claims that he missed the final because the power went off in the dorm, shutting down his alarm clock. The professor, knowing this is probably a lie and also knowing that the student has missed almost every class during the semester, decides to have a little fun.
>
> "All right," the professor says, "I'll give you an oral final exam. Right now. And your entire grade for the semester depends on how well you do. Is that acceptable?"
>
> "OK," the student replies.
>
> "Good. Here is your final exam: Tell me everything you know about French history."
>
> The student thinks for a moment and answers, "King Louis got his head cut off and Napoleon was Emperor."
>
> "Is that *everything* you know about French history?"
>
> "Yes. That's everything"
>
> "Then I'll have to give you an F for the course."
>
> "No," the student says. "You have to give me an A. You asked me to tell you everything I know about French history and that is exactly what I did."
>
> The student got his A.

CLASSROOM METHODS

An extended course allows an instructor the time to use methods other than traditional lecture/demonstration. Group work, active learning, extended discussions, unplanned pursuits of unexpected threads—all are more possible in an extended course than within the confines of a one-shot class or workshop. For example, in an extended class students might view a video of a complete *X Files* episode as a springboard for discussing censorship, secrecy, urban myths, and disinformation. Or students might increase their understanding of copyright issues by participating in a role-playing exercise in which some students play the part of recording-industry executives, some play recording artists, and some play (this is a stretch) music-loving college students. If an interesting, possibly unexpected, question arises in the middle of a lecture, the instructor of an extended course can afford the luxury of sending students on a ten- or 20-minute search mission to find and report back on possible answers. An entire class session can be given over to a guest lecturer with special knowledge of an information-related topic.

While the list of possibilities can go on and on, the real point here is that instructors need to remember that lecture and demonstration, while both have their place, should not be the only weapons in a teacher's arsenal. As with assignments, being creative when it comes to classroom methods is rewarding both to the instructor and to students.

READINGS

One possibility for readings is to require one or more course textbooks. A traditional how-to-do-research book might fit the bill, but there are also less obvious choices. For example, one librarian successfully used David Brinn's science-fiction novel *Earth* as a textbook for an information literacy course. Requiring one or two books should not be a problem, but before requiring a whole armload of books it is wise to consider both the cumulative cost of the books and the amount of time reading them will require; otherwise, you may walk into an open rebellion on the first day of class.

A second possibility for readings is to put together a "reserve reading" collection of articles, book chapters, Web pages, and so on. Whether the format of such a collection is electronic, print, or some combination of the two, be sure to attend to any copyright issues that might attach to the selected readings.

TESTS

For some instructors, tests do not lend themselves to the subject of information literacy. And, unless an institution requires that instructors give tests, there is no reason that tests must be part of the grading mix in an information literacy course. Should an instructor choose to use tests—essay, multiple choice, fill in the blank, true/false, short answer, take home—it is important that students get, in writing, the necessary information about the tests, including when the tests will be administered, how they will impact the final grade, and the rules for taking them (open or closed book, make-up tests, cheating, etc.).

TIME-MANAGEMENT FOR INSTRUCTORS

Teaching even one extended class will take a bite out of anyone's time. Besides the actual hours spent in the classroom, there is the time required to develop the course, to prepare for each meeting of the class, to meet with students outside of class, and to grade assignments. Ideally, administrators will grant release time to instructors who take on an extended course (or two) in addition to their regular duties. If there is no release time, then the instructor must work overtime and/or the instructor's colleagues must pick up the slack. Neither scenario is sustainable over the long term.

Instructors must also consider their own time pressures when planning assignments and readings for a class. Most instructors are eager and want their courses to be sufficiently rigorous, but overloading a course wears out instructors as well as students. A good practice is to take a look at syllabi from other courses on your campus that are of a similar level and adjust the readings and assignments in your course to an acceptable level. As you do this, though, remember that it is not a contest. If Econ 201 requires three textbooks and six papers, requiring four textbooks and seven papers for Lib 203 does not automatically make Lib 203 the better course.

USING COURSEWARE WITH THE EXTENDED INFORMATION LITERACY CLASS

Courseware packages (such as *WebCT* and *Blackboard*) can be used to create course Web sites, distribute course readings and assignments, give exams, communicate with students, and so on. If your institution has adopted a courseware package, it is certainly worth investigating its use in conjunction with an information literacy class. While the sophisticated technology of courseware lends itself to the whole information literacy zeitgeist, instructors with a high degree of technological savvy may find that they would rather do it themselves than use courseware.

8 BECOMING AN EFFECTIVE INSTRUCTOR OF ELECTRONIC INFORMATION LITERACY

There are thousands of things that go into making an effective teacher of electronic information literacy. Most, if not all, of these should fall into one of the following general areas: subject knowledge, technical knowledge, understanding students, and teaching.

KNOW YOUR SUBJECT

Without a doubt, knowledge of Information (with a capital *I*) is crucial for teaching information literacy. Every single thing an instructor knows about Information—from its history, sociology, economics, politics, management, and future trends to how to find, evaluate, and apply it—is a plus. No one can effectively plan instruction, design assignments, or perform well in the classroom without such knowledge.

Earning an advanced degree in librarianship or information science is, of course, one important way to expand your knowledge of Information, but there are other ways as well:

- Take additional information-related courses beyond the MLS/MIS degree. As more and more library schools and information-science programs offer online courses, taking additional courses need not burden the working librarian/instructor with the hassle of temporarily relocating to, or traveling back and forth from, the home institution. Note, too, that library schools and information-science programs are not the only source of potentially useful courses that relate to the study of information. Perhaps a research-methods class taught by the History Department would be of benefit? Or a course on copyright taught by the School of Business? If the thought of taking an advanced course for credit is not appealing, there is always the option of auditing.

- As an alternative or supplement to extended courses, information literacy instructors should take advantage of workshops and other short-duration educational and training opportunities such as those offered in conjunction with national and regional conferences. Information-literacy instructors tend to gravitate to workshops that focus on instruction, but sessions on topics that expand attendees' knowledge of Information—"How to Become a Super Web Searcher" or "Online Business Information Sources for the Non-Business Librarian"—can be as, or more, beneficial to the development of a good information literacy instructor than are straight how-to-teach courses. Also, do not forget to take advantage of in-house learning opportunities offered by your colleagues—sometimes the best teachers in the world are just down the hall or across campus.

- Information literacy instructors who are really serious about furthering their education in the field should consider the immersion programs sponsored by the Association of College and Research Libraries' Institute for Information Literacy. These annual programs "provide instruction librarians with the opportunity to work intensively for four-and-a-half days on all aspects of information literacy." See www.ala.org/acrl/nili/immersion.html for details on these programs.

- Keeping on top of all the new and changing information resources is a huge job. Instructors tend to focus only on those resources that are available to their students—after all, when you have limited time with students there is not a lot of point in teaching them about grapes they cannot reach—but it is always beneficial to an instructor's overall knowledge to keep up on the widest possible range of information resources, regardless of availability. Listservs can be good sources for current information on emerging information resources, and various library, information-science, and discipline-related publications (both print and online) can help you keep up with new information resources. An essential listserv for any information literacy instructor is *ILI-L* (Information Literacy Instruction Listserv). Created in May 2002, *ILI-L* is the heir of *BI-L*, a pioneer library listserv launched by Martin Raish in 1990. Information about *ILI-L* is available at www.ala.org/acrl/is/ilil.html. To subscribe send the text **subscribe** *ILI-L* **your firstname your lastname** in the body of the message to listproc@ala.org.

- Conducting actual research is a fantastic way to expand your knowledge of Information and sharpen your hands-on research skills. The subject of your research can be anything—local history, raising orchids, teaching effective electronic searching to the *Google Generation*—because it is the act of using information tools and resources, not the subject itself, that produces the true benefit. Using the fruits of your research to create a finished information product, which could be something as formal as a published journal article or as informal as a personal Web page, serves to round out the learning experience. If nothing else, an instructor who uses research to produce books or articles or Web sites can say to students, "I don't just teach this stuff. I do it for real, too."

KNOW INFORMATION TECHNOLOGY

The creation of Web sites mentioned above implies knowledge of how to author Web pages, and that is certainly one technology with which information literacy instructors should be comfortable. Because information technology changes so fast, keeping up is difficult and knowing what new trends to follow is almost impossible. There is nothing more frustrating then investing a lot of time in mastering the Next Big Thing in technology only to see it sink without a ripple. The best advice is to pick your technology battles carefully. One clue that a particular technology is worth learning is when you see it being adopted by the students you teach. If your students are all instant messaging like crazy or using tablet computers, then it is clearly time for you to get familiar with these technologies.

Obviously, enrolling in formal technology courses, workshops, and certificate programs (such as those that lead to certification as a network administrator) are all options for improving your store of technological knowledge. And while no law says that an information-literacy instructor has to be a programmer, mastering a bit of PERL or C++ is not a bad thing.

A side benefit of technological skills is that having them can be a way to win the respect of students. If you can help one student fix a bug in a program he or she is writing or show another how to configure their Web browser to access the campus proxy server, those students are likely to think of you as something more than another resident dinosaur in the campus book museum.

UNDERSTAND YOUR STUDENTS

While it is safe to say that the more an information literacy instructor knows about information technology the better, it is important to remember that the technologically astute instructor must never forget what life is like for the person who knows very little about technology. Similarly, it is important to never forget what life is like for the person who knows very little about Information. Instructors who so lose touch with their students that they constantly teach over the head of everyone who sets foot in their classrooms are not effective teachers. There are steps instructors can take to stay in touch with students:

- Working at various library service points—not only the reference desk, but also such points as the circulation desk, the periodicals room, and the interlibrary loan office—is a good way to understand how students use information and where their knowledge falls short.
- You can learn a lot about the roadblocks and frustrations students experience by occasionally using the library as if you were a rank-and-file student engaged in actual research. Instead of using the computer in your private office to do a database search, go over to the library computer cluster during a busy time and experience what it is like to wait along with everyone else for the next available public workstation. (And when you actually get to use that public workstation, think about how it compares to the computer you normally use. Is it so locked down that you find it impossible to work effectively? Is it slow enough to make you tear out your hair?) Try out some of your library's other services and resources and experience its ambiance: When was the last time you used your library's public photocopiers? Do you know what it is like to try to do an hour or two of focused work while sitting in one of your library's public areas? Have you ever set foot in your library after 9:00 p.m.?
- Although not an option for everyone, teaching an extended course (either for the library or for some other department at your institution) will provide insights into student knowledge, attitudes, and behaviors that you cannot get any other way.
- Most important of all, conduct regular assessments of student outcomes. This is the only way to compile data on what your students do and do not know about informa-

tion. See Chapter 12 of this book for more on the subject of assessment.

TEACHING: CONTINUALLY WORK TO IMPROVE IT

Nobody is so good that their teaching cannot be improved upon. In fact, the best teachers are so good because they are constantly working to improve their teaching. Chapter 6 of this book presents a number of suggestions for improving your classroom performance as well as techniques that you can use to break out of the straight-lecture rut. Attending classes and workshops on teaching, reading (selectively) the teaching literature, and paying attention to feedback from students can all lead to improved teaching.

Reviewing videotapes of yourself in the classroom or having someone you trust (other than your supervisor) observe your teaching and provide feedback are proven techniques, but of course observation works both ways. Ask permission to sit in on classes taught by your colleagues. If someone on your campus is noted as a great classroom teacher, sit in on a class or two to learn from—and perhaps be inspired by—a master.

In every region of the country there are a few libraries that stand out for the quality of their information literacy programs. Learning everything you can about how these institutions earned and maintain their reputations is worth the effort, and chances are you will come across a few good ideas that you can adapt for your own program. Even if you do not have the time and resources to make an extended trip to observe firsthand one of the outstanding information literacy programs in you region, you can at least visit its Web site and exchange a few e-mails with key players in its information literacy program.

Finally, nobody can teach well when they get stale. If you teach the same thing in the same way long enough, you will sooner or later lose your spark. Going over the same old handouts, examples, exercises, slide presentations, and anecdotes eventually becomes wearisome beyond endurance. In spite of your best efforts to hide it, students will sense that you have no enthusiasm for what you are teaching and tune you out in a minute. The only way to keep fresh is to make changes as soon as you feel yourself getting stale. Try new teaching techniques, tear up your existing lesson plan and start over from scratch, redo your slide presentation, or develop a new active-learning exercise—anything to make what you do in the classroom new and interesting to you. It may seem counterintuitive to change something that has worked well ("If it ain't broke, don't fix it"), but the fact is that stale teaching is broken teaching.

9 EXTENDING YOUR REACH WITH PRINT PUBLICATIONS, ONLINE TUTORIALS, AND WEB-CASTING

Distance education is, arguably, the most significant educational trend of the early twenty-first century. It seems as if every college and university in North America is offering classes, if not entire degree programs, via distance education. From a purely educational perspective, distance education appeals because it has the potential to provide quality education to large numbers of both traditional and nontraditional students; in particular, distance education is seen as a way of reaching working students who cannot stop their busy lives to attend traditional classes. From a financial perspective, distance education appeals as a cost-efficient way to provide instruction. Small surprise, then, that many state governors and legislatures have jumped on the distance education bandwagon.

Will distance education eventually conquer the world of learning? Perhaps. But there are a few things working against total victory:

- Distance education requires different sets of skills than those required for traditional classroom teaching, making it difficult for some teachers to make the transition.
- Distance education is resisted by those who see it as a "McDonaldization" of education that will, in the end, devalue the teaching profession and reduce the quality of instruction.
- Some students resist distance education because the technology behind it is difficult or unreliable; similarly, some students feel that distance education is simply not as good as what you get in the presence of a live instructor.
- Although distance education is hailed as a cost saver, holding distance education programs to high educational standards can shrink or eliminate any cost savings.

WHAT IS DISTANCE EDUCATION?

Distance education brings instruction to students who are geographically distant from the place where the instruction originates. Distance education can be either asynchronous or synchronous. Asynchronous distance education allows learning to take place at any time the student chooses, as is the case with the old-fashioned correspondence course. On the other hand, synchronous distance education demands that instructor and students "meet" during specific times even though they may be miles apart geographically. Two-way live telecourses are a prime example of synchronous distance education. While asynchronous distance education has the advantage of being convenient for students with irregular schedules, synchronous distance education is more interactive and more like traditional classroom learning.

Even when the medium for distance education is as low-tech as sending paper documents through the mail, true distance education requires some level of learner participation as well as some measurement or certification of what has been learned. If I watch Ken Burns's *The Civil War*, I am merely watching educational television. But if I watch *The Civil War*, use technology to interact with a remote instructor and other students, and complete graded assignments based on the television series, I am participating in distance education.

DISTANCE EDUCATION FORMATS

Under the loosest definition of distance education, the printed book could be considered a format for distance education. After all, the instructor (the author of the book) imparts knowledge to students (the readers) who may be remote both geographically and chronologically. But if the definition of distance education requires measurement of what is learned, the oldest form of dis-

---

Distance Education Defined

You can find several definitions of distance education, as well as lots of other useful information on the topic, by visiting the University of Wisconsin's *Extension Distance Education Clearinghouse* at www.uwex.edu/disted.

tance education is the traditional correspondence course. Although we might not think of correspondence courses as dependent on technology, they began to flourish only when advances in technology allowed for inexpensive mail service. Similarly, later distance education formats—such as courses conducted via audiotape, broadcast television (or radio), or videotape—did not come into their own until improved technology made them practical and affordable. Today the distance education formats getting the most attention are, not surprisingly, those that are powered by digital technology: Web-based instruction, Internet chat, Web videoconferencing, and so on.

One characteristic of distance education is that mixing formats is quite common. For example, students taking a course via distance education could read a printed textbook to get a grasp of the foundational knowledge of the course, watch videotaped lectures to get the instructor's take on the subject, and subscribe to a course listserv to interact with the instructor and other students taking the course. Or branch-campus students learning how to use the main-campus library might read a printed guide to the library, complete a Web-based library tutorial, and then participate in a telephone conference with a main-campus librarian for answers to specific questions about using the library. The point of the above examples is not the specific distance education formats used but, rather, the idea that various formats—both low-tech and high-tech, new and old—can be combined in imaginative ways to provide effective, affordable instruction.

Returning for a moment to the question of what is or is not a distance education format, you could make the argument that the live digital reference technologies currently finding their way into libraries are also a distance education format. While this argument is as true as the argument that providing reference service at a traditional library reference desk can (or should) be a form of teaching, both are limited in the number of students they can reach because they both require one teacher (librarian) per student.

What About Courseware?

Many campuses have adopted courseware packages such as those produced by *Blackboard* and *WebCT*, the current leaders in the field. Courseware does many jobs, but part of what it does falls under the rubric of distance education. For example, instructors can use courseware to create course Web sites, distribute course readings and assignments, give exams, communicate with students, and so on.

Although courseware packages such as *Blackboard* and *WebCT* offer some features for free, the full packages are so costly that their adoption is generally an institution-wide decision. For more information on these products, start with a visit to their Web sites:

> *Blackboard*
> www.blackboard.com/
>
> *WebCT*
> www.webct.com/

It is worth noting that *Blackboard* and *WebCT* are not the only courseware packages on the market. In addition, there is the argument that, at least for those who are adept at Web design, do-it-yourself courseware is preferable to turnkey packages.

THE LIBRARY WEB SITE AS DISTANCE EDUCATION TOOL

Library Web sites can be powerful distance education tools. While Web site design is a topic in its own right, it is worthwhile to outline here a few of the ways in which a Web site can serve the interests of distance education:

GENERAL INFORMATION

What general information about your library is important to remote students? Just for starters you might consider:

- Library phone numbers.
- Hours.

- Physical location.
- Driving directions.
- Floor plans.
- Basic instructions on using the online catalog and databases.
- Policies (circulation, remote-access, ILL, etc.).

It is likely that you can think of many more items that belong on such a list. Whatever you include, make sure this information is easy to find on your library Web site. Also useful to those who are far from the library are online forms for such things as obtaining a library card or requesting an interlibrary loan. Forms are especially useful when they can be completed and submitted online rather than having to be printed out and mailed or hand delivered.

Teaching Students How to Take Advantage of Distance Services

One of the common librarian complaints about digital-reference and ask-a-librarian services is that they get little use compared to the traditional reference desk. A good way to boost usage of such services is for instruction librarians to show students that such services exist and show students how to take advantage of them. Points to cover include:

- The difference between live digital-reference services (often chat based) versus ask-a-librarian services (often e-mail based).
- What services are available.
- Many digital-reference services require some affiliation with the sponsoring library.
- How to use chat. (Be prepared—students may be able to teach you a thing or two about chat.)
- Strategies for getting the most out of such services.
- What types of questions work well in a digital-reference setting, what questions are better asked via e-mail, and what questions are best asked in a face-to-face setting.

IN-HOUSE PUBLICATIONS

Any library in-house publication that is available in print should also be available via the Web. If your library produces a large number of print publications, the purchase of Adobe's *Acrobat* software could be well worth the cost. (*Acrobat 5.0* retails for $250, though it may be less with an educational discount.) With *Acrobat*, you can easily convert documents created with word-processing or desktop-publishing software into .pdf documents that can be read, printed, or saved by anyone who has the free Adobe *Acrobat Reader* software. Converting documents to .pdf is much less labor intensive than creating .html versions of print documents, and with the .pdf format you have more control over the final appearance of the document than is possible with the .html format. For a book-length treatment on the topic of serving distant users via the Web, see Donnelyn Curtis's *Attracting, Educating, and Serving Remote Users Through the Web: A How-To-Do-It Manual for Librarians* (New York: Neal-Schuman, 2002).

WEB-BASED TUTORIALS

Librarians have been developing Web-based tutorials since the earliest days of the Web. Besides the obvious advantage of being available from anywhere at any time, Web-based tutorials can be far more interactive than any paper-based tutorial or pathfinder. For example, students taking a Web-based library tutorial might read a few lines of instruction on searching the online catalog and then click on a link that puts them in the live catalog where they can practice what they have just read. Web-based tutorials can also make use of graphics, animation, sound, and video to enhance both effectiveness and stickiness. (In Web jargon, *stickiness* refers to the ability of a Web site to keep visitors' interest so they do not wander off to other Web sites.) Sophisticated Web-based tutorials can test what students have learned and collect data on how students actually use (or do not use) the tutorial. In the ideal case, a Web-tutorial would be so seamless that the users would think they were simply doing their research, not taking a tutorial.

Before embarking on creating a Web-based tutorial it is important to consider the downside of such a project:

- Initially creating a Web-based library tutorial is a lot of work. Such projects typically require a team to complete them and should involve significant usability testing as they are being developed.
- Keeping a Web-based tutorial up to date will require an ongoing commitment. Tutorials that are not kept up to date quickly turn into Times New Roman ruins.
- Getting students to take a Web-based tutorial is hard. Getting them to complete it is harder. Typically, Web-based

library tutorials work best when completing the tutorial is one of the requirements for a graded class.

If you chose to create a Web-based tutorial, usability testing is vital. Get real users—actual members of your target audience—to try out the tutorial as it is being developed. Listen to their feedback and make changes as you go. Although it deals with Web site design instead of tutorial design, Jacob Nielsen's *Alertbox* column of March 19, 2000, "Why You Only Need to Test With 5 Users" (www.useit.com/alertbox/20000319.html), provides a practical model of user testing and iterative design that could easily be applied to developing a Web-based tutorial.

There are a number of "authoring" software packages on the market that are designed to ease the chore of developing a Web-based tutorial. In truth, the only way to know if any of these packages are right for you is try them out. Many offer free trials. A list of authoring software packages follows:

Macromedia Authorware
www.macromedia.com/software/authorware

Macromedia Flash MX
www.macromedia.com/software/flash/

Presedia Express Trainer
www.presedia.com/products/trainer.htm

Qarbon ViewletBuilder
www.qarbon.com/products/viewletbuilder

RoboDemo
www.ehelp.com/products/robodemo/

Snagit
www.techsmith.com/products/snagit/default.asp

Screenwatch
www.screenwatch.com/screenwatch.html

Wanadu iCreate
www.wanadu.com/new/site/products.html

There are many examples of Web-based information literacy tutorials on the Web. One of the most highly developed is *TILT*, a product of the University of Texas System Digital Library. *TILT* is available at tilt.lib.utsystem.edu.

Is Your Library Thinking Locally?

Libraries—and library Web sites—fail to serve the needs of remote learners when libraries forget about those students who rarely, if ever, set foot on campus. Any of the following on a library Web site is a red flag that the library is thinking locally:

- Phone numbers are listed in formats such as "Ext. 1734." (Which is great if you happen to be using a campus phone.)
- Web site visitors are informed that they can pick up library in-house publications at the reference desk but are not offered the option of accessing the full text of those publications online.
- The street address and/or geographical location of the library are not given or are hard to find. If the address is given, postal codes and/or the state or province are left off. (Is this library in Vancouver, Washington, or Vancouver, British Columbia?)
- Acronyms are used (often repeatedly) without ever being spelled out: "The ERC Collection is located on the third floor of the SVR."
- The name of the library is given but the institution with which it is affiliated is not specified: "Jones Library proudly serves the University community. . . ."
- To obtain remote-access to the library's electronic resources, students must first come to the library.
- Library forms for such things as obtaining a library card or requesting an interlibrary loan are either not available on the Web site or must be printed out and mailed in. (Forms that can be completed and submitted online are much more useful.)
- Links that allow Web site visitors to contact the library via e-mail are hard to find or are entirely absent. (When users submit e-mails, are they replied to promptly?)

VIDEOCONFERENCING FOR DISTANCE EDUCATION

The goal of providing distance education via videoconferencing technology is to recreate for remote students the same experience (or nearly the same experience) they would have if they were sitting in a classroom with a live instructor. In its most refined form, videoconferencing allows for real-time transmission of sound, video, and data from an instructor to remote students and vice versa. Not long ago, videoconferencing was too expensive for all but an elite group of educators. However, new Internet-based technology has lowered the cost of videoconferencing to the point where it has become an option for growing numbers of institutions.

A full treatment of the technologies and techniques necessary to provide instruction via videoconferencing could fill (and have filled) many books. The purpose of this chapter is merely to introduce these technologies and techniques. The list of selected readings at the end of this chapter provides a starting point for those who want in-depth information.

H.320: TRADITIONAL VIDEOCONFERENCING

Traditional videoconferencing, which came into its own in the 1980s and 1990s, is based on the International Telecommunication Union (ITU) standard H.320. Traditional videoconferencing takes place over dedicated network connections—an arrangement that is analogous to making a telephone call. During a typical telephone call, you and the person on the other end monopolize a single line (or, more precisely, a single circuit). This allows the two of you to talk to each other in real time without delays and without interference from other users of the telephone system. Similarly, traditional videoconferencing over a dedicated line allows for two (or more) sites to interact with little to no time delay and with little loss of sound or image quality. Even with a dedicated connection, however, H.320 audio and video must be compressed in order to move across the network at reasonable speeds. This is why the quality of traditional videoconferencing, though quite good, is not up to what you would expect to see on an ordinary cable television in a private home. The biggest drawback to traditional videoconferencing, however, is not its quality but rather its cost. The charges for monopolizing a dedicated network connection can run to hundreds of dollars per hour, which is why traditional videoconferencing is more associated with the boardroom than the classroom.

H.323: VIDEOCONFERENCING OVER THE WEB

Videoconferencing over the Web—a technology new enough to still be considered emerging in 2003—is based on the International Telecommunication Union (ITU) standard H.323. Instead of using a dedicated network connection, sounds and video transmitted in compliance with H.323 travel over the Web just like e-mail messages and Web pages. Because everything that travels on the Web is cut up into tiny data packets, sent to its destination via unpredictable (and often Byzantine) routes, and then reassembled once it reaches its destination, H.323–compliant audio and video must endure this same fate. If network problems cause too many of the audio and video packets to arrive late or not at all, there is a loss of quality in the transmission; if such problems are serious enough, the whole videoconference can come to a crashing halt.

Despite the inherent weakness of the Web as a highway for time-critical audio and video transmission, there is immense interest in videoconferencing over the Web because, unlike dedicated network connections, the Web is free (or at least very cheap). In addition, the potential market for videoconferencing over the Web has resulted in more companies entering into the business of manufacturing videoconferencing hardware and software, driving down the cost of such equipment. For some idea of how videoconferencing prices have plunged, consider that in the early 1980s, when videoconferencing was pretty much limited to Fortune 500 companies, getting started in videoconferencing meant an initial investment of $500,000 to $1,000,000 plus annual networking charges in the neighborhood of $35,000 per year. Twenty years later, anyone can get an H.323–compliant desktop videoconferencing system for a few hundred dollars and pay no fees to transmit over the Web.

WHAT DO I NEED TO DO VIDEOCONFERENCING OVER THE WEB?

The following is a basic list of what you will need. Optional items are so noted.

WEB CONNECTION

Of course you cannot send anything over the Web without a connection. The higher the network bandwidth (on both the sending and receiving ends), the better the quality of the transmission. The minimum connection speed for H.323–compliant videoconferencing is 128Kbps, so forget about that 56K modem.

VIDEO CLIENT

Also called a "terminal end station," a video client can be either software or hardware. Two of the more widely used software video clients are Whitepine's *CU-SeeMe* and Microsoft's *NetMeeting*, but any H.323–compliant client can do the job. Hardware video clients are almost always superior to software clients because they come with their own processor and thus do not need to share the processing power of a PC that may be doing several jobs at once. Manufactured by a number of different companies, hardware video clients typically come as part of a turnkey desktop or room system. (See sidebar on turnkey systems on page 185.)

CODEC

To speed up the transmission, both H.320– and H.323–compliant data is compressed before being sent and then decompressed when it arrives at its destination. A codec (short for **compression/decompression**) is a piece of hardware or software that compresses and decompresses data. The faster the codec, the more quickly data is processed and the more likely the videoconference will run in real time (or close to it). As with hardware video clients, hardware codecs have their own processors and are almost always faster than software codecs residing on a PC. Software codecs are less expensive than the hardware versions and are often found on desktop videoconferencing systems. Chances are you will never purchase a codec as a separate piece of hardware or software; rather, it will come as part of a videoconferencing hardware or software package.

DIGITAL VIDEO CAMERA

A digital video camera is necessary to capture the images you wish to transmit. Deluxe cameras can cost tens of thousands of dollars, while small Webcams designed to sit on top of a computer monitor cost less than $100. Some Web retailers even offer refurbished Webcams for under $20.00. As you might expect, the image quality and number of features drop along with price.

Room lighting can contribute to, or take away from, the quality of the images broadcast by a digital video camera. Rooms with windows need blackout shades to block out strong sunlight. Adjustable lighting is desirable.

MICROPHONES AND SPEAKERS

You will need microphones and speakers if you plan to transmit and receive audio. Microphones and speakers range from expensive, high-quality devices to budget PC mikes and speakers (or headphones) that cost less than $10 each. During a videoconferencing session, sound is often more important than video, so microphones and speakers are one area where it does not pay to scrimp. Seeking out an audio expert for advice on microphones, speakers, and how to set them up in your classroom is a good idea.

The sound quality of rooms with lots of windows or glass walls will be improved by covering "bouncy" glass surfaces with sound absorbing materials. Heavy drapes offer one such solution.

MONITORS

A monitor of some sort is necessary to see transmitted video. An ordinary computer monitor can do the job, but you can also employ large-screen television or data-projection units when video will be viewed by a group.

MULTIPOINT CONTROL UNIT (OPTIONAL)

Though not necessary, a Multipoint Control Unit (MCU) is a good thing to have when connecting multiple sites in a single videoconference. The MCU switches from one input stream to another during a videoconference, either automatically or on command from a human operator. For example, if a student at Branch Campus B asks a question, the MCU can switch to that student so everyone can hear the question and see who is asking it.

ALTERNATE VIDEO SOURCES (OPTIONAL)

Video need not be limited to what can be captured with a video camera. Typical alternate sources of video include:

- **Computer Workstation**
  The feed from a computer workstation (often the instructor's workstation) can be transmitted so that whatever is on the workstation's screen (database search, *PowerPoint* presentation, etc.) can be viewed by remote audiences.
- **Document Camera**
  A document camera is useful for displaying printed items (photographs, pages from books, handwritten pages, etc.) to remote learners. Although manufactured by a number of different makers, document cameras are often generically referred to as "Elmos" because ELMO is the dominant brand in the field.
- **VCR/DVD**
  An ordinary VCR or DVD can be used to transmit prerecorded video.
- **Electronic Whiteboard**
  While it is always possible to simply point a digital camera at an ordinary whiteboard, an electronic whiteboard encourages collaboration and gives you the option of saving what has been written on the board. Saved files from

an electronic whiteboard can be made available to students (local and remote) for later viewing.

Turnkey Videoconferencing Systems

Turnkey videoconferencing systems are convenient because all the hardware and software comes in one neat package. They are certainly the easiest way to get into videoconferencing. In addition, purchasers can add or leave off extra features to fit their needs and budgets.

Turnkey videoconferencing systems come in two configurations: desktop and group. Desktop configurations are designed for a single user or a very small group of users clustered around a desktop PC or even a laptop. Desktop systems can be had for around $500. Group (also called "room") configurations are intended to serve an entire room and are appropriate for a classroom setting. Group systems start at around $7,000.

Leading Manufacturers of Videoconferencing Systems

Manufacturer	Web Site
PolyCom	www.polycom.com
Sony	www.sony.com
Tandberg	www.tandberg.net
VCON	www.vcon.com
Vtel	www.vtel.com
Zydacron	www.zydacron.com

T.120

Yet another ITU standard, T.120, makes it possible to use the Web for both application sharing and data collaboration.

- **Application Sharing**
  Application sharing occurs when those on the receiving end can only see the data item in question. An example of this would be when the instructor allows remote learners to access (read, save, and print) a Microsoft *Word* document containing the course syllabus or handouts for the day's lecture.
- **Data Collaboration**
  Data collaboration occurs when those on the receiving end can not only access the data in question, but can make

additions and changes to it just as if they were sitting at the instructor's workstation. An example of data collaboration would be when both local and distant learners are given access to an electronic whiteboard on which they create a brainstorming list.

Microsoft's *NetMeeting* is the tool most often used to support T.120 applications.

STREAMING MEDIA

Yet another way to transmit classroom audio and video to remote learners is to present live or prerecorded instruction via streaming media. Unlike videoconferencing, streaming media is not designed to be a two-way medium; however, live streaming media can become highly interactive if remote learners have the option of contacting the instructor during the transmission via telephone, e-mail, chat, or FAX.

VIEWING STREAMING MEDIA

If you have ever accessed a nonstreaming video file on the Web, you know that you cannot start viewing the video until the entire file has downloaded. This can take a long time even with a short video; and, once downloaded, video files take up a lot of space on a hard drive. With streaming media, you do not have to wait for the entire file to download to begin viewing it; instead, you receive only a small amount of data at one time. This data is buffered (held in temporary memory) for a few seconds before being processed into sound and video. Streaming media can run on lower bandwidth connections than are required for either H.320 or H.323 videoconferencing (though the larger the bandwidth, the better). When you have finished viewing streaming media, no file remains on your workstation's hard drive.

Other than a PC, a Web connection, a soundcard, and speakers (or headphones), all you need to see and hear streaming media is the appropriate software. In most cases this means either the free *Windows Media Player* from Microsoft (www.microsoft.com) or the free *RealPlayer* software available from *RealNetworks* (www.real.com). In addition to the free *RealPlayer*, *RealNetworks* sells a $20 version offering more capabilities.

To access a streaming-media production, you typically go to a specified Web page and click on a link that points either to a pre-recorded or live streaming-media production. Clicking on the link invokes your streaming-media player (*RealPlayer* or *Windows Media Player*), and in a few seconds the sound and video begin.

PRODUCING STREAMING MEDIA

In order to produce streaming media for remote learners, you will need a digital camera, microphone(s), and software that allows you to serve streaming media. Chances are good that the server software you use will be *RealServer*, a product of industry-leader *RealNetworks*. The *RealServer* software comes in a free version that allows up to 25 remote connections at one time. The free version is great for learning how to stream and is perfectly adequate for those who never expect to host more than twenty-five connections at one time. *RealServer* software that supports 40 simultaneous connections costs $695, with the price increasing along with the number of connections. While it is possible to run *RealServer* off an ordinary PC, it is better to have a robust dedicated server both to run the software and to store any streaming media presentations that you want to make available for later use. An adequate server can be had for under $2,000. One of the great advantages of storing streaming-media productions on a server is that students can access stored productions at their convenience (asynchronous instruction).

LIVE VERSUS EDITED STREAMING MEDIA

As with most audio/video media, streaming media can be recorded live or it can be recorded in a number of takes and edited. Streaming-media productions that are recorded live have all the missteps and errors inherent in any live production, but they have the advantage of being easy and cheap to produce—the digital cameras roll, the instructor instructs, and when it is done you have your production. Edited productions, on the other hand, can be as close to perfect as you are willing to make them. Tight editing keeps productions short in length and small in file size—both of which are desirable. But edited productions cannot be streamed live, and repeated takes and editing can be time consuming and expensive. For a good description of how one library created an edited streaming-media production, see Cox and Pratt's "The Case of the Missing Students" in the list of information resources for distance education which appears at the end of this chapter.

TELE-TEACHING TECHNIQUES

The term *tele-teaching* describes teaching via videoconferencing technology as well as via cable or broadcast television. What follows is an outline of issues particular to tele-teaching.

Planning

As with any form of teaching, tele-teaching works best when you plan well. Formulating your instructional goals and objectives is vital. Goals and objectives are easier to formulate if you are aware of your students' prior knowledge and skills, but gaining this awareness is more difficult when students are at a distance. The same holds true for measuring educational outcomes, as well. Good planning also takes into consideration all the little details that normally can be taken care of at the last minute in a regular classroom. For example, in a tele-teaching situation you need to carefully plan the creation and distribution of class handouts, not simply warm up the photocopier ten minutes before class and hand copies to students as they walk in the door.

It is also important that a tele-teaching plan include time for active learning. Although there is a temptation to "get my money's worth" by filling the entire tele-teaching time with lecture and demonstration, this is often deadly for audiences. Take advantage of the two-way nature of the medium by encouraging remote users to ask questions, participate in brainstorming sessions, present mini-reports, demonstrate how they searched Database-X, and otherwise get involved. There is no law against short periods of "dead air" in tele-teaching, so do not be afraid to take breaks during which students at every site (remote and local) conduct group exercises and then report the results.

In some tele-teaching situations the technical people may inform you that your class *will* end at some specific time—ready or not. This means that carefully planning the timing of your class is essential. Plotting the segments of each class session on a spreadsheet can help you exactly fit what you want to teach into your allotted time. Time limit or no, it is a good idea to block your class content in to segments of approximately ten minutes and set aside time in between segments for question-and-answer sessions or active-learning exercises. If this pace seems familiar, that is because it is approximately the pace of network television programs: the segments are the "program" and the in-between activities are the "commercial breaks." Be sure, too, to allow some extra time for segments or activities that run long, student questions, and unexpected time over runs.

Preparing Students

Just as instructors need to be prepared to become tele-teachers, students need to be prepared to become tele-students—especially if they have never taken a tele-class. Remote students may need encouragement to develop the sense that they are as important as on-site students. They also need to master the basics of the tele-classroom, such as speaking into the microphone, looking directly into the camera, and not talking over the instructor or students at other sites.

Managing the Class

Managing a tele-class is even more of a juggling act than managing a regular class. As the instructor you may be responsible for making the technology work and controlling who or what appears on the video and audio feeds. You will need to pay sufficient attention to your remote students while not ignoring those students in the room with you. Knowing your students' names is more important when tele-teaching than in a traditional classroom, as is allowing students sufficient time to ask questions or otherwise respond.

Copyright

The fair-use copyright rules that apply to face-to-face classroom instruction *probably* do not apply to distance-education classes. This means that you will need to get permission to use copyrighted material that you could use without a care in a regular classroom. For an excellent treatment of this complex topic, see Gretchen McCord Hoffmann's *Copyright in Cyberspace* (New York: Neal-Schuman, 2001).

Sound

If you are not wearing a clip-on microphone, be sure you are close to a microphone when you speak. Always speak in a normal tone of voice—you need not shout to be picked up by a microphone. One of the more difficult sound problems associated with tele-teaching is that people will unintentionally talk over each other. (If you have ever seen a television program in which two (or more) political pundits with opposing views try to speak at the same time, you know how disconcerting this can be.) It takes a bit of practice getting used to the time delays that result as sound data moves across a network. A three-second delay is to be expected, so instructors and students must learn to wait a few beats to give the other person a chance to speak.

Appearance

Many things you wear in ordinary life do not look good on television. Avoiding certain television fashion no-nos will help keep students focused on the topic instead of on the blinding glare from your wedding ring. When tele-teaching:

- Wear medium blue, brown, or gray clothing.
- Do not wear solid dark colors, clothes with lots of white, or bright colors.
- Do not wear clothing with complicated patterns such as herringbone or tiny stripes.
- If you are using a clip-on microphone, wear clothing with lapels or other surfaces on which to clip the mike.
- Do not wear large pieces of glare-producing metal jewelry or jewelry that is noisy or otherwise distracting.
- Avoid glasses with tinted lenses. Contact lenses are preferable to glasses.
- Do not wear dark makeup.

Movement

Just as some clothing does not work well on television, certain ordinary movements do not translate well to the small screen.

- Avoid rapid movements of your hands, head, or body. On compressed video, such movements appear as distracting swirls.
- Do not rock or tip your chair, pace, or tap your pencil. Avoid talking with your hands.
- Do not block the whiteboard or other visuals.

- Look directly into the active camera when addressing your audience.
- Stay close to a microphone when speaking.

While all the above rules apply, for variety it is best not to remain fixed in one spot for an entire class period. Plan to change your location from time to time—ideally when the camera is not on you.

Selected Information Resources for Distance Education

Allan, Barbara. 2002. *E-learning and Teaching in Library and Information Services*. New York: Neal-Schuman.
A practical guide to online learning.

Cox, Christopher, and Stephen Pratt. 2002. "Case of the Missing Students, and How We Reached Them with Streaming Media." *Computers in Libraries* (March): 40–45.
Describes how one library created an edited streaming-media instructional video.

Goodson, Carol. 2001. *Providing Library Services for Distance Education Students: A How-To-Do-It Manual*. New York: Neal-Schuman.
Gives a librarian's perspective on distance-education delivery systems and trends.

Horton, William K. 2000. *Designing Web-Based Training: How to Teach Anyone Anything Anywhere Anytime*. New York: Wiley.
Anyone interested in creating a Web-based tutorial will benefit from this practical guide. Contains many examples.

Lee, William W., and Diana L. Owens. 2000. *Multimedia-Based Instructional Design: Computer-Based Training, Web-Based Training, Distance Broadcast Training*. San Francisco: Jossey-Bass/Pfeiffer.
Applies the instructional-design approach to computer-aided instruction, tele-teaching, and Web-based training.

Mantyla, Karen. 1999. *Interactive Distance Learning Exercises That Really Work!: Turn Classroom Exercises into Effective and Enjoyable Distance Learning Activities*. Alexandria, VA: American Society for Training & Development.
A good source for active-learning exercises that work in the distance-learning environment.

Noah, Carolyn B., and Linda W. Braun. 2002. *The Browsable Classroom: An Introduction to E-Learning for Librarians*. New York: Neal-Schuman.

Selected Information Resources for Distance Education *(continued)*

Palloff, Rena M., and Keith Pratt. 1999. *Building Learning Communities in Cyberspace: Effective Strategies for the Online Classroom*. San Francisco: Jossey-Bass.

An essential primer on developing a course for distance-education. Practical information from experienced educators.

Palloff, Rena M., and Keith Pratt. 2001. *Lessons From the Cyberspace Classroom: The Realities of Online Teaching*. San Francisco: Jossey-Bass.

Another practical guide to course development from Palloff and Pratt.

Rhodes, John. 2001. *Videoconferencing for the Real World: Implementing Effective Visual Communications Systems*. Boston: Focal Press.

Though the focus is on videoconferencing technology, there is also a useful section on videoconferencing applications.

Simonson, Michael R. 2000. *Teaching and Learning at a Distance: Foundations of Distance Education*. Upper Saddle River, NJ: Merrill.

Discusses both the theory and practice of distance education.

University of Minnesota Video Network Services. "Video Conferencing." Twin Cities, MN: University of Minnesota Office of Information Technology. (February 2003) Available: umtv.cee.umn.edu/UMITV/index.htm.

A rich source of information and practical tips for anyone interested in tele-teaching.

Video Development Institute. "The Videoconferencing Cookbook 3.0." Atlanta, GA: Georgia Institute of Technology. (February 2003) Available: www.vidnet.gatech.edu/cookbook.

A handy, accessible guide to understanding videoconferencing. Updated approximately once a year.

Wilcox, James R. 2000. *Videoconferencing & Interactive Multimedia: The Whole Picture*. 3rd ed. New York: Telecom Books.

Will appeal to the technology buff who wants to understand the nuts and bolts of videoconferencing. Also does a nice job of relating the history of videoconferencing.

PART IV
MANAGING THE SUCCESSFUL ELECTRONIC
INFORMATION LITERACY PROGRAM

10 DESIGNING AND EQUIPPING THE ELECTRONIC CLASSROOM

Even with all the recent advances in distance education, it looks like the classroom will be around for some time to come. What is different today is that many traditional classrooms have been transformed—to one extent or another—into electronic classrooms. The basic elements of the electronic classroom are:

- Physical Space.
- Furniture.
- Technology.

THE PHYSICAL SPACE

The physical-space considerations for an e-classroom include: size, privacy, acoustics, lighting, boards and screens, attractiveness, and comfort.

Size: Ideally, an e-classroom is big enough to accommodate the largest groups of students expected to be instructed at one time. In practice, if a classroom can accommodate all but the very largest groups in need of instruction, the room is about the right size. For example, if 90% of your instruction is for groups of 25 or fewer students, then a room that accommodates 25 is good enough. For the other 10%, it is best to come up with some way of taking instruction to those larger groups in their usual classrooms or breaking large groups into smaller sections that can be accommodated in the e-classroom.

When estimating the square footage needed for an e-classroom, the rule of thumb is to allow about 35 to 45 square feet per workstation. This will leave enough space for workstations, aisles, and an instructor's workstation. Aisles should be wide enough for two adults to walk shoulder to shoulder. By lining up workstations in cheek-by-jowl rows, it is possible to get away with less than 35 feet per workstation, but there will be little room for books or note taking and the space will feel crowded. When planning an e-classroom, do not forget to allow space for such things as an instructor's workstation, a networked printer (if there will be printing in the e-classroom), a projector stand (unless the projector is ceiling mounted), and any other peripherals that might be needed.

Privacy: An e-classroom should be private enough so students are not distracted by other users of the building and vice versa. If any valuable equipment (computers, projectors, etc.) is kept in the classroom, the room must be lockable. Lockable storage cabinets are useful for securing both expensive equipment as well as all the little items that tend to walk away when left out—whiteboard markers and erasers, reams of printer paper, laser pointers, and so on.

Acoustics: Noise should not leak into—or out of—the classroom. One of the drawbacks of using folding walls to create an on-demand classroom is that most folding walls do not provide enough noise insulation.

Unless the room is exceptionally large or will be used as a videoconferencing room, it should not require microphones and speakers. If these are required, it is worth bringing in audio experts to consult on equipment and installation.

Lighting: In the early days of computer-projection equipment, it was crucial that an instruction room could be blacked out; otherwise, the audience was not going to see much of what was projected onto the screen. Today, computer-projection equipment has improved to the point where ambient light is not so great a problem. Even so, room-darkening blinds or curtains are desirable for e-classrooms and absolutely necessary for videoconferencing rooms. When designing a new room, keep in mind that not all window treatments block light to the same extent, so make sure that whatever blinds or curtains you install will darken the room sufficiently.

A good lighting scenario for an e-classroom is a combination of fluorescent lights plus incandescent lights controlled by a dimmer switch; this way, when the room needs to be darkened, the instructor can turn off the fluorescent lights and dim the incandescent lights to the point where students can see what is being projected while still having enough light for note taking or keyboarding. (Only incandescent lights can be dimmed; fluorescent lights are either off or on.) In an e-classroom it is essential that all lights in the room are controlled from switches located inside the room itself rather than be under the control of a remote master switch.

An added bonus of being able to control lighting in an e-classroom is that institutional lighting is typically too bright for extended computer use. If an e-classroom has only fluorescent lighting, outfitting the overhead lights with diffusers (such as parabolic wedge louvers) will prevent light from traveling horizontally into eyes or screens. Glare can also be reduced by:

- Positioning VDTs so they are parallel to overhead lights and perpendicular to windows.
- Using neutral (not bright) wall colors.
- Eliminating or covering shiny-surfaced objects.

Boards and Screens: Even in the computer age, being able to write something so that everyone in the room can read it is still a valuable teaching tool. Whiteboards are a better solution than blackboards because they are easier to read and do not produce chalk dust, a substance that is harmful to both humans and computer equipment. Another plus is that whiteboards can double as projection screens. If whiteboards are to be used to their fullest, they require proper accessories: fresh whiteboard markers, special whiteboard erasers, and a supply of cleaning solution. Avoid using whiteboard markers that have begun to fade, and be sure to clean whiteboards regularly. (Here is a whiteboard tip: If someone accidentally writes on a whiteboard with a non-whiteboard marker, take a genuine whiteboard marker, trace over the unwanted writing, let dry, and erase. This will usually remove all traces of the non-whiteboard marker.)

Flip charts are useful auxiliaries to whiteboards. They are especially good for group work or brainstorming sessions because as the sheets fill up they can be torn off and taped to a wall or pinned to corkboard for later review.

Projection screens are better than whiteboards or walls for projecting computer images, overheads, and the like. The surfaces of good quality projection screens do not produce glare or contain irregularities that distort images and, unlike whiteboards, screens do not get covered with writing. Projection screens vary greatly in price depending on their size and whether or not they are motorized. While built-in, motorized screens are the most desirable, simple pull-down screens can do the same job for much less money.

Attractiveness: Keeping a classroom attractive is important because a messy or dismal room sends that message that instruction is an afterthought. Do not allow a classroom to turn into an auxiliary storage room. Even if a complete remodeling of a run-down classroom is a budget buster, lobby for a new paint job and a few nicely framed prints or posters to give the room some appeal.

Comfort: Computers generate considerable heat, so an e-classroom needs heating, ventilation, and air conditioning (HVAC) sufficient to handle the extra load. Ideally, an e-classroom should have its own thermostat. Retrofitting HVAC is expensive, so be sure to consult with an HVAC expert when planning a new e-classroom.

ELECTRONIC CLASSROOM LAYOUT

Imagining perfect electronic classroom layouts is simple. After all, in your imagination your designs are not constrained by such realities as the size of the room you actually have to work with, its shape, the limitations imposed by technology, or that fact that different instructors have different teaching styles and preferences for classroom layout. Room size, shape, and technology are all design obstacles that you must work around; often, this is best done by sketching the room on graph paper and penciling in various layouts. Another technique (which is often best used in combination with the graph paper approach) is to take a roll of masking tape and a tape measure into the electronic classroom-to-be and lay out imaginary workstations to get a feel for how it all might work when it is furnished for real. Will there be enough room for the maximum number of computers and students you want the classroom to accommodate? Will you be able to get power and network connections to every computer in the room without creating trip hazards? Will there be good lines of sight? Will the aisles be wide enough for someone in a wheelchair to corner? Where will the instructor's station go? How about the computer projector and the screen?

Overcoming the physical limitations of a room can be tricky, but it is an easy task compared to working out differences in teaching styles. The fact is that it is likely that some of the instructors who use the electronic classroom will prefer a traditional instructor-centered classroom in which every seat faces the instructor. This layout reinforces the idea of student as passive receptor of knowledge and discourages all interactions except those between students and instructor. On the other hand, some instructors are likely to prefer a student-centered layout in which the instructor is not the focal point. Such a layout encourages active learning and interactions between students as well as between students and instructor. Unless you are lucky enough to have a wireless laptop classroom with furniture that easily reconfigures from one layout to another, no single layout is going to please everyone and an arbitrarily imposed layout may actually discourage

Figure 10–1: Electronic Classroom Layout 1

The electronic classroom layout shown here is a traditional instructor-centered layout. The advantages of this layout is that it focuses students' attention on the instructor. The disadvantages are that it is not well-suited for group-active learning, does not allow the instructor to see what is on the students' screens, and makes it difficult for the instructor to assist any student one-on-one.

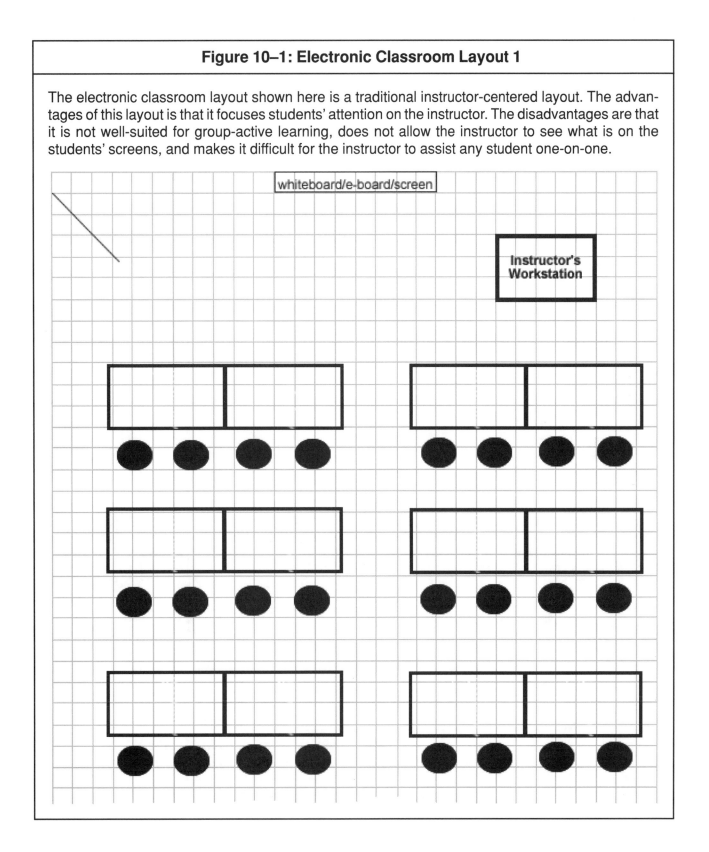

Figure 10–2: Electronic Classroom Layout 2

The horseshoe layout shown here is useful when power and/or network connections are available only along the walls of a room. This layout is more instructor-centered than student-centered and does not lend itself to active learning. It is easier for the instructor to approach and interact with individual students in this layout than in Layout 1, but it is still difficult for the instructor to see what is on any student's screen. There will be a great deal of wasted space in the center of any room laid out in this manner.

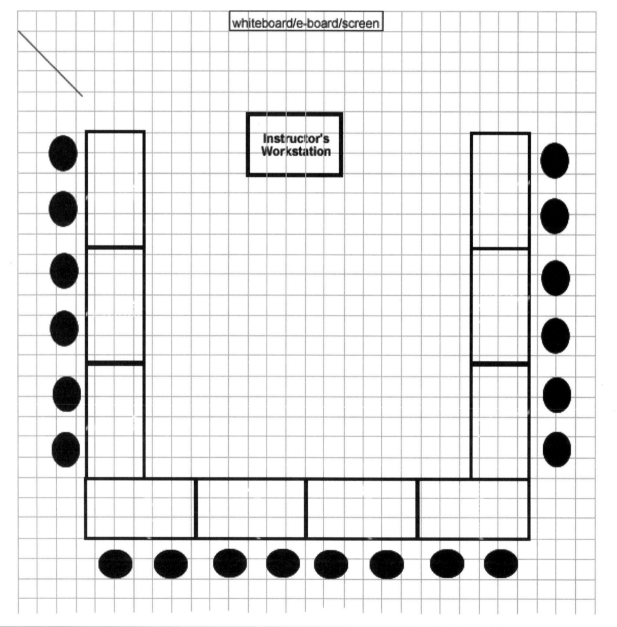

Figure 10–3: Electronic Classroom Layout 3

As with Layout 2, this is a useful layout when power and networking are all located along walls. The big advantages of this layout are that it allows the instructor to see what is on students' screens and to easily approach them when they need help. Instructors who like to roam could make good use of this layout. Because students all face away from both the instructor and the projection screen, this is not a good layout for any instructor who relies heavily on lecture and demonstration; at the same time, neither does it lend itself particularly well to active learning.

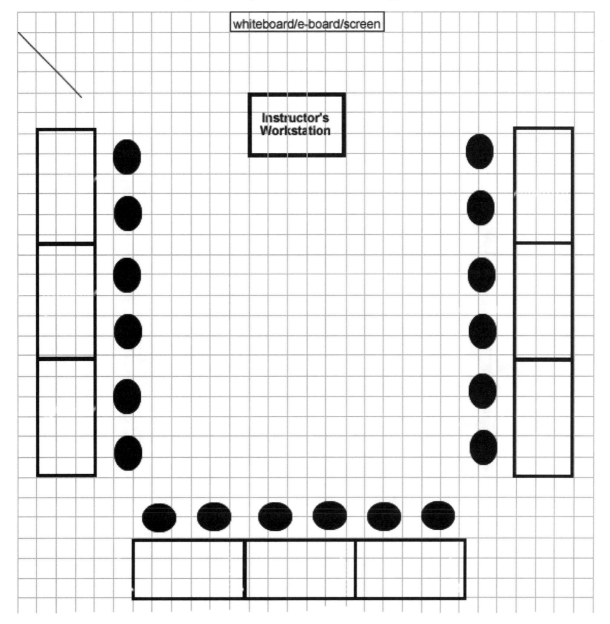

Figure 10–4: Electronic Classroom Layout 4

The layout shown here is designed to foster a student-centered, active-learning environment. When lecture-demonstration is used in this classroom, one-fourth of the students will find themselves facing in the wrong direction, and this is not a good layout unless access to power and network connections is distributed across the room or the room is equipped with wireless laptops. Indeed, laptops are the best (some would argue the only) option in this layout as full-sized computers will tend to isolate students from each other and discourage student-to-student interactions. This layout can work with square as well as round tables.

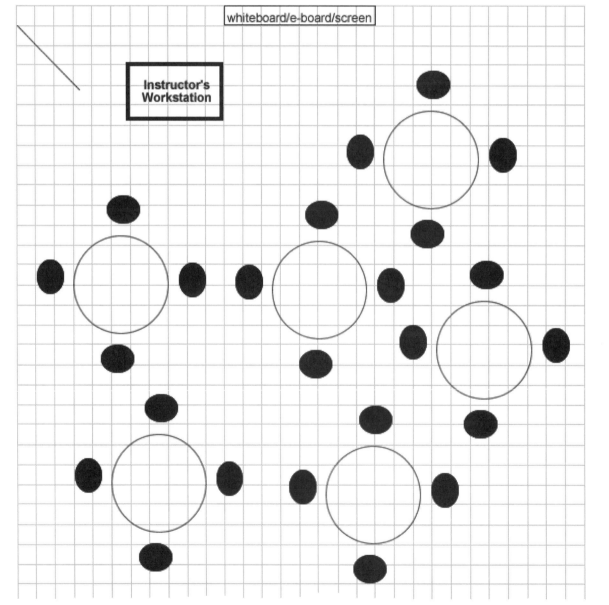

instructors from using the classroom. The somewhat obvious solution to this problem is to bring as many instructors as possible into the discussion of how the electronic classroom should be laid out. As various instructors express their preferences, it is possible that a compromise can be reached; in the ideal case, instructors who favor the traditional teaching style may have their eyes opened and choose to cast their lot with the student-centered, active-learning side.

Four highly representational electronic classroom layouts are shown on pages 199–202. The hypothetical room used for these layouts is a perfectly square 30' x 30'. Then each layout is rendered on a one-square-foot grid. The square tables shown in each layout are 2.5' deep by 6' wide and are intended to seat two students each. (Students are represented by the dark circles.) The round tables used in the final layout are 60" diagonal tables and are intended to seat four students using laptops.

Recommended Reading

The subject of designing electronic classrooms can be (and has been) a book in itself. One notable book on the topic is Lisa Janicke Hinchliffe's *Electronic Classroom Handbook* (New York: Neal-Schuman, 2001).

FURNITURE

Furniture for an e-classroom should support and protect computer equipment, be comfortable, and contribute to the overall learning environment by improving the attractiveness of the room. To a considerable extent, furniture is as important to the e-classroom as the technology that makes the room electronic in the first place.

Next to having no furniture at all, the worst scenario is an e-classroom filled with old library tables. Not only are such tables too high for comfortable keyboarding, they harbor unsightly booby traps of dangling cords and cables and cause high-riding computer monitors to block the view of everyone who does not happen to be a scholarship basketball player. Any instructor involved in the planning of an e-classroom must make it clear to administrators that 1) money for proper furniture is as important as money for technology and 2) the initial cost of the furniture might well exceed the initial cost of the technology.

Though the initial outlay is greater, durable, well-built furniture will prove a better long-term bargain than the shoddy stuff. Try to select flexible furniture rather than furniture that is too specifically designed to accommodate a particular piece of equipment. Computer furniture invariably outlasts computer equipment, so buy with the idea that whatever technology is sitting on the furniture on Day One is going to look quite different ten years down the road. Aesthetics are important, too, so try to purchase the best-looking furniture the budget will allow. Though it is easier said than done, avoid flavor-of-the-month styles that will look dated soon after the goods arrive in the building.

ERGONOMICS

If students will be using e-classroom computers for less than one hour at a sitting, then ergonomics, though still important, is not an overriding concern. However, ergonomics is crucial when computers will be used for longer periods.

Workstation Ergonomics

The general rule for computer workstations is that the height of the desktop should be approximately 27" above the floor. When desktops are too high, it is possible to use a keyboard tray to correct the situation, but the two caveats to this are that 1) the tray must have space for both the keyboard and the mouse because both devices should always be on the same level, and 2) the keyboard tray must be **rock solid**, as bouncy keyboard trays cause muscle strain. Providing each user with 4' by 4' of desktop surface provides plenty of room for a computer plus notebooks, books, and so on. It is possible to get by providing each user with a desktop that is 2.5' wide by 2.5' deep, but there will be little room for anything other than a computer.

Monitor Ergonomics

No instructor likes to teach in a classroom where every head is blocked by a computer monitor. The worst situation arises when bulky monitors sit on top of desktop CPUs that, in turn, sit on overly high tables. Avoid this problem by using tower CPUs along with furniture that allows a tower CPU to sit securely beneath the desktop. Split-level desktops on which monitors sit lower than keyboards are another possible solution. Though split-level desks put monitors somewhat lower than the ideal level for ergonomic comfort, they are fine for a few hours of computing. Finally, there are the glass-topped desks that allow monitors to sit entirely below the desktop. The advantages of such desks are that they provide a clear line of sight between the students and the instructor and leave plenty of space for note taking. The disadvantages are that such desks are ergonomic disasters, make it hard to get at the computer equipment for maintenance, and are more expensive than traditional desks or tables.

Regardless of the furniture, it is important that users can adjust the angle of computer monitors to reduce glare and avoid neck strain. Flat-panel monitors are a plus in the e-classroom because they are easy for users to adjust for both angle and distance. (The distance between the computer user's eyes and the monitor should be somewhere between 18 and 24 inches.)

Chair Ergonomics

Chairs should be height adjustable and provide good back support. Recessed arms that are at the same height as the desktop are ideal. Computer task chairs that roll and swivel are better than rigid chairs, as one key to comfortable computing is the ability to make frequent changes in one's sitting position. As for padding, the "0–1–2–3 Rule" applies: brief tasks require chairs with 0 inches of padding; tasks that take 30 to 60 minutes require 1 inch of padding; tasks that take 1 to 2 hours require 2 inches; tasks that take more than 2 hours require 3 inches. Seat pans should be slightly concave and have a rounded "waterfall" edge that does not cut off circulation to the legs.

A relatively new type of chair on the market is the tablet-arm chair designed to support a laptop computer. Tablet-arm chairs are attractive because they can be easily arranged and rearranged to accommodate a variety of learning situations. They especially lend themselves to a wireless classroom where power and network cords are not a concern. One concern about tablet-arm chairs is that they typically do not have room for anything more than a laptop; if users want to take notes or consult a book, they either have to set the laptop on the floor (where it can get kicked or stepped on) or configure themselves into a position that would cripple a contortionist. Besides the comfort level of the seat itself, it is crucial that tablet-arm chairs provide a solid surface for the laptop computer. Just as with a keyboard tray, a wobbly tablet arm will wear out a user in short order. And even if a tablet arm is solid when new, it is worth considering how long it will stay that way under the stress and strain of daily use.

Miscellaneous Furniture Desirables

Nothing looks worse than cables hanging about as if there has just been an explosion at the spaghetti factory; even worse, untamed cables are a trip hazard. Consider furniture that helps manage cables via built-in power plugs and network jacks, cable trays, hollow legs, and so on.

If classroom computer equipment needs to be secured against theft, look for furniture to which security cables can be readily attached.

Look for furniture that positions computer equipment in such a way that it is not constantly being kicked, toppled, or otherwise banged around.

Furniture that makes it easy for technicians to get at the computer equipment and cables will save backaches and ease maintenance chores. A technician should not have to dismantle a piece of furniture to work on a CPU. Similarly, computer users should be able to reach disk drives without straining.

WHAT ABOUT THE ADA?

When it comes to e-classrooms, the most important thing to remember about the Americans with Disabilities Act (ADA) is that a classroom need only provide "reasonable accommodation" to persons with disabilities. In a nutshell, this means that only some—not every—desk in a classroom needs to be ADA-compliant.

Probably the biggest ADA concern in an e-classroom is wheelchair accessibility. As a general rule, for a workstation to be wheelchair accessible the bottom of the desktop should be at least 27 inches above the floor while the top of the desktop should be no more than 34 inches above the floor. Desktops that can be raised and lowered by means of a crank are an option, though any such workstations need to provide a truly solid desktop without any wobble or play. A less expensive and more certain option is to purchase at least one workstation that is permanently at an ADA-compliant height. Even when there are no wheelchair users in a class, extra-high workstations will be appreciated by the aforementioned scholarship basketball players. If you feel unsure about ADA issues, note that furniture vendors can be reliable sources of information on ADA compliance.

Wheelchair-accessible workstations should be marked with the blue-and-white international symbol for accessibility, and wheelchair users should have priority use of such workstations. While wheelchair-accessible workstations should not be segregated, they should be placed close to classroom entrances so that there is no need to pass through the entire classroom to get to the workstations. To allow room for maneuvering wheelchairs, provide 36 inches between the back of the wheelchair-accessible desk and the front of any wall or desk behind it; if someone will be seated directly behind the wheelchair (back-to-back seating), allow 60 inches between desks.

The Dual-Purpose Lab/Classroom

One way to stretch technology budgets is to use a single room as both a public-access computer lab and an e-classroom. This approach makes sense because the expensive computers that go into the e-classroom get more use if they can be used as lab computers when not being used for instruction. There are, however, drawbacks to such an arrangement.

E-classroom computers often allow users more privileges than do non-classroom computers. For example, classroom computers may grant users the privilege of downloading files from the Internet to the hard drive, or the privilege of accessing a utility (such as *Explorer* or the DOS prompt) that allows users to delete, rename, or move files on the hard drive. While such privileges may create few problems in the controlled setting of a classroom, granting those same privileges to largely unsupervised public-access users is a recipe for disaster.

E-classroom computers may also have certain software programs that are licensed only for instructional use. Granting users the privilege to access such software in a non-classroom setting violates the license agreement.

While neither of the above problems is insurmountable, they must be satisfactorily solved before an e-classroom can be opened up as a public-access computer lab.

Other problems that must be considered when setting up dual-purpose e-classrooms:

- E-classrooms may contain equipment (computer projectors, laser pointers, whiteboard markers, etc.) that must be locked up every time the room is opened to public access. There must be a place to lock up these items and staff responsible for the locking up.
- E-classroom furniture (especially chairs) may not be comfortable for periods lasting more than an hour or so. Also, the forward-facing layout of most e-classrooms is not ideal for a lab setting.
- E-classroom computers often print to an in-room printer which may not be robust enough for heavy public-access printing or which may not be integrated into the library's pay-to-print system (if such a system is in place).
- Evicting public-access users so that a class can begin may lead to conflicts.
- Public-access users may feel they should be allowed to use "extra" e-classroom computers during less-than-capacity class sessions.
- E-classroom areas are often not readily visible to library staff, leaving the computers in them more susceptible to intentional harm and making it more difficult for users to get staff help when they need it.
- Instructors who want to rehearse or prepare for classes have less access to the room when it is also used as a lab.

TECHNOLOGY

Of course there can be no e-classrooms without technology. Because technology is both complicated and costly, it is important to plan wisely when upgrading an existing classroom or creating a new e-classroom from the ground up.

POWER

Technology has come a long way in the last 20 years, but there is still no such thing as wireless power. Unless e-classroom computers run on battery power (see "The Laptop Option" later in this chapter), computers require adjacent power sources. Running extension cords across open floor space is never an option as the cords present both trip and fire hazards; besides, extension cords should never be used with computers in any case. Before installing 20 or more computers in an existing room, consult with an electrical expert to make sure that the building's electrical system can handle the extra power demand.

When power outlets are found only along walls, as is often the case in older buildings, computers will need to go along the walls as well. This necessitates a horseshoe or hollow-square classroom layout, neither of which may be ideal. The cheapest way to provide new power outlets is to install interior power poles and drop electrical wires down from the ceiling. Interior power poles are undesirable in an e-classroom because they block views, though they are less offensive if run down existing support columns. A more attractive solution is to install new power outlets in the floor, though this can be an expensive solution, especially if the floor is concrete. Floor outlets allow great flexibility in deciding where computers will be placed, but, just as with wall outlets, once floor outlets are installed the computers that use them must sit adjacent to the outlets. For this reason it is important to plan the location of floor outlets carefully and to allow for future needs (such as expansion).

There must be some kind of surge protector between all electronic equipment and the power source into which it is plugged. Surge protectors range in price from $10 to well over $100, but whatever the cost it is important to use surge protectors that will clamp (limit) a voltage spike to less than 400V. The package label on a surge protector will give its clamping-voltage rating—the lower the clamping-voltage level, the more protection the surge protector offers. Surge protectors are often included in power strips, though do not assume that this is always the case or assume that a power-strip surge protector will have a sufficient clamping-voltage rating. Whether they offer surge protection or not, power strips are useful in and of themselves because they accommodate multiple plugs and make it easy to cut off power to an entire workstation for maintenance or other purposes. It may be possible to accommodate more than one workstation with a single power strip, but no more than one workstation per power strip is a better option.

A superior alternative to surge protectors is an uninterruptible power supply (UPS). An uninterruptible power supply not only protects computers and their peripherals against power surges, but also continues to supply power in the case of an outage. While the length of time a UPS will continue to supply power is limited, an adequate UPS will provide enough time to safely shut down all computers before its power reserves run out. There are small UPS systems designed to support a single computer workstation, as well as larger ones that can support an entire network.

NETWORKING

There is not much point in creating an e-classroom for teaching information literacy if the computers in it are not networked. Traditional hardwired networks require that each computer be connected to a network drop via a cable. The number of drops needed, their location (wall, ceiling, or floor), and cable control raise location and proximity concerns similar to those raised by power outlets.

THE WIRELESS NETWORKING OPTION

Of course it is now possible to free the e-classroom from the tyranny of the cable by choosing to go wireless. Imagine a wireless classroom equipped with 25 wireless-capable laptops. With laptop batteries fully charged, students can sit anywhere in the room and enjoy network access with no network cables or power cords to get in the way. Students can be seated in rows, in a horseshoe, in groups, or whatever configuration best lends itself to the instruction at hand. The instructor can freely roam the classroom with a laptop or other wireless device instead of being trapped at an instructor's station at the front of the room. In the near future, the instructor may even be able to roam and project at the same time via a wireless connection between laptop and projector.

What is the catch? The catch is that, under the present reality, wireless networks are not as fast as traditional wired networks. Without sufficient wireless capacity, one student downloading an MP3 could shut down an entire wireless classroom. Which is not to say that wireless classrooms cannot work; they can, but only if they are well planned. Planning a wireless classroom should involve input from experts in wireless technology. In some cases this may mean in-house technical support staff; in others, it may mean hiring outside consultants with wireless expertise.

Wireless Standards

Before getting too deep into wireless, it helps to know the standards. The IEEE family of standards for wireless is known as 802.11.

As of 2003, the leading standard for wireless is 802.11b (also known as "Wi-Fi"). At its best, 802.11b offers speeds of 11Mbps (MegaBits Per Second), though speed drops off the further a user is from the source of the signal. The maximum range for 802.11b is about 300 feet, though interference from anything that might absorb the signal (such as water or fabrics) or interfere with the signal (such as cellphones and microwaves) will reduce that distance and/or slow the speed of transmission.

Creating a Wireless E-Classroom

A typical scenario for creating a wireless e-classroom is to install a "wireless overlay" by plugging wireless access points into existing network jacks. A wireless access point is simply a transmitter that sends out a signal that can be picked up by any computer equipped with a wireless adapter. Wireless adapters, which are comparable to antennas, come in several forms. Desktop computers typically employ wireless adapters that snap into the PC much like an internal modem card. Laptops use wireless cards that pop in and out of the same slot that accepts other laptop cards such as network and modem cards. Both desktops and laptops can also employ external wireless adapters that connect via a USB port and sit on the desktop next to the computer. As wireless becomes increasingly popular, it is more common for off-the-shelf laptops and desktops to come with built-in wireless adapters.

The wireless capacity of an e-classroom depends on the power,

Figure 10–5: Wireless Standards			
Standard	*Speed*	*Band*	*Compatible with 802.11b?*
802.11b (Wi-Fi)	1–11 Mbps	2.4GHz	—
802.11a	6–54 Mbps	5Ghz	No
802.11g	6–54 Mbps	5Ghz	Yes

number, and location of the wireless access points that serve it. Often the best location for wireless access points is up high, typically behind a wall or ceiling where existing network connections are unlikely to be found. And while it might seem like creating sufficient wireless capacity is simply a matter of installing n number of wireless access points and cranking them up to full power, the truth is that a room needs to be tuned so that competing access points do not interfere with each other. Such tuning is more of an art than a science and best left to wireless experts.

A different scenario for creating a wireless e-classroom crops up when the building the e-classroom is in, or the campus it is on, is already wireless. In such a case, the task becomes determining if the e-classroom has the necessary wireless capacity to support the desired maximum number of users and, if not, how to increase capacity to that level. Again, this is a job best left to the experts.

COMPUTERS

The whole idea of an e-classroom is to provide enough computers so that every student can get hands-on practice using computers to find information. Just about any up-to-date desktop computer will do the job, but it is best to acquire the fastest, most powerful computers the budget allows on the grounds that such computers will have longer useful lives than slower, less powerful machines. Bear in mind, though, that at the current rate of technological change even the best computers are likely to have a useful life of from three to five years. And five years is really stretching it.

As mentioned above, for reasons of visibility and user comfort, tower CPUs are preferable to desktop models and flat-panel monitors are preferable to traditional CRT monitors.

The Laptop Option

In recent years laptops (aka "notebooks") have dropped enough in price to have become an option for the e-classroom. There are several advantages to laptops:

- When fully charged, laptops can be used without power cords for all but the longest instruction sessions.
- Wireless/cordless laptops offer tremendous flexibility in how the e-classroom can be laid out and the ways in which students and instructors can interact and collaborate.
- Laptops stored in carts provide a mobile e-classroom that can be readily moved from room to room or split between

two rooms when more than one instruction session is booked for the same time slot.
- In areas prone to flooding or violent windstorms, a cartful of laptops has the advantage of being easy to move to higher floors or interior rooms on short notice.

Of course the laptop has some disadvantages as well:

- Laptops are much easier to steal than desktop computers.
- Students may have problems using laptop keyboards or mice. In some cases it may be necessary to provide traditional keyboards and mice along with a laptop.
- Laptops are more expensive than desktops and are harder to repair.
- Making sure that laptops are fully charged and ready for use requires some extra planning and effort.

Some laptop manufacturers—including *Gateway* (www.gateway.com) and *Dell* (www.dell.com)—offer turnkey mobile wireless computer labs that typically consist of wireless laptops and a mobile storage cart designed for both storage and recharging. It is also possible to create a mobile classroom by purchasing component parts separately.

Software Packages

At minimum, computers in the e-classroom require Web browser software. *Netscape* or *Internet Explorer* are the most popular choices and students are likely to be familiar with one or both. Since both Web browsers are free, it is easy to install both browsers and allow students to choose their preferred browser. Reasons for not offering both major browsers are 1) to prevent confusion that might arise when the instructor and students are using different browsers and 2) because one or more critical information resources work better with one browser or the other.

Adding additional software packages (word processors, spreadsheets, etc.) to e-classroom computers is a plus because it allows students to experience the full power of an integrated scholar's workstation. The minus is that additional software packages are potential distracters—instead of paying attention to what is being taught during an information literacy instruction session, a student might use a word-processing package to write a letter or open a paint program to doodle. Of course Web browsers offer the greatest potential distraction of all—the entire Internet. One approach to the distraction issue is to install only those software packages that are absolutely necessary for instruction and to block access to Web sites that offer the opportunity to check e-mail, chat, surf, play games, and so on. Note well that the latter task is easier conceived of than carried out, as the chore of staying on top of such sites is never ending.

As mentioned in Chapter 6, classroom control software can be used to keep students "on task." See www.ala.org/acrl/is// projects/control.html for a list of classroom-control software packages. As also mentioned in Chapter 6, an alternative approach is to consider extracurricular surfing, e-mailing, and so forth as challenges that can be overcome by good teachers who present their subject in effective and compelling ways.

Computer Security

Computer security is a book in itself. For the information literacy instructor, the main point to consider is how to balance computer security with students' need to carry out a number of different computer functions as part of the process of becoming computer literate.

There are two general types of computer security: software based and hardware based. Software-based security operates on the principle that computer users are granted various levels of permission to access files and run programs based on the user's status. These levels of permission are set by an administrator, enforced by the security software, and protected by passwords. For example, those who log in using the "Public User" password may find the computer has been tightly locked down. Public users may have permission to access a Web browser and a few selected software packages but cannot access system files, download from the Net, or save files to the hard drive. On the other hand, those who log in using the "Power User" password may find they have permission to do everything public users can do plus download to the hard drive, burn CDs, and access additional software programs. The *Windows NT* operating system is designed to provide security based on user types and their respective privileges, but it takes considerable knowledge of *Windows NT* to install and administer security. *Fortres Grand Corporation* (www.fortres.com) produces several popular software-based security solutions that are known for being simple to install and administer. *Fortres' Clean Slate* software, a relatively new product, is attractive to managers of e-classrooms because instead of restricting users from carrying out certain functions on the computer, *Clean Slate* simply undoes all the changes that users have made every time the computer is rebooted.

Hardware-based security solutions operate in a way that is similar to *Clean Slate*. Once the security hardware is installed, users can do anything at all to the computer, including deleting critical system files, changing passwords, and downloading viruses, but, because all such user-initiated changes are written to the security hardware rather than to the computer hard drive itself, upon reboot all changes disappear and the computer returns to its original configuration. *Centurion Guard* (www.centuriantech.com) is the leading provider of hardware-based security.

Because both *Clean Slate* and hardware-based security solutions do not short-circuit the learning process by preventing users from carrying out the computer functions that are essential when one is finding, saving, and using information, such solutions are better for the e-classroom than those solutions that tightly lock down the computer.

Display

The two main options for displaying what is on the instructor's computer are projectors and e-boards.

Projectors

From about the mid-1990s onward, computer-projection equipment improved tremendously in quality while dropping significantly in price. When considering any projector, it is always best if you can test-drive a working model prior to purchase; ideally, you should test it in the room or rooms where you intend to use it for instruction.

Computer projectors come in 1) larger-sized models designed to be mounted on ceilings or to reside more-or-less permanently on A/V stands and 2) small portable models that travel easily. Ceiling mounting is a great option for larger projectors because it eliminates the need for aisle-clogging A/V stands and protects the projector from damage and theft. Small, portable projectors are a good option for the mobile classroom, but they tend to cost more than similar-quality large projectors and are more susceptible to theft and damage.

Whether the projector is small or large, a few points to consider are:

> **Ease of Use:** With the present state of projection technology, hooking up a projector to just about any computer should involve no more than attaching a cable and, perhaps, pushing a function key (usually F5). The operator should not need to reboot the computer or reset the screen area in order for the image on the computer's screen to project. Anyone who can run a computer should be able to use at least the basic functions of a projector with no more than a few minutes of training and practice.

Keystone Correction: Good projectors should adjust to eliminate keystoning—the trapezoid effect that occurs when a projected image is angled upward toward a screen or wall surface.

Remote Control: A good remote control should allow the operator to do everything that can be done by pushing the control buttons on the projector itself. Remote controls are especially important for ceiling-mounted projectors. A remote mouse is a nice feature, though not absolutely necessary.

Zoom: Make sure that the projector's zoom feature will allow the unit to sit the desired distance from the surface on which it will project while still projecting an image of appropriate size. For example, if the projector will be mounted on the ceiling at a distance of ten feet from a 6' x 6' screen, the zoom should allow the operator to adjust the projected image to fit nicely on the screen.

Auxiliary Devices: A projector should be able to accommodate such auxiliary devices as VCRs and DVD players.

Image Quality: Images should be clear and visible even with significant ambient light in the room. Image quality is largely determined by a projector's brightness and resolution.

A projector's brightness is measured in ANSI lumens. Top-of-the-line projectors will weigh in at up to 3,500 lumens, while bargain basement models will muster less than 1,000 lumens. Brightness is good, so try to acquire a projector capable of at least 1,000 lumens or higher.

The number of pixels determines the "native" resolution of a projector—the more pixels, the sharper, more detailed the image. Projectors with XGA (1024 x 768), SXGA (1280 x 1024), or WXGA (1366 x 768) resolution should work with most PCs and notebooks currently on the market. Avoid projectors with VGA (640 x 480) and SVGA (800 x 600) resolutions, as the worst problems occur when the projector's resolution is lower than the screen resolution of the computer attached to it. In any case, it is worth determining in advance if the resolution of a projector you intend to buy is compatible with the computers you intend to use it with.

Wireless: Although the technology is not quite ripe at the time of this writing, in the near future it will likely be possible to acquire projectors that use some type of wireless technology (such as *Bluetooth*) to communicate with a computer. Ideally, a wireless projector will easily switch between displaying what is on the instructor's computer to displaying what is on a student's computer.

E-Boards

The term *e-board* takes in a couple of emerging technologies: plasma screens and intelligent whiteboards.

Plasma screens are essentially large, flat computer monitors designed to hang on a wall. The images on plasma screens look great even in a brightly lit room and there is no projection beam to shine in the instructor's eyes or cast shadows on the wall. Plasma screens also lend themselves to videoconferencing. The downsides of plasma screens are that they are, at present, much more expensive than computer-projection devices and are not big enough for a really large room, such as a lecture hall.

Intelligent whiteboards do a couple of useful things. First, they allow users to capture whatever is on the screen, including handwritten notes or drawings. For example, an instructor could display a record from a database on an intelligent whiteboard, use special markers to make notes or circle key areas on the record, and then save the whole thing as a file that could be distributed to students in electronic form or printed on paper. Secondly, intelligent whiteboards can function as giant touch screens, largely freeing the instructor from moving back and forth between projected image and computer. For example, to advance a PowerPoint presentation to the next slide, the instructor merely taps the intelligent whiteboard.

There are two types of intelligent whiteboards on the market. The first requires a traditional computer projection unit to display the image that appears on the whiteboard. The second (as exemplified by the 3M Wall Display system) comes with its own projection unit that swings out from the whiteboard. As with plasma screens, the downside of intelligent whiteboards is their high cost compared to computer projection units. Intelligent whiteboards also require special markers that are more expensive than ordinary whiteboard markers.

11 MARKETING ELECTRONIC INFORMATION LITERACY INSTRUCTION

So you have worked hard to develop a solid information literacy program? Great. The last thing you want now is for the services you offer to become some of the best kept secrets on campus. The only way to avoid this dubious distinction is to get out and market your program and services to students, faculty, and administrators.

STUDENTS

Marketing information literacy directly to students is a bit like wishing on a star: it does no harm and it might make you feel better, but there is no scientific proof that it gets results. The surest way to get students to take advantage of an information literacy program is to arrange it so that their participation is a required part of their course work. This is typically done by marketing to faculty (see below). The next best way to engage students is to provide information literacy services that *make their lives easier*. If you can develop such services—workshops, Web tutorials, and so on—then marketing these services to students is worth the effort. However, if students cannot see how a service will make their lives easier, or if using a service creates yet another hardship for students, then all the marketing in the world will not make it a success. Witness the recent experience of the high profile online library that spent millions marketing itself to college students nationwide only to see them stay away in droves.

Too often, what an information literacy professional sees as a service that will be irresistible to students proves to be quite resistible, thank you very much. The best way to avoid putting a huge effort into developing a service only to see it flop with students is to test the service with student focus groups as it is being developed and to make changes based on what you hear and (most importantly) observe during testing.

Library Marketing in Depth
For a more complete, hands-on guide to library-oriented marketing than could possibly be presented here, see Suzanne Walters' *Library Marketing That Works!* (New York: Neal-Schuman, 2003).

FACULTY

Marketing to faculty has two components. One component is marketing information literacy services, while the other is marketing the broad concept of information literacy.

Success in marketing of information literacy services is largely measured by the extent to which faculty include those services as required parts of their courses. As with students, faculty are most attracted to information literacy services that *make their lives easier*: "None of my students has a clue how to find articles in engineering journals. Can you help [make my life easier so I do not have to come to grips with something that I know in my heart is important but with which I do not wish to (or perhaps cannot) deal]?" Because their students' lack of information literacy is the thing that makes faculty aware that information literacy services are needed, marketing to faculty is mostly a matter of making them aware that information literacy services exist and being ready to provide those services when they are needed. Awareness marketing can be done through flyers, mailings, campus newsletters (print and electronic), information fairs, faculty orientations, Web sites, and all the other usual channels of communication, but perhaps the most powerful awareness tool is good old-fashioned personal contact.

A good information literacy professional must be a persuasive and dogged salesperson who constantly makes the rounds with faculty: handing out business cards, serving on campus-wide committees, attending campus events that attract faculty (lectures, performances, and the like), listening to endless gripes about library services over which an information literacy professional has little or no influence, and talking one-on-one with faculty about information literacy problems and solutions. If a faculty member tells you, "You should have been an insurance salesman," take it as a compliment.

To be fair, most faculty care about student learning as much or more than they care about having their own lives made easier.

With this in mind, a very important way to win the hearts and minds of faculty is to provide information literacy services that are truly effective. When faculty see good results after their students attend an information literacy session or complete an information literacy assignment that you created, those faculty will jump on your information literacy bandwagon. For those hesitant or dubious faculty who have never taken advantage of your information literacy services, providing them with student-outcomes data is a good way to sharpen their interest in information literacy. (See Chapter 12 for more on the topic of assessment.)

Some of the best resources and opportunities for marketing information literacy services to faculty include:

- **Subject-Specialist Librarians.** Subject specialists can be great information literacy sales reps because of their close contact with faculty and knowledge of the particular information literacy needs within their specialties. Do not forget that subject-specialist librarians often get invited to department meetings and might be able to arrange for you to give an information literacy pitch to an entire department.
- **Reference Desk Contacts with Faculty.** While that faculty member you have just helped with an impossible reference question is still gushing thanks, take the opportunity to strike with your pitch for information literacy. People respond remarkably well when they feel they owe a debt of gratitude.
- **Lousy Library Assignments.** The faculty member who gives 100 students a horrible library assignment—

  > Use *Index Ponderous* to find the citation to my seminal 1976 article concerning the number of angels that can dance on the head of a pin. *Index Ponderous* is located next to the watercooler on the third floor of the library and has brown covers. When you actually locate my article in the bound periodicals, take a single-edged razor blade and carefully. . .

  —may not have a clue about what is going on in the library or the world of information, but at least he cares enough to give his students an assignment that takes a stab at information literacy; for this reason, such a faculty member might be amenable to an overture from a librarian:

Gee Professor Fossilman, I would love to get together with you to polish up that wonderful assignment your students are working on. After all, those *wee* little problems your students encountered occurred because we silly old librarians simply forgot to tell you that *Index Ponderous* changed from brown covers to red [in 1978], was shifted from the third to the fourth floor of the library [five years ago], and has been pretty much replaced by *IPOnline* [which the library is paying a fortune to subscribe to at the inflexible insistence of your department chair].

More seriously, offering to help any faculty member with an information-related assignment, whether it be creating a new one from scratch or updating an old one, is a great way to make contact, build trust, and increase the use of information literacy services.

- **New Faculty.** Pitching information literacy services to faculty before they have had a chance to get set in their ways is a great tactic. By all means get on the program for new-faculty orientations and make appointments to meet with every new faculty member who will let you in the door.

Marketing the broad concept of information literacy is not as easy as marketing specific services. For one thing, the concept of information literacy does not produce for faculty the tangible benefits that well designed and executed information literacy services can produce. For another, information literacy is yet another competitor among the growing pack of literacies clamoring for recognition and support: media literacy, math literacy, financial literacy, plain-old literacy, and so on.

Faculty typically specialize in one subject and tend to be oriented towards the notion of a subject as an area of knowledge with its own body of literature, research methods, academic department, and so on. To people conditioned to think this way,

---

Further Reading on Collaborating with Faculty

See Rosemary M. Young and Stephena Harmony's *Working with Faculty to Design Undergraduate Information Literacy Programs: A How-To-Do-It Manual for Librarians* (New York: Neal-Schuman, 1999).

this thing called "information literacy" may seem, at best, to be a rather fuzzy concept or, at worst, yet another academic fad that will be forgotten as soon as the next flavor of the month comes along. This is why, when a faculty member asks, "Just what do you mean by information literacy, anyway?" it is a good idea to have a definition on hand (see Chapter 1).

Because faculty are scholars (or at least should be), providing them with a scholarly article or two that defines and defends information literacy can be a good strategy. It is especially important that the article or articles you present to faculty get across the idea that information literacy is as much about critical thinking as it is about skills (library or computer).

Most faculty have enough to read as it is, so it is best to be selective when choosing recommended readings. (Side note: If you really want faculty to read an article, splurge and provide them with a copy of the full text rather than a citation; there is no guarantee that they will read any full-text article you give them, but it is all but a certainty that they will never bother to track down a citation.) An article that is both provocative and informative, such as "Information Literacy as a Liberal Art" (Shapiro and Hughes), might do the trick, or you might want to consider something more neutral, such as "Information Literacy in a Nutshell" (Institute for Information Literacy). When choosing any article or Web page for faculty, it is important to carefully consider your audience and to select readings that will best appeal to their mindsets.

Like just about everyone else in the world, faculty have been exposed to a great deal of hype about electronic information, and this no doubt contributes to faculty skepticism about the need for information literacy programs:

- "Isn't everything available online now?"
- "All these kids are born computer whizzes. They should be teaching us."
- "Will we really need libraries ten years from now?"

Faculty who ask these kinds of questions are as much in need of a good dose of information literacy as their students, which is why Chapter 2 of this book is titled, "Teaching Students (and Others) Why Information Is Not All 'Just a Click Away.'"

The most effective way to get faculty sold on the broad concept of information literacy is to get them involved in planning information literacy programs. While it is certainly more expeditious to keep planning for information literacy in-house rather than, for example, forming a campus-wide information literacy planning committee, too often the programs that emerge from in-house planning hold great appeal for librarians and little for faculty. Bringing non-librarians in on the planning slows progress, raises questions that range from the irrelevant to the uncomfortable, and ends up taking the program down roads you never intended to travel. That said, the end result may not only be a stronger information literacy program, but also a higher level of faculty buying in to the broad concept of information literacy than could ever be achieved without their participation in the planning process. In the ideal, faculty participation could eventually lead to the Holy Grail of an articulated, campus-wide, across-the-curriculum program of information literacy in which the library is a key, but never a lone, player.

ADMINISTRATORS

Regardless of title—department head, director, dean, principal, academic vice president, provost, president, chancellor, or grand pooh-bah—the typical academic administrator is a person with plenty on his or her plate. Faculty and staff constantly bombard their administrators with problems, complaints, fires in need of dousing, and—most of all—pleas for a share of whatever funds and resources the administrator controls. At the same time, administrators feel constant pressure from *their* higher-ups to do more, more, more with less, less, less. Uneasy lies the head that wears the crown. What most administrators would really like, in fact, is someone who could *make their lives easier.*

Before jumping into the ways information literacy can make the lives of administrators easier, it is worth noting that almost all academic administrators come from the ranks of faculty and, as such, harbor some of the same skepticism towards information literacy as do faculty. For this reason, everything said above about winning over faculty applies to administrators with the caveat that some administrators have been out of the classroom so long that their need for education on the realities of electronic information is even greater than that of the rank-and-file faculty. Anyone who has been in the information business for long has heard tales (some no doubt apocryphal) of the administrator who announces that there soon will be no need for a library budget "now that everything is on the Web."

If faculty's primal information literacy need is services that teach their students how to do research for specific courses or assignments, the administrator's primal information literacy need is data that will keep from his or her door the wolves of accountability: the school board, the state legislature, the regional accrediting body, and so on. For this reason, anyone who can put together an effective information literacy program and back it up with outcomes assessment data that show the program is effective is likely to be counted among the administrator's friends.

It is worth remembering why it is important to be on an administrator's friends list:

- Administrators can provide direction and leadership by making the institution's information literacy goals clear to those responsible for information literacy, and this type of communication flows more easily when the administrator and the information literacy professionals have a cordial relationship based on confidence in each other. Of course it is quite possible that a key administrator may be unsure of what the institution's information literacy goals should be or unaware of what various accrediting bodies expect in the area of information literacy. In such cases it is important that the information literacy professionals are able to communicate up to the administrator, and, again, this is easier when a good relationship is already in place.
- Administrators who have been sold on the idea of information literacy can become powerful instruments for ensuring that information literacy becomes a key part of the institution's mission, plans, and policies. Cutting to the chase: If your goal is to see information literacy implemented campus wide and across the curriculum, it helps to have the provost in your back pocket before you begin your crusade. Getting key faculty to sit on, and actively participate in, a campus-wide information literacy planning committee is a lot easier when the invitation comes from on high instead of from a rank-and-file librarian.
- Most importantly, administrators can provide the funding for the staff, facilities, and professional development opportunities needed to develop and maintain a high-quality information literacy program.

In a perfect world, administrators would provide those responsible with developing an information literacy program with the up-front funding and resources they need to make their program happen. In the real world, however, information literacy programs usually need to give before they get. That is, before an administrator is going to put money into expanding or creating an information literacy program, the information literacy program needs to provide proof (typically in the form of positive student outcomes) that it can deliver the goods. The Catch-22 involved here hardly needs to be stated. (But let's not let that spoil our fun):

> To provide positive information literacy outcomes, we need administrative support. To get administrative support, we need to provide positive information literacy outcomes.

The way this scenario usually plays out is that the information literacy people give something (student outcomes) to the administrator in order to get a reward (resources) that allows them to expand their program and, as a result, give more to the administrator. In theory, the giving and the getting can spiral on and on forever, though the reality is that some point of equilibrium is eventually reached. The trick in making this game work is to not give too much on the first go-round. If you tell an administrator that you need support but turn around and produce the desired results before any support is forthcoming, the shrewd administrator is unlikely to reach for the checkbook. Why, after all, pay for something you are getting for free?

This all sounds far too cynical, and it probably is. Most administrators are not bloodless Machiavellians and most do care about more than the bottom line. Still, it takes real resources to create an information literacy program that will produce meaningful student outcomes, and administrators need to understand that information literacy, like information itself, is not free. Librarians have historically been too willing to tighten their belts and make good things happen without additional resources; this should not be the case with information literacy, especially given that fact that information literacy is being mandated by accrediting bodies right along with math, science, reading, and all the other subjects that line up for their share of the institution's resources.

Of course resources for information literacy can always be boosted by outside grants or gifts. As with any academic area, the availability of grants for information literacy efforts varies from place to place and year to year. Applying for a grant can be a Herculean task, and there is no guarantee that all the effort put into applying will bear fruit. If your institution has a support system for grant seekers, such as an office for grants, your first step should be through the door of that office. Without such a support system, your best bet is to read a good book or two on grant getting and start pounding the pavement in search of grant opportunities. Peruse the Web sites and publications of library professional organizations, as these often carry information about information literacy grants. Various federal Web sites are also worth visiting, with the Department of Education's site (www.ed.gov) being a logical starting point.

If grants for information literacy are hard to find, the situation for gifts is worse. Most individuals and organizations that give to libraries want their names on buildings, rooms, or major collections, not on intangibles like information literacy programs. That said, a nice endowment will do wonders for any information literacy program lucky enough to bag such a rare bird.

REFERENCES

Institute for Information Literacy. "Information Literacy in a Nutshell: Basic Information for Academic Administrators and Faculty." Chicago: Association of College and Research Libraries. (February 2003) Available: www.ala.org/acrl/nili/whatis.html.

Shapiro, Jeremy J., and Shelley K. Hughes. "Information Literacy as a Liberal Art." *Educom Review*. (February 2003) Available: www.educause.edu/pub/er/review/reviewarticles/31231.html.

12 ASSESSING ELECTRONIC INFORMATION LITERACY INSTRUCTION

Assessment of information literacy divides into two parts. The first part is assessment of student outcomes, while the second part is assessment of program performance. (As a point of clarification, the terms *assessment* and *evaluation* are used more-or-less interchangeably in the literature of information literacy. From unscientific observation, *assessment* seems to be the current term of choice and is used throughout this chapter.)

ASSESSMENT OF STUDENT OUTCOMES

WHY ASSESS STUDENT OUTCOMES?

Assessment of student outcomes is not an absolutely essential part of information literacy. Indeed, it would be quite possible to run a top-notch information literacy program and never do a bit of assessment. However, without assessment any moves made to improve the quality of instruction would have to be based on guesswork; additionally, those running the program would not be able to demonstrate that their program was, in fact, effective. To put a positive spin on it, there are two reasons why assessment is so important that it does not matter that you could, in theory, live without it:

1. Assessment provides guidance for improving information literacy programs.
2. Assessment allows those who teach information literacy to demonstrate to administrators (and others) that their efforts are effective and worthy of support.

Given the importance of assessment, why is it more often not done than done? The answer is that the pressures facing real-world instructors often push assessment to the back burner:

Look. Each semester three reference librarians teach about forty information literacy sessions just for freshman writing alone. With all of our other duties, it's a miracle we get all the classes taught as it is. Why in the world would we want to take on a big, hairy assessment project on top of all that? So we can write it up in some library journal that nobody reads? Get real.

First of all, there is no doubt that assessment should not be done just for publication. If assessment does not help to improve and/or justify instruction, it is not worth doing. Another time when assessment is of no value is when those doing the assessment have already decided what the outcome is going to be before the assessment has begun. Approaching assessment honestly—prepared to take the bad news as well as the good—is arguably the most important factor in obtaining useful information from any assessment effort.

Secondly, assessment should not become so huge a burden that it interferes with actually providing instruction. The reality is, though, that assessment is a burden. For starters, good assessment is not a one-time or occasional activity; it is an ongoing, permanent activity that never stops demanding time and resources. Also, it is quite possible to put more time and energy into assessing instruction than went into planning and carrying out the instruction in the first place. To avoid this perverse inversion of effort, always remember that the effort that goes into assessment must be in proportion to the effort that goes into the instruction itself. An information literacy endeavor that involves a dozen instructors and serves hundreds of students a semester is worthy of a pretty serious assessment effort; a one-shot instruction session that involves one instructor and 15 students is not.

Finally, even though assessment is a great deal of work, assessment can actually cut down on your workload by showing you where you need to put your efforts and where your efforts are not effective. For example, if your library has offered drop-in *ERIC* workshops for the last ten years, an assessment of those workshops might tell you that they are not effective and are not really needed, thus allowing you to put your efforts into areas where the need for, and impact of, instruction is greater.

CUTTING ASSESSMENT DOWN TO SIZE

So how do you keep assessment from turning into the tail that wags the dog? The first step is to accept the fact that assessment does not have to be perfect to be useful. Sure, if the fairy godmother of assessment hands out a grant that allows you to employ control groups, longitudinal studies, double-blind scoring, and all the other bells and whistles that go into a textbook assessment effort, by all means take the money and shoot for perfection. Back in the real world, a less-than-perfect assessment effort is better than no assessment at all. Think of it this way: Would you rather base future instructional decisions on assessment data that is, let's say, about 80% accurate, or would you rather base those decisions on no data at all? And no data is exactly what you will have to work with if you postpone assessment until that far-off day when you can do it textbook perfect.

All of which is not to say that you should do sloppy assessment. Everyone wants the best possible data, and high quality data comes from doing the best possible assessment. The key word here is *possible*. If having a control group is not possible, then do your assessment without one. If following a cohort of students for four years will overtax your resources, then do the best you can without a longitudinal study. In any case: Do the best you can with what you have.

Another way to keep assessment efforts down to manageable sizes is to use random sampling. One of the key ideas of the science of statistics is that given a population of size n, studying a random sample of that population can provide significant information about the entire population. That is, if 250 freshman writing students sit through your information literacy sessions, you need to obtain information from only a random sample of that population, not all 250 students.

EXPERT ASSISTANCE

When considering random sampling, the first questions that come to mind should be: "How do I obtain a true random sample?" and "How many students out of a population of size n do I need to sample to get significant data?" Good questions. And unless you have training in statistics (bully for you if you do), they are questions you should ask of an expert. If you are fortunate enough to work at an institution that provides expert consultants for faculty and staff who are conducting assessment, by all means take advantage of that assistance; if that option is not available to you, then you will either need to talk an expert into assisting you for free or pay an expert to serve as a consultant.

Whether or not an expert is paid, it is important to get that expert involved in your assessment effort at the earliest point possible. If an expert has a hand in your research design right from the start, you are likely to come out with meaningful numbers at the end of the assessment; if you do your own research design, collect a pile of data, and bring it all to a statistics expert to number crunch, more often than not he or she will send you back to the drawing board and all your work will have been for naught.

Human Subjects

When you assess student outcomes, you will most likely need to get prior clearance from whatever person or office in your institution is responsible for human-subjects research. Generally, this involves nothing more than presenting the human-subjects czars with a description of how you plan to assess students while protecting their privacy. Failing to get clearance to assess human subjects can result in serious consequences, so be sure you do not overlook this small, but important, part of the assessment process.

AN ASSESSMENT PLAN

Another way to keep assessment from gobbling up more than its share of time and energy is to develop an overall assessment plan. Too often, assessment of information literacy is a legacy program—a few individuals collecting statistics here, someone else doing a bit of outcomes assessment there. Without a unifying assessment plan, bringing all these diverse efforts together in order to come up with some meaningful data is just about impossible. Some points to consider when developing an assessment plan include:

- How does assessment fit in with the mission of our institution?
- What are the goals and objectives of our assessment program?
- How can we develop outcomes assessments that, all in one go, provide information we can use for multiple purposes, such as: improving instruction, maximizing our instructional efforts, building administrative support for the information literacy program in particular and for the library in general, and providing data that we can submit to accrediting bodies?
- Whose outcomes should we assess? Freshmen writing students, students in sophomore core courses, students in capstone courses, graduate students, alumni, or combinations of the above? How can we use random sampling to keep assessment manageable?
- What methods will we use to assess outcomes? (See below.)
- What criteria will we use to interpret the assessment data we collect and to determine whether or not we are achieving our goals?

- What mechanisms can we put in place to periodically review and revise our assessment efforts?

METHODS OF ASSESSMENT

One area where an expert can help in the early stages of an assessment effort is to suggest a workable method of assessment. (For a more detailed description of various assessment methods, see Joseph Prus and Reid Johnson. 1994. "A Critical Review of Student Assessment Options," *New Directions for Community Colleges* no. 88 (Winter): 69–83.)

There are several standard methods to consider, including:

Tests

Tests that assess students' level of information literacy can take many forms—multiple choice, essay, fill in the blank, take-home, and hands-on simulations—and be administered in print or online. The key to using tests, of course, is to design a meaningful test that can be scored consistently. Essay tests have the potential to provide the truest measure of student outcomes, but they are also the most difficult tests to score with any consistency. One approach to scoring essay tests is to write up some fairly specific scoring guidelines and then have two scorers independently score each essay. If the two scores fall within a predetermined range, they are averaged; if the scores are too far apart, a third reader determines the final score of the test.

Administering a pretest and a posttest is a good way to measure what students have learned. This method simply involves giving students a test prior to instruction, giving them the same test afterwards, and then comparing the scores.

Student Research Projects

Although this method of evaluation requires cooperation from classroom instructors and raises some (surmountable) privacy issues, examining student research projects (such as term papers, bibliographies, case studies, research logs, and so on) can be a valuable evaluation tool. The goal is to determine whether or not the sources the students used in their research projects reflect an understanding of what they were taught about information literacy. For example, you might examine student bibliographies to see if they reflect the use of a variety of information finding tools (Web search engines, subject periodical databases, library catalogs, etc.); or if they reflect an understanding of the difference between, and appropriate uses of, scholarly versus popular literature. Another approach might be to have information literacy instructors rate student bibliographies (using a set of written standards to achieve as much consistency as possible) and then compare these ratings to the final grades that classroom instructors gave to the completed projects.

Extending this method even further is the evaluation of student portfolios—collections of student work done over time rather than as a single project. The student-portfolio method lends itself particularly well to longitudinal studies.

The "Default" Control Group

When you are assessing student outcomes and lack a true randomly selected control group, the following idea often surfaces: "Let's identify those students who, for one reason or another, did not participate in information literacy instruction and use them as the control group." There is some sense in this approach, but there are pitfalls. Because there are a number of reasons students may have missed out on the information literacy instruction—illness, hubris, laziness, schedule conflicts—such a control group is far from random and the numbers that result from studying such a group may be very skewed.

Student Feedback

Asking students what they think of the information literacy instruction they received can be a valuable evaluation tool. You can ask students for feedback in written or oral form. Focus groups are an option for oral feedback. While student feedback will provide some useful insights for instructors, there is always the problem that what students feel they did or did not gain from information literacy instruction does not always reflect what they really gained. That is, the student who says, "The instruction was great," may really have learned very little, while the student who says, "The instruction sucked," may actually have learned a lot.

Automated Assessment

Any online tutorial that you adopt for information literacy instruction should include a component for automated assessment. The simplest sort of automated assessment might do no more than tell you what percentage of those who started the tutorial actually completed it, while more sophisticated assessment mechanism might (with due regard for privacy) track users of the tutorial and compile statistics on their successes, failures, missteps, and so on.

Longitudinal Studies

Though time consuming and somewhat difficult to pull off, longitudinal studies give perhaps the truest picture of how information literacy instruction impacts students. The idea of a longitudinal study is to follow a cohort of students during their time at your institution (and, ideally, afterwards) to see how information literacy correlates to academic success and (again in the ideal) success after graduation.

Observation

Observation of how students use information, though vulnerable to observer bias, has its place in evaluation. For example, it is significant if reference librarians notice a sudden upsurge in the use of an information resource that was recently emphasized in information literacy sessions.

ASSESSMENT OF PROGRAM PERFORMANCE

The second part of assessing information literacy is assessment of program performance. Student outcomes are clearly an important—or maybe the most important—element of program assessment. After all, if students who are touched by the information literacy program become more information literate, it strongly suggests that the overall information literacy program is doing something right. There are a number of questions that should be answered by program assessment:

- Is the information literacy program in step with the mission of its parent institution?
- Does the program have an agreed-upon definition of information literacy?
- Does the program have clear goals and objectives and is it achieving them?
- Do the goals and objectives of the information literacy program have real impact on the way frontline instructors teach information literacy?
- Does the program have the necessary administrative support (including financial support) to carry out its goals and objectives?
- Does the program enjoy widespread support among both library and non-library instructors?
- Is the program assessing student outcomes in an organized, consistent, and effective way?
- Do student outcomes show that the information literacy program improves students' level of information literacy and their overall academic performance?

There are certainly other questions that might be asked when assessing an information literacy program, and any of the above questions could be restated. In any case, answering these types of questions, though not easy, is important. Program evaluation of this type is most often self-evaluation in that those doing the evaluation are the very people who oversee the program and do the instruction. Bringing those involved together to review outcomes assessment data, ask hard questions about the program, and brainstorm solutions to problems is perhaps the most common way to do program assessment; on the other hand, if time and resources afford, bringing in an outside expert as a reviewer or moderator can increase the objectivity of program assessments.

RESOURCES FOR ASSESSMENT

The Web is home to a number of good resources for information on assessing information literacy. Many of these resources contain not only information, but also bibliographies that point to additional Web and print resources. Also listed below are two recent print publications on information literacy assessment.

Association of College & Research Libraries. "Information Literacy Competency Standards for Higher Education: Standards, Performance Indicators, and Outcomes." Chicago: ACRL. (February 2003) Available: www.ala.org/acrl/ilstandardlo.html.
Presents five standards and 22 performance indicators for assessing information literacy.

ERIC Clearinghouse on Assessment and Evaluation. "Ericae.net." College Park, MD: University of Maryland, Department of Measurement, Statistics and Evaluation. (February 2003) Available: ericae.net.
This is the Web site of the ERIC Clearinghouse on Assessment and Evaluation. Among other features, this site offers 550 selected full-text books and articles on educational assessment.

Hernon, Peter, and Robert E. Dugan. 2002. *Action Plan for Outcomes Assessment in Your Library*. Chicago: American Library Association.
This volume presents a comprehensive plan for librarians interested in assessment, including assessment of information literacy programs. The authors provide "data-collection tools for measuring both learning and research outcomes that link outcomes to user satisfaction."

Indiana University Bloomington Libraries. "Assessment Plan for Information Literacy." Bloomington, IN: Indiana University Bloomington Libraries. (February 2003) Available: www.indiana.edu/~libinstr/Information_Literacy/assessment.html.
This document is an example of a detailed plan for assessing information literacy.

Merz, Lawrie H., and Beth L. Mark, comps. 2002. *Assessment in College Library Instruction Programs*. Chicago: Association of College and Research Libraries.
This publication includes the results of a survey to learn how information literacy is being assessed in nearly 300 college and university libraries. Also includes examples of information literacy assessment tools.

Pausch, Lois M., and Mary Popp. "Assessment of Information Literacy: Lessons from the Higher Education Assessment Movement." Chicago: Association of College & Research Libraries. (February 2003) Available: www.ala.org/acrl/paperhtm/d30.html.
This ALA/ACRL paper "reviews higher education assessment

methods; identifies useful theories and practices; describes assessment programs in academic libraries; and makes recommendations for changes in library education and for future research."

Ragains, Patrick. "Assessment in Library & Information Literacy Instruction." Reno, NV: University of Nevada, Reno. (February 2003) Available: www2.library.unr.edu/ragains/assess.html.
This Web site includes such categories as "Bibliographies on Assessment of Library and Information Literacy Instruction" and "Pretests of Students' Library & Information Literacy Skills."

APPENDIX:
USEFUL RESOURCES FOR
INFORMATION LITERACY

The resources listed below are annotated except where the title of the resource makes its purpose so obvious that annotation would be redundant.

Allan, Barbara. 2002. *E-learning and Teaching in Library and Information Services*. London: Facet.
A practical guide to online learning.

American Association of School Librarians. "AASL." Chicago: AASL. (February 2003) Available: www.ala.org/aasl/index.html.
The following sections of the AASL Web site—"National Guidelines and Standards," "Position Statements," and "Resource Guides"—all provide access to resources that deal with information literacy.

Anderson, Kari J. 1999. *"LOEX" of the West: Collaboration and Instructional Design in a Virtual Environment*. Stamford, CT: JAI Press.

Association of College & Research Libraries. "ACRL Institute for Information Literacy." Chicago: ACRL. (February 2003) Available: www.ala.org/acrl/nili/nilihp.html.
The ACRL Institute for Information Literacy champions the cause of information literacy throughout the realm of higher education. One of its main roles is preparing librarians to become effective information literacy teachers. The IIL sponsors annual immersion programs to give librarians the tools they need to build information literacy programs at their home institutions.

Association of College & Research Libraries. "Characteristics of Programs of Information Literacy that Illustrate Best Practices." Chicago: ACRL. (February 2003) Available: www.ala.org/acrl/guides/bestprac.html.
A practical list of best practices for information literacy programs.

Association of College & Research Libraries. "ILI-L (Information Literacy Instruction Listserv)." Chicago: ACRL. (February 2003) Available: www.ala.org/acrl/is/ilil.html.
ILI-L is the heir of BI-L, a pioneer library listserv launched by Martin Raish in 1990. To subscribe to ILI-L send the text **subscribe ILI-L your firstname yourlastname** in the body of the message to listproc@ala.org.

Association of College & Research Libraries. "Information Literacy Competency Standards for Higher Education." Chicago: ACRL. (February 2003) Available: www.ala.org/acrl/ilintro.html.
Includes a very complete definition of information literacy as well as a list of five standards and 22 performance indicators for assessing information literacy.

Association of College & Research Libraries Instruction Section. "Instruction Section." Chicago: ACRL. (February 2003) Available: www.ala.org/acrl/is.
The mission of the ACRL Instruction Section is to enhance "the ability of academic and research librarians to advance learning, teaching and research with respect to information literacy in higher education."

Barclay, Donald A. 1993. "Evaluating Library Instruction: Doing the Best You Can with What You Have." *RQ* 33, no.2 (Winter): 195–202.
Describes an evaluation effort and argues that the inability to do "perfect" evaluation should not prevent evaluation from going forward.

Barclay, Donald A. 1992. "Understanding the Freshman Writer: The Pedagogy of Composition and Its Relevance to Bibliographic Instruction." *Proceedings of the Sixth National Conference of the Association of College and Research Libraries, Salt Lake City, Utah, April 1992.* Chicago: ACRL.
A historical overview of using freshman writing classes to provide students with bibliographic instruction.

Barclay, Donald A., and Darcie R. Barclay. 1994. "The Role of Freshman Writing in Academic Bibliographic Instruction." *Journal of Academic Librarianship* 20: 213–217.
A survey of the extent to which freshman writing classes are used to provide bibliographic instruction.

Behrens, Shirley J. 2002. "A Conceptual Analysis and Historical Overview of Information Literacy." *College & Research Libraries* 55: 309–322.
A historical overview of the concept of information literacy from the 1970s to the 1980s.

Birks, Jane, and Fiona Hunt. 2003. *Hands-On Information Literacy Activities*. New York: Neal-Schuman.

Bradley, Phil. 2002. *Internet Power Searching: The Advanced Manual, Second Edition*. New York: Neal-Schuman.

Brandt, D. Scott. 2002. *Teaching Technology: A How-To-Do-It Manual for Librarians*. New York: Neal-Schuman.

Bundy, Alan L. 1999. "Information Literacy: The 21st Century Educational Smartcard." *Australian Academic and Research Libraries* 30, no.4: 233–250.

California State University System. "CUS Information Competence Project." San Luis Obispo, California: California State University System. (February 2003) Available: www.lib.calpoly.edu/infocomp/project.
Web site for a California State University systemwide project to implement information competence through interactive teaching materials. The focus is on teaching ten core information literacy competencies.

Ciolek, T. Matthew. "Information Quality." The *WWW Virtual Library*. (February 2003) Available: www.ciolek.com/WWWVL-InfoQuality.html.
Links to sites focusing on locating and evaluating reliable information on the Web.

Cooke, Alison. 1999. *Neal-Schuman Authoritative Guide to Evaluating Information on the Internet*. New York: Neal-Schuman.

Cox, Christopher, and Stephen Pratt. 2002. "Case of the Missing Students, and How We Reached Them with Streaming Media." *Computers in Libraries* (March): 40–45.
Describes how one library created an edited streaming-media instructional video to serve remote and commuter students.

Craver, Kathleen W. 1997. *Teaching Electronic Literacy.* Westport, CT: Greenwood Press.

Curtis, Donnelyn, ed. 2002. *Attracting, Educating, and Serving Remote Users Through the Web: A How-To-Do-It Manual for Librarians.* New York: Neal-Schuman.

Doggett, Sandra L., and Paula Kay Montgomery. 2000. *Beyond the Book: Technology Integration into the Secondary School Library Media Curriculum.* Englewood, CO: Libraries Unlimited.

Eisenberg, Mike, and Bob Berkowitz. "*Big6.*" Fayetteville, NY: Big6 Associates. (February 2003) Available: www.big6.com.
A commercial endeavor, *Big6* is a system for teaching information and technology skills for K-12 students.

Eisenberg, Michael, and Robert E. Berkowitz. 2000. *Teaching Information & Technology Skills: The Big6 in Secondary Schools.* Worthington, OH: Linworth Publishing.

ERIC Clearinghouse on Assessment and Evaluation. "Ericae.net." College Park, MD: University of Maryland, Department of Measurement, Statistics and Evaluation. (February 2003) Available: ericae.net.
This is the Web site of the ERIC Clearinghouse on Assessment and Evaluation. Among other features, this site offers 550 selected full-text books and articles on educational assessment.

Goodson, Carol. 2001. *Providing Library Services for Distance Education Students: A How-To-Do-It Manual.* New York: Neal-Schuman.
Gives a librarian's perspective on distance-education delivery systems and trends.

Grassian, Esther, and Joan Kaplowitz. 2001. *Information Literacy Instruction: Theory and Practice.* New York: Neal-Schuman.

Harmon, Charles. 2000. *Using the Internet, Online Services, and CD-ROMs for Writing Research and Term Papers, Second Edition.* New York: Neal-Schuman.

Hernon, Peter, and Robert E. Dugan. 2002. *Action Plan for Outcomes Assessment in Your Library.* Chicago : American Library Association.

This volume presents a comprehensive plan for librarians interested in assessment, including assessment of information literacy programs. The authors provide "data-collection tools for measuring both learning and research outcomes that link outcomes to user satisfaction."

Hinchliffe, Lisa Janicke. 2001. *Electronic Classroom Handbook.* New York: Neal-Schuman.

Hoffmann, Gretchen McCord. 2001. *Copyright in Cyberspace: Questions & Answers for Librarians.* New York: Neal-Schuman.

Horton, William K. 2000. *Designing Web-based Training: How to Teach Anyone Anything Anywhere Anytime.* New York: Wiley.
Anyone interested in creating a Web-based tutorial will benefit from this practical guide. Contains many examples.

Hutchins Library. "Bibliographic Instruction Program Evaluation." Berea, KY: Berea College. (February 2003) Available: www.berea.edu/library/BIEVAL/Pre-test-Post-test.html
A good example of a pretest/posttest evaluation of instruction.

Indiana University Bloomington Libraries. "Assessment Plan for Information Literacy." Bloomington, Indiana: Indiana University Bloomington Libraries. (February 2003) Available: www.indiana.edu/~libinstr/Information_Literacy/assessment.html.
This document is an example of a detailed plan for assessing information literacy.

Institute for Information Literacy. "Information Literacy in a Nutshell: Basic Information for Academic Administrators and Faculty." Chicago: American Library Association/Association of College and Research Libraries. (February 2003) Available: www.ala.org/acrl/nili/whatis.html.
A good resource to share with faculty and administrators.

Iowa City Community School District. Mary Jo Langhorne, ed. 1998. *Developing an Information Literacy Program K-12: A How-To-Do-It Manual and CD-ROM Package.* New York: Neal-Schuman.

Jones, Debra. 1998. *Exploring the Internet Using Critical Thinking Skills: A Self-Paced Workbook for Learning to Effectively Use the Internet and Evaluate Online Information*. New York: Neal-Schuman.

Kent State University. "Project SAILS." Kent, OH: Kent State University. (February 2003) Available: www.library.kent.edu/sails/projdescription.html.
Project SAILS (Standardized Assessment of Information Literacy) in an effort to develop "an instrument for programmatic level assessment of information literacy skills that is valid and thus credible to university administrators and other academic personnel." Includes citations and links to resources dealing with the assessment of information literacy.

LaGuardia, Cheryl, and Christine K. Oka. 2000. *Becoming a Library Teacher*. New York: Neal-Schuman.

Lee, William W., and Diana L. Owens. 2000. *Multimedia-based Instructional Design: Computer-based Training, Web-based Training, Distance Broadcast Training*. San Francisco: Jossey-Bass/Pfeiffer.
Applies the instructional-design approach to computer-aided instruction, tele-teaching, and Web-based training.

Librarians Association of the University of California. "Information Literacy Background." Berkeley, CA: LAUC. (February 2003) Available: library.berkeley.edu/~smcdanie/infoliteracy.html.
Links to sites dealing with accreditation as well as current information literacy projects in California.

Library Instruction Round Table. "Library Instruction Round Table." Chicago: LIRT. (February 2003) Available: www3.baylor.edu/LIRT.
The American Library Association's Library Instruction Round Table (LIRT). LIRT represents all types of libraries and "advocates library instruction as a means for developing competent library and information use as a part of lifelong learning."

Loertscher, David, and Blanche Wool. 2002. *Information Literacy: A Review of the Research*. 2nd ed. San Jose, CA: Hi Willow.

Mantyla, Karen. 1999. *Interactive Distance Learning Exercises That Really Work!: Turn Classroom Exercises into Effective and Enjoyable Distance Learning Activities.* Alexandria, VA: American Society for Training & Development.

Martin, Allan, and Hannelore Rader, eds. 2002. *Information and IT Literacy: Enabling Learning in the 21st Century.* London: Facet.

Maughan, Patricia Davitt. 2002. "Assessing Information Literacy Among Undergraduates: A Discussion of the Literature and the University of California-Berkeley Assessment Experience." *College and Research Libraries* 62, no.1: 71–85.

Merz, Lawrie H., and Beth L. Mark, comps. 2002. *Assessment in College Library Instruction Programs.* Chicago: Association of College and Research Libraries.
This publication includes the results of a survey to learn how information literacy is being assessed in nearly 300 college and university libraries. Also includes examples of information literacy assessment tools.

Milbury, Peter. "Information Literacy And Library Skills Resources." Chico, CA: School-Libraries.Org. (February 2003) Available: www.school-libraries.org/resources/literacy.html.
Links to Web sites focusing on information literacy.

Mintz, Anne P. 2002. *Web of Deception: Misinformation on the Internet.* Medford, NJ: CyberAge Books.

Noah, Carolyn B., and Linda W. Braun. 2002. *The Browsable Classroom: An Introduction to E-Learning for Librarians.* New York: Neal-Schuman.
A how-to guide for distance education.

Notess, Greg R. 2002. "Dead Search Engines." *Online* 26, no.3: 63–64.
Describes the rise, fall, and transformation of Web search engines.

Notess, Gregg R. "Search Engine Showdown: The Users' Guide to Web Searching." Bozeman, MT: Gregg R. Notess. (February 2003) Available: searchengineshowdown.com.
An excellent site for comparisons of Web search engines as well as information on their workings, controversies, and so on.

Palloff, Rena M., and Keith Pratt. 1999. *Building Learning Communities in Cyberspace: Effective Strategies for the Online Classroom.* San Francisco: Jossey-Bass.
An essential primer on developing a course for distance education. Practical information from experienced educators.

Palloff, Rena M., and Keith Pratt. 2001. *Lessons from the Cyberspace Classroom: The Realities of Online Teaching.* San Francisco: Jossey-Bass.
Another practical guide to course development from Palloff and Pratt.

Pausch, Lois M., and Mary Popp. "Assessment of Information Literacy: Lessons from the Higher Education Assessment Movement." Chicago: Association of College & Research Libraries. (February 2003) Available: www.ala.org/acrl/paperhtm/d30.html.
This ALA/ACRL paper "reviews higher education assessment methods; identifies useful theories and practices; describes assessment programs in academic libraries; and makes recommendations for changes in library education and for future research."

Plotnick, Eric. 2000. "Definitions/Perspectives: Information Literacy." *Teacher Librarian* 21, no.1: 27–29.

Prus, Joseph, and Reid Johnson. 1994. "A Critical Review of Student Assessment Options." *New Directions for Community Colleges*, no.88 (Winter): 69–83.

Ragains, Patrick. "Assessment in Library & Information Literacy Instruction." Reno, NV: University of Nevada, Reno. (February 2003) Available: www2.library.unr.edu/ragains/assess.html.
This Web site includes such categories as "Bibliographies on Assessment of Library and Information Literacy Instruction" and "Pretests of Students' Library & Information Literacy Skills."

Rhodes, John. 2001. *Videoconferencing for the Real World : Implementing Effective Visual Communications Systems.* Boston: Focal Press.
Though the focus is on videoconferencing technology, there is also a useful section on videoconferencing applications.

Shapiro, Jeremy J., and Shelley K. Hughes. "Information Literacy as a Liberal Art." *Educom Review* (February 2003) Available: www.educause.edu/pub/er/review/reviewarticles/31231.html. Persuasively argues that information literacy is a lot more than simple library or computer skills.

Simonson, Michael R. 2000. *Teaching and Learning at a Distance: Foundations of Distance Education.* Upper Saddle River, NJ: Merrill.
Discusses both the theory and practice of distance education.

Snavely, Loanne, and Natasha Cooper. 1997. "The Information Literacy Debate." *Journal of Academic Librarianship* 23 (January): 9–14.

Sonntag, Gabriela. 2001. "Report on the National Information Literacy Survey: Documenting Progress throughout the United States." *College and Research Libraries News* 62, no.10: 996–1001.

University of California, Los Angeles Library. "The Information Literacy Initiative @ UCLA." Los Angeles: UCLA Library. (February 2003) Available: www.library.ucla.edu/infolit.
Information on a significant information literacy initiative undertaken by a major university library. Includes the full text of "Information Competence at UCLA: Report of a Survey Project," a 1999 survey that "documented deficiencies in UCLA students' understanding of resources and methods, and assessed the general level of information literacy as low."

University of Minnesota Video Network Services. "Video Conferencing." Twin Cities, MN: University of Minnesota Office of Information Technology. (February 2003) Available: umtv.cee.umn.edu/UMITV/index.htm
A rich source of information and practical tips for anyone interested in tele-teaching.

University of Texas System Digital Library. "*TILT.*" Austin, TX: University of Texas System Digital Library. (February 2003) Available: tilt.lib.utsystem.edu.
A working example of a well-developed information literacy tutorial.

University of Washington Information Literacy Learning. *"uwill."* Seattle, WA: University of Washington Libraries. (Febrary 2003) Available: www.lib.washington.edu/uwill.
The Web home of a developing initiative to support faculty in teaching information competencies within the context of courses. Includes links to information literacy resources and examples of courses involved in the *uwill* pilot project.

University of Wisconsin-Extension. "Distance Education Clearinghouse." Madison, WI: University of Wisconsin. (February 2003) Available: www.uwex.edu/disted.
An outstanding resource for anything relating to distance education.

Video Development Institute. "The Videoconferencing Cookbook 3.0." Atlanta, GA: Georgia Institute of Technology. (February 2003) Available: www.videnet.gatech.edu/cookbook.
A handy, accessible guide to understanding videoconferencing. Updated approximately once a year.

Walters, Suzanne. 2003. *Library Marketing That Works!* New York: Neal-Schuman.

Ward, Dane. "Information Literacy: The Key Web Sites." San Jose, CA: National Forum on Information Literacy. (February 2003) Available: www.infolit.org/related_sites/index.html.
Links to Web sites focusing on information literacy plus a number of full-text documents on the topic.

Washington Library Media Association. "Information Literacy." Bellevue, Washington: WLMA. (February 2003) Available: www.wlma.org/Instruction/infolit.htm.
Presents information on the role of the school librarian in information literacy, information literacy models, and sample information literacy curricula.

Washington State Library. "LibrarySmart." Olympia, WA: Washington State Library. (February 2003) Available: www.librarysmart.com.
An example of a well-developed online information literacy project. The "Resources for Library Staff" link on this site is worth following.

Wilcox, James R. 2000. *Videoconferencing & Interactive Multimedia: The Whole Picture*. 3rd ed. New York: Telecom Books. Will appeal to the technology buff who wants to understand the nuts and bolts of videoconferencing. Also does a nice job of relating the history of videoconferencing.

Wolinsky, Art. 2002. *Internet Power Research Using the Big6 Approach*. Berkeley Heights, NJ: Enslow Publishers.

York College of Pennsylvania Library. "YCP Information Literacy." York, PA: York College of Pennsylvania. (February 2003) Available: www.ycp.edu/library/ifl.
Web site for Information Literacy 101, a core course at York College. Includes links to information literacy resources intended for college students.

Young, Rosemary M., and Stephena Harmony. 1999. *Working with Faculty to Design Undergraduate Information Literacy Programs: A How-To-Do-It Manual for Librarians*. New York: Neal-Schuman.

INDEX

3M Wall Display, 216
802.11 (wireless standard), 210

ABI/Inform, 53
accessibility barriers, 48, 118
accreditation, vii-viii
accuracy, 82-83, 128
active learning, 150-152, 164, 172, 188, 198
administrators, 222-225
Adobe Acrobat, 177-178
advertising, 23, 26, 64, 131
affiliation, 80-81
Agricola, 50-51, 120-121
Alta Vista, 52, 52, 63, 129, 131
alternate video sources, 184
amazon.com, 32
American Association of School Librarians, 11
American Council on Science and Health, 66
American Library Association, 18
American Memory, 18, 22
Americans with Disabilities Act, 206-207
analogies, 149-150
anecdotes, 147-149
application sharing, 185
archaic terminology, 46, 47, 48, 117
artificial intelligence, 42
Ask Jeeves, 60, 68, 104, 129
ask-a-librarian services, 177
assessment (of program performance), 227, 233-236
assessment (of student outcomes), 7-8, 144, 170-171, 188, 219, 223-224, 227-233
assessment methods, 231-233
assessment plans, 239-231
assignments, 161-163
Association of College and Research Libraries, 10
Association of College and Research Libraries Institute for Information Literacy Immersion Program, 168

Association of Research Libraries, 34
asynchronous distance education, 174, 187
audience, 70, 76, 82, 110, 128
authoring software, 179
authority, 79, 126

Backstreet Boys, vii
bad information, 19-20
basic and advanced search interfaces, 58, 63, 130
Bertelsman Media Worldwide, 28, 97
bibliographic databases, 24, 53, 61, 129
bibliographic instruction, 4
BI-L, 168
BioMed Central, 71
Blackboard (courseware), 166, 176
book reviews, 83-84
Boolean Logic, 54, 55, 93-95
boredom, 145
brainstorming, 151
Brinn, David, 164
Bush, President George W., 19

capitalization, 44
censorship, 18, 48, 118
Center for Science in the Public Interest, 66
Center for the Public Domain, 35, 107
Centurion Guard, 214
chairs, 205
changes in terminology, 46
chat, 177
cheathouse.com, 32, 105
cheating, 28-33, 105-106
Chronicle of Higher Education, 28
citation indexes, 85
citing sources, 30-31
classroom methods, 163-164
classrooms, electronic, *see* electronic classrooms
CNN, 20

codec, 183
common knowledge, 30, 106
common words, 59-60, 104
computer workstations, 204
computer monitors, 184, 204
computer security, 213-214
computer skills, vii, 4, 6-9
computer viruses, 49, 108, 118
conflicts of interest, 82, 127
continuing education, 167
control groups, 232
controlled vocabulary, *see* fixed vocabulary
copyright, 19, 23, 33-37, 47, 107-108, 117, 189
corporate authors, 79, 126
correspondence courses, 174, 175
cost, *see* economics of information
course approval, 154-156
course description, 155
courses, extended, *see* extended courses
courseware, 166, 176
coverage, 85, 128
crime, 38, 49, 108, 118
critical thinking, 4, 6, 10-12
cross references, 56
currency, 77-79, 125
CU-SeeMe, 182

dailypress.com, 68
data collaboration, 185-186
databases, 53, 62, 99, 130
date of creation, 45-46, 77, 116
deceptive practices, 49, 118
defaults, 54-55, 56, 100
DIALOG, 50
Digital Millennium Copyright Act, 36
digital reference technologies, 175, 177
digital video cameras, 183
directories, Web, *see* Web directories
display features, 55, 59, 103
distance education, 173-192
document cameras, 184
Dogpile, 129
dot.com, vii, 23-24
dramatic techniques, 146-147

dual-purpose lab/classroom, 201
DVD players, 184, 215

Earth (novel), 164
eBay, vii
e-boards, 216
EBSCO, 24, 27, 97
economics of information, 19-20, 21-28, 45, 74, 96-97, 116
electronic classrooms, 151, 195-216
  acoustics, 196
  attractiveness, 197
  comfort, 198
  furntiure, 203-204
  layout, 198-203
  lighting, 196
  privacy, , 196
  size, 195
electronic information literacy skills, 9-10
electronic information literacy, definition, 3-13
electronic searching, 41-64
electronic white boards, 184-185, 216
ELMO (document camera), 184
Embase, 27
Encyclopedia Britannica, 23, 26-27
ergonomics, 204-206
e-Scholarship, 71
ethics, 12, 28-39, 105-108
evaluating information, 27, 65-89, 109-115, 125-128
evaluation (of student outcomes), *see* assessment (of student outcomes)
extended courses, 153-166, 170

faculty, 218-222
fair use, 36-37, 108, 189
fallacies, logical, *see* logical fallacies
false drops, 46-47, 57, 63, 68, 98, 117
fee-based information services, 24
feedback (electronic searching), 50-51, 120-121
feedback (from students), 153
fields, 53
FirstGov, 63, 131
fixed vocabularies, 48, 56, 101, 118
flip charts, 197

Ford Motor Company, 23
format, 47, 117
Fortress Clean Slate, 213
free information, *see* open-access information
freshness, 63, 130
full-text information, 24, 53, 61, 129
funding, 80, 127

Galen, 78, 126
general information literacy course, 154
gifts, 224-225
goals, 13, 188
Google, 63, 129, 131, 169
grades, 17
grading, 157
grants, 224-225
gray literature, 45, 116

H.320 (videoconferencing standard), 181,
    183, 186
H.323 (videoconferencing standard), 181-
    182, 183, 186
handouts, 141-142
handwriting, 46
Harvey, Paul, 146
help menus, 52, 54, 58, 64, 99, 130
historical distance, 46, 117
hits, 43, 57, 98, 120
homonyms, 47, 117
human subjects, 230
humor, 147-148
HVAC, 198
hype, 16, 221

Ideal, 24
ILI-L, 168
"I'll Sleep When I'm Dead", 145
impact factors, 85-86
improving your teaching, 171-172
independent confirmation, 83-85, 128
indexing, 62
information cynicims, 66
Information Literacy Competancy Standards
    for Higer Education, 10-11
Information Literacy Instruction Listserv, 168

information literacy, definition, 3-13, 221, 234
information need, 68, 76, 77, 82
information roadblocks, 45-50, 116-119
information technology, 169
in-house publications, 177-178
Institute for Scientific Information, 85-86
intellectual property, 33, 35, 108
intelligent whiteboards, 216
invisible Web, 64, 129-130
iterative search, 50-53, 120-122

jargon, 43, 47, 117, 147
JSTOR, 18
junk science, 65-67
Junkscience.com, 66

keystone correction, 215
keyword searching, 55, 100

lab/classroom, 207
language barriers, 47-48, 117
laptop computers, 202, 211-212
learning objectives, *see* objectives
Lesko, Matthew, 147
lesson plans, 138-141, 172
Lexis-Nexis, 19, 24, 27, 61
library assignments, 219-220
library instruction, 4
Library of Congress, 18, 22, 61
lighting, 183
limits, 56, 57, 102
Lippincott, Williams & Wilkins, 27
literature review, 69
litigation, 45, 116
logical fallacies, 86-89, 112-114
lost information, 46, 117
Lycos, 63, 129, 131

marketing electronic information literacy, 156,
    217-225
MD Consult, 24
MEDLINE, 25-26
metadata, 49, 57, 102, 130
metasearch engines, 64, 132
methods of assessment

automated assessment, 233
focus groups, 232
longitudinal studies, 233
observation, 233
student feedback, 232
student portfolios, 232
student research projects, 231-232
tests, 231
microphones, 183-184, 189, 196
monitors, computer, *see* computer monitors
Mouserobics, 7, 57
multipoint control unit, 184
myths (about information), 15-20, 21, 133, 221, 222

Napster, 29, 33, 34
National Lampoon, 29
National Library of Medicine, 25
natural language searching, 60, 104
Neal-Schuman, vii
NetMeeting, 182, 186
networking (computer), 209-211
new faculty, 220
New York Times v. Tasini, 47
NewsIndex, 63, 131
Nielsen, Jacob, 179
Nine Information Literacy Standards for Student Learning, 11-12
Nixon, President Richard, 36
notebook computers, *see* laptop computers

objectives, 138-139, 188
objectivity, 72, 110
observation (of teaching), 171
open Web, 63, 76, 84
open-access information, 22-23, 25-27, 61, 74. 96, 129
outcomes, 13
Ovid, 24, 25-27

paraphrase, 30
parody, 49, 118
pay for positioning, 64, 131
Peanuts (comic strip), 15
peer review, 70, 73, 76, 109

Pfizer, 19
physical location, 46, 116
plagiarism, 18, 28-33, 105-106
plasma screens, 216
Polly, Jean Armour, 18
posttest, 231
power, 209
power, pacing, and pitch, 145-146
PowerPoint, viii-ix, xiii-xv, 143-144
precision, 48, 51, 123-124
Presley, Elvis, 36
pretest, 231
primary sources, 114-115
print information, 76, 80, 112, 127
privacy, , 48, 118
private information, 48, 118
professional development, 167-169
Project Gutenberg, 22-23, 26-27
projection screens, 197
projectors, 214-216
proprietary information, 24-27, 61, 96-97
proximity operators, 55-56, 101
PsycLit, 137, 143
public domain, 35-36, 107
public-access computers, 207
publications, in-house, *see* in-house publications
publishers, 71, 80, 110, 126-127
PubMed, 25-26, 122
purpose, 81-82, 127

quick-and-dirty searching, 42-43

Raish, Martin, 168
Random House, 28
random sampling, 229
rarity, 46, 116
RealPlayer, 186-187
RealServer, 187
recall, 48, 51, 123-124
records, 53, 99
Reed Elsevier, 27, 97
refereed journals, 70
reference desk, 170, 219
remote controls, 215

reserve reading, 164
review articles, 84
reviews, 83-84
revision, 50-51
Rolling Stone, 29

satire, 49, 118
saving searches, 59
scholarly information, 69-75
scholarly information process, 73, 109-111
scholarly journals, 75, 111
schoolsucks.com, 32, 105
Schultz, Charles, 15
Schuyler, Michael, 20
Science Direct, 24, 27
scope, 54, 100
search engines, 49, 53-54, 57, 61-64, 129-132
search history, 59, 103
search strategy, , vii
searching, electronic, *see* electronic searching
searching, quick-and-dirty, *see* quick-and-dirty searching
secondary sources, 114-115
secrecy, 19, 48, 118
SEDS: Students for the Exploration and Development of Space, 68
self publication, 70, 71, 80, 127
September 11, 2001, 19
skills, computer, *see* computer skills
skills, electronic information literacy, *see* electronic information literacy skills
slang, 47, 117
slide presentations, 143-144, 172
software, 212-213
speakers (sound systems), 183-184, 196
spelling, 44, 45, 47, 50, 117
spiders, 62, 130
Springer, 28
stagecraft, 146-147
statistical consultants, 229
stickiness (on the Web), 178
stopwords, 59, 103
streaming media, 186-187
student questions, 140

students, understanding, *see* understanding students
subject categories, 56-57, 63, 102, 130
subject headings, 56, 57, 101
subject knowledge, 167-169
subject-specialist librarians, 219
subject-specific information literacy course, 154
subscriptions, 23, 24
surfing the Net, 18
surge protectors, 208-209
syllabi, 156-161
synchronous distance education, 174
synonyms, 43, 47,117
syntax, 63, 130
systematic reviews, 84

T.120 (technical standard), 185-186
teaching style, 198-199
teaching, improving yours, *see* improving your teaching
tele-teaching, 186-191
terminology, changes in, *see* changes in terminology
term-paper mills, 29, 32-33
tests, 165
textbooks, 164
time management, 165
truncation, 58-59, 103
turnitin.com, 33
turnkey videoconferencing systems, 185
tutorials, Web-based, *see* Web-based tutorials

UCITA (Uniform Computer Information Transaction Act), 18
uncollected information, 46, 117
understanding students, 170-171
universal search interface, 61, 122
updating, 78-79, 125
usability testing, 178-179
user interfaces, 63, 64, 130
user interfaces, basic and advanced, *see* basic and advanced user interfaces

vague words, 59-60, 104
vanity press, 71, 80

VCRs, 184, 215
Viagra, 19
video client, 150, 182-183
videoconferencing, 180-186
videoconferencing systems, turnkey, *see* turnkey videoconferencing systems
videotaping, 146, 171
Vindigo, 20
viruses, computer, *see* computer viruses
vocal techniques, 145-146

Washington State Library, 20
Web conventions, 57, 102
Web directories, 63, 130-132
Web search engines, *see* search engines
web sites (and distance education), 176-177
Web-based tutorials, 178-179, 233
Webcams, 183
WebCrawler, 62, 129

WebCT, 166, 176
wheelchairs, 206-207
whiteboards, 197
whiteboards, electronic, *see* electronic whiteboards
whiteboards, intelligent, *see* intelligent whiteboards
Wi-Fi (wireless standard), 210
Windows Media Player, 186-187
Windows NT, 213
wireless technology, 209-211, 216
Wolters Kluwer, 27, 97
workshops, 168
workstations, computer, *see* computer workstations

Zagat, 20
Zevon, Warren, 145
zoom, 215

ABOUT THE AUTHOR

Currently the Assistant University Librarian for Public Service at the fledgling University of California, Merced, Donald A. Barclay has previously worked as a librarian at New Mexico State University, the University of Houston, and the Houston Academy of Medicine–Texas Medical Center Library. He has authored or co-authored several books for Neal-Schuman Publishers: *Teaching Electronic Information Literacy* (1995), *Managing Public-Access Computers* (2000), and *The Medical Library Association Consumer Health Reference Service Handbook* (2001). The latter was named an "Outstanding Academic Title" by *Choice: Current Reviews for Academic Libraries*. In addition to his writing on library-related topics, Donald has also co-authored three anthologies dealing with the literature of the American West. He is a graduate of Boise State University and the University of California, Berkeley, where he earned advanced degrees in English and library and information studies. He lives in Merced, California with his wife Darcie R. Barclay, a psychologist, and their daughter, Tess.

HOW TO USE THE COMPANION CD-ROM

Open the CD-ROM by inserting the disk into your computer's "D" drive and click the "D" symbol to open, or open office documents, then select "D' drive.

Folders offer downloadable and customizable versions of the PowerPoint presentations supporting the instruction material in *Teaching and Marketing Electronic Information Literacy Programs*.

Please see the complete description of "How to Use The 12 Ready-To-Go PowerPoint Presentations" on page xiii.